OUTSMARTING THE COMPETITION

■ ■ ■ ■ ■ ■ ■ ■ ■ ■ ■ ■ ■

Practical Approaches
to Finding and Using
Competitive Information

■ ■ ■ ■ ■ ■ ■ ■ ■ ■ ■ ■ ■

John J. McGonagle, Jr.
and
Carolyn M. Vella

Sourcebooks, Inc.
Naperville, Illinois

Sourcebooks, Inc.
P.O. Box 372
Naperville, IL, 60566
(708) 961-2161.

Cover design: Creative Mind Services
Editorial: Lynn Brown, Joyce Petersen and Pat Schorr
Design and Production: Monica Paxson

Published in conjunction with the Partners in Publishing Program

 KENDALL / HUNT PUBLISHING COMPANY
2460 Kerper Boulevard P.O. Box 539 Dubuque, Iowa 52004-0539

0-8403-6449-0 hardcover; 0-8403-6450-4 paper

This publication is designed to provide accurate and authoritative information in regard to the subject matter covered. It is sold with the understanding that the publisher is not engaged in rendering legal, accounting, or other professional service. If legal advice or other expert assistance is required, the services of a competent professional person should be sought.
From a Declaration of Principles Jointly Adopted by a Committee of the American Bar Association and a Committee of Publishers.

Library of Congress Cataloging-in-Publication Data

McGonagle, John J.
　　Outsmarting the competition : practical approaches to finding and using competitive information / John J. McGonagle, Jr. and Carolyn M. Vella.
　　　　p.　　cm.
　　Includes bibliographical references, index
　　ISBN 0-942061-06-3 (hardcover) -- ISBN 0-942061-04-7(pbk)
　　1. Business intelligence.　2. Competition.　I. Vella, Carolyn M.
I I. Title.
HD38.7.M39　　1990
658.4'7--dc20
　　　　　　　　　　　　　　　　　　　　　　　　　　　90-31866
　　　　　　　　　　　　　　　　　　　　　　　　　　　　CIP

Printed and bound in the United States of America.
10 9 8 7 6 5 4 3 2

Table of Contents

Table of Contents

Acknowledgments

We would like to thank the editors of a number of business publications for printing our articles about competitive intelligence. We have benefited from their insight and would like to acknowledge the consent of their publications to reprint or adapt materials in those articles for use in this book:

Carolyn M. Vella and John J. McGonagle, Jr., "Competitive Intelligence," in *The Secured Lender*, Vol. 45, no. 1, January/February 1989. Copyright 1989 by The National Commercial Finance Association. Reprinted with permission.

Carolyn M. Vella and John J. McGonagle, Jr., "Competitive Intelligence in Financial Services," in *SourceBank*, Vol. 1, no. 1 and 2, May/June and July/August 1988. Copyright 1988 by Financial Sourcebooks, a division of Sourcebooks, Inc. Reprinted with permission.

John J. McGonagle, Jr., "Getting Information Out of the Federal Government," in *Information Broker*, Vol. 5, no. 4, July/August 1987. Copyright 1987 by Burwell Enterprises. Reprinted with permission.

Portions of this book are based on continuing professional education materials originally developed by us and The Helicon Group, Ltd., for Andersen Consulting, Arthur Andersen & Co. Those materials are copyrighted 1989 by Arthur Andersen & Co. They are reprinted and adapted here with permission and with all rights reserved.

Acknowledgments

Some materials in the book have appeared in other publications and are reprinted here with the permission of the authors, specifically

> Portions of Chapter 3 are adapted from "A Competitive Intelligence Ethics Policy," copyright 1989, *The Information Advisor,* The Winters Group, Rochester, New York. Reprinted with permission. All rights reserved.

> Throughout the book, we have quoted from and reprinted material originally presented by The Conference Board, Inc., in *Competitive Intelligence,* Research Report No. 913, copyright 1988, The Conference Board, Inc. These are reprinted with permission. All rights reserved.

In addition, the authors would like to note their specific appreciation to the following:

> Dominique Raccah of Sourcebooks, Inc., and Lynn Brown for their enthusiasm and help in structuring this book.

> George Tuller, an M.B.A. student at Moravian College, for reading parts of the manuscript "cold" and giving his frank evaluations.

> Jon Pretti, formerly associated with Andersen Consulting, for his suggestions on presenting examples of CI in action.

> Dr. Ronald Garst of the Defense Intelligence College, and Madhu Bhide of Toshiba America, Inc., for their suggestions on approaches to gathering and analyzing raw intelligence.

Trademark Acknowledgments

ABI/Inform is a registered trademark of Data Courier, Inc.

CompuServe is a registered trademark of CompuServe Inc.

COMPUSTAT and CORPORATE REGISTER are registered trademarks of Standard & Poor's Corp.

DIALOG and OneSearch are service marks of Dialog Information Services Inc.

Disclosure is a registered trademark of Disclosure, Inc.

Dow Jones News/Retrieval is a registered trademark of Dow Jones & Company, Inc.

InvesText is a registered trademark of Technical Data International.

Japan Economic Newswire Plus is a trademark of Kyodo News International, Inc.

NEXIS is a registered trademark of Mead Data Corporation.

ORBIT is a registered trademark of Maxwell Online, Inc.

PTS Marketing and Advertising Reference System and PTS New Product Announcements/Plus are trademarks of Predicasts, Inc.

VU/TEXT is a registered trademark of VU/TEXT Information Services, Inc.

WESTLAW is a registered trademark of West Publishing Company.

Introduction

Business survival and growth often depend on ensuring that you have accurate, current information about your competitors *and* a plan for using that information to your advantage. The key is determining what you need and where to find it. And the best tool for doing that is called competitive intelligence (CI).

Demystifying CI

CI is not mysterious. Although it has only recently been talked about openly, CI is something that many successful businesses have been doing for some time. CI is not something only the giant international corporations do. Every manager and executive—of either a small local service business or a giant manufacturing firm—can and should be obtaining CI regularly.

This book introduces you to competitive intelligence, also known as competitive information. CI is a vast subject. In this book, we focus on what CI is and how you can use it in your everyday business dealings. This book is written for every executive, manager, or CI specialist involved in gathering or using CI.

Introduction

■ ■ ■

CI uses public sources to locate and develop information on competition and competitors. You must remember, *public* is *not* the same as *published*—it is a substantially broader concept. In an open society such as ours, businesses place a lot of information in the public domain. Aggressive and effective CI can provide much more information on markets, businesses, and businesspeople than you might imagine.

The vast amount of data that is public may be illustrated by the problems facing the U.S. pharmaceutical industry overseas. According to industry sources, drug "piracy" is a severe problem for many industrialized nations, and in particular for the United States. Foreign pirates obtain information about American drugs from a wide variety of sources. Foremost among them are patent records, as well as the files of the U.S. Food and Drug Administration. This agency reportedly received 34,000 Freedom of Information Act requests in 1982, the last year for which data is available. As the president of the Pharmaceutical Manufacturers Association put it, these pirates can copy new drugs "faster than we can get them into the market because all the data about a drug is published."[1]

Locating important data *and* converting it into useful information is the task of CI. The ever-increasing availability of online databases makes CI a resource usable by any business of any size. This is true whether the information you need is on potential acquisition targets, the market for a particular product, the identities of key personnel working for a competitor, the emergence of a new technology, or the financial strength of a particular firm.

But do not think that you must use online databases to produce CI. These databases are just one of the many tools available to you. For example, CI can involve observing the number of cars in a competitor's factory parking lot while you are driving to work, checking out local news stories sent by a clipping service, reading names of committee members in a trade association directory, and talking to your personnel office about new employees and where they worked before, so that you can then interview them.

CI is much more than collecting unconnected facts, however. It is the process by which you decide *what* you need to know about your competitors, *where* to get the raw facts you need, and *how* to make sense of what you find or don't find.

History of CI

It is difficult to chart the history of CI, largely because those practicing it have been reluctant to tell their competitors that they are doing it. That kind of information is potentially important CI in itself.

From what we have seen, several trends have led to the use of CI on a wider basis in the United States:

■ A number of the largest transnational corporations have been conducting some types of CI for decades, primarily in the area of political risk evaluation. As you can imagine, a bank or oil company facing the possibility of nationalizations of assets may be quickly motivated to set up its own early warning system.

■ In the U.S., the antitrust laws have been interpreted to bar competitors from exchanging data in order to fix prices or divide markets. This interpretation of the antitrust laws has prevented many trade associations from collecting and releasing specific information on identified companies. Companies seeking such information have had to develop it themselves.

■ Competition from non-U.S.-based firms has grown substantially. Over time, it has become clear that the more successful firms have been requiring their managers to collect some CI on a regular basis. It can be said, with little risk of exaggeration, that the average Japanese plant manager is expected to know more about how competitors operate than

Introduction

his or her U.S. counterpart, the average U.S. marketing director, and the typical U.S. corporate planner combined.

■ Strategic planning in corporations became more sophisticated in the 1980s. Most corporations recognized, at least implicitly, that they had to know *something* about their competitors in order to develop a corporate business plan.

■ Online databases have exploded onto the business scene during the past 10 years. Emerging from their status as tools used only by librarians, lawyers, and magazine researchers, these databases enable more people to have prompt access to more raw data. A few years ago, these databases were little more than electronic indexes to articles. Now, they contain the full text of wire service stories and reports in local business papers, as well as stock analysts' reports commissioned especially for online users.

As these trends developed, CI emerged as an accepted and effective business tool for managers and executives alike. It is the goal of this book to take another step toward making that tool available.

About This Book

To assist our readers, each chapter is self-contained, with endnotes listing all sources. We also include a list of publications for further reading and a varied list of CI resources in Appendix B of the book. They will draw your attention to media and organizations of particular relevance to CI topics and help you dig more deeply into topics of greatest interest to you. These selective resources reflect our perception of useful materials available at the time this book was written. We include a glossary of key terms in Appendix A, and a comprehensive index concludes the book.

In addition to the exhibits of forms, samples, and worksheets developed for this book, we have included three additional features: CI Clips, CI Closeups, and CI Alerts.

■ CI Clips are short quotations from a wide variety of sources, all intended to illustrate some key point in the book and to provoke your thinking about CI.

■ CI Close-ups are short summaries of actual cases involving the need for or the use of CI.

■ CI Alerts are reprints of public information about companies that illustrate how revealing news articles, help-wanted advertisements, speeches, press releases, and even in-house publications can be for your CI efforts.

Other boxed items define new terms or give maxims we have distilled over the years about CI.

When we make reference to a source for raw data, we are doing it only to illustrate a point. We do not recommend particular databases, data sources, or vendors. Similarly, when we mention the name of a specific company in an example, we do not intend that to be either an endorsement or a criticism of that company.

Throughout the book, you may find that we sometimes make reference to military or political examples. This is *not* because CI is identical to military and political intelligence and espionage. Rather, we cite such cases because the military and political offices of many countries have developed some of the techniques now being used by CI, and many people have felt freer to write about military and political intelligence cases than about CI cases. Hopefully that will change.

We have included a number of references to practices in Japan and by Japanese firms. These references reflect the fact that Japanese firms, overall, have been using CI for a much longer period of time than have American firms, and the Japanese have been more willing to acknowledge what they do and how they do it. We are merely taking advantage of that openness.

Introduction

Notes

1. Christopher Elias, "Big Profits, Extensive Research Are Industry's Best Medicine," *Insight,* August 24, 1987, pp. 38-40.

Part I

The Big Picture

Chapter 1
Competitive Information as Part of Your Business

Chapter 2
How CI Can Improve Your Business

Chapter 3
Ethical and Legal Issues

Competitive Information as Part of Your Business

Competitive intelligence, or CI, is sometimes also called *competitive information*. Actually, competitive information is the result of competitive intelligence. CI consists of two phases. First is the use of public sources to develop data (raw facts) on competition, competitors, and the market environment. Second is the transformation, by analysis, of that data into information (usable results). Generally, CI results deal with specific competitors or with the competition in general. For convenience, this book calls the whole two-phase process CI.

> **Competitive Intelligence (CI):** *The use of public sources to develop information about the competition, competitors, and market environment.*

A key maxim of CI is that 90 percent of all information that you and your business need to make key decisions and to understand your market and competitors is already public or can be systematically developed from public data.

CI is *not* business espionage. Business espionage is the collection of information by illegal means, such as breaking and entering, "hacking," or the collection of information that is illegal to have, such as possession of classified U.S. government files.

What *Is* Public Information?

To understand CI, you need to understand what is meant by *public*. Here the term is taken in its very broadest sense—not only what the U.S. Department of Commerce releases or what you can find in *The Wall Street Journal*. *Public* is not the same as *published*; it is a much broader concept.

In CI, *public* means all information you can legally and ethically identify, locate, and then access. It ranges from a document released by a competitor as a part of a lawsuit to the text of a press release issued by your competitor's advertising agency describing that client's proposed marketing strategy as it extols the virtues of a new product or the opening of a new plant. Chapter 3 of this book explores the ethical and legal issues of CI in detail.

The widespread use of computers and the development of thousands of online databases in the last 10 years have added a whole new dimension to the concept of public information. The Congressional Office of Technology Assessment (OTA) described just how powerful the online database can be in the search for good CI. Discussing the vast improvements in the press's ability to research its reports, OTA concluded:

> Databases. . . are powerful tools for the press. Researching stories, investigating the background of subjects and sources, corroborating information, drawing out latent connections between people and events, and constructing "mosaics" of information from disparate sources, will all become more practicable, and in some cases, possible for the first time.

> It is safe to say that, by the end of this decade, every recent news story, news picture, wire service report, and major press release will be commercially searchable from the reporter's workstation, subject only to the cost his newspaper is willing to incur.[2]

The same is true, perhaps even to a greater extent, for businesses. In fact, as an illustration of the vast improvements that are possible using these databases, OTA chose a business example:

> The new power to aggregate information was illustrated [in 1987] when two prominent businessmen were competing publicly to buy a major U.S. newspaper company. An enterprising journalist ran a check on both of their names in. . . [the] NEXIS® database, and learned that one of them, who lived in Indiana, was married to the sister of the investment banker representing the target newspaper's interests. He also learned that the Indiana man had just returned from a weekend with his wife in Mexico City, where the competitor lived. The two men announced a few days later that they

5

were joining forces to buy the newspaper together, leading the journalist to report that the businessmen were colluding, rather than competing.[3]

Who Uses CI?

The use of CI among United States businesses is rapidly growing, and rightly so, for four key reasons:

1. More American businesses realize how important CI is. These businesses have begun to learn just what a vast amount of information on their competitors can be made available to them. They also appreciate that this kind of information can help them compete more effectively.

2. Some American businesses know just how devastating CI, as developed and used by their foreign and domestic competitors, can be. Some of these companies have learned only from bitter experience.

3. As American industries and service sectors mature, growth has slowed, and CI provides effective ways to retain market share in periods of decline.

4. The pace of change in business has quickened in certain sectors (like high tech), and CI helps companies learn and cope with changes and surprises in technology, competitors, materials, and the economy.

These trends are reflected in the results of a survey of over 300 companies by The Conference Board, Inc. That survey found that 68 percent of the companies stated that, over the next few years, their efforts in monitoring competitor activities would increase. Only 1 percent said they would decrease, and 32 percent said they would "hold at about the same level."[4]

> *Can I name five of my major competitors?*
>
> *Can I name their major products or services?*
>
> *What will they be doing in the next six months?*
>
> *Who is doing my job at each competing firm?*
>
> *What is he or she doing now?*
>
> *If you can answer any of these questions, you are already using some CI.*

Today, every business needs good CI to compete, and many companies require it to survive.

■ New and developing businesses need good CI just to get started and to grow. With requirements for solid business planning gradually being imposed by those providing venture capital (and ultimately by banks), companies will soon need good CI to get significant financing.

■ Medium-sized businesses need CI both to help them determine which new markets to enter and to help them expand their current markets. Such businesses also should be using CI whenever they consider merging with another company, acquiring another company, or being acquired.

■ For the largest businesses, CI can be an important aid in monitoring and controlling their own activities in a wide variety of markets and lines of business. CI can provide senior management with information that is critical to management operations because, to a very real extent, good information is power for the largest businesses.

Although CI's use is still in its infancy, The Conference Board survey showed that 68 percent of the middle-line managers in the surveyed corporations felt that it was "very important" to monitor their competitor's activities. Another 30 percent thought it was "fairly important," and only 2 percent felt it was only "slightly important."[5]

CI CLOSEUP: "Lost Profits"

Several years ago, Serpintina Glass Inc., a speciality glass company, put out a bid to repair stained glass windows in a church. Without checking out competitors' prices, the company bid $18,000. The next lowest bid, the company was later shocked to learn, was $76,000.[6]

When Should You Use CI?

Understanding and using CI is most important when your business faces any of these threats.

■ Competition increases from firms outside your industry's traditional boundaries.

■ Competition, both actual and potential, increases from non-U.S.-based firms.

■ Consumers and customers become increasingly sophisticated and knowledgeable, demanding more and openly comparing products, services, and sources.

■ Changes occur continuously in the nature and variety of the products and services you must offer to continue to compete.

■ Significant changes occur in the ownership or senior management of firms in your industry, which may bring in new operating or marketing philosophies.

> *Are you seeing more competition from firms outside your industry?*
>
> *Are you seeing more non-U.S. competition?*
>
> *Are your customers getting more sophisticated and knowledgeable?*
>
> *Do you have to keep changing your products or services to compete?*
>
> *Have any of your major competitors experienced significant changes in ownership or management recently?*
>
> *If the answer to any of these questions is yes, you need good CI—now!*

The experiences of three different industries—insurance, retail banking, and business services—can help put this in focus.

Insurance companies are a prime example of the growing importance of CI and have become highly sensitive to the need for a program to analyze their competitors. That sensitivity has developed for several reasons.

■ A few insurance companies have, for a number of years, consistently tracked competitive insurance policies. Expanding an existing product tracking system to track competitors was a logical step for them.

■ Due to employee mobility in the insurance industry, employees accustomed to using CI bring that experience with them to new employers.

■ Insurance companies are increasingly diversifying into non-insurance businesses, and the firms need CI to help understand new lines of business.

The Big Picture
■ ■ ■

■ Insurance companies find themselves increasingly in competition with other financial services firms, such as banks and securities brokers. Insurers are learning that they must find out about these competitors before they start losing important markets.

The *retail banking* industry's use of CI is more advanced than that used by commercial and asset-based lenders. Again, there are several historical reasons for this advancement.

■ Retail banking has become more competitive, in terms of geography, consumer sensitivity, and the number and variety of participants. For example, if a bank wants its credit card operations to be more competitive, it must understand what American Express and Sears are doing. When retail bankers have done that kind of CI, they have discovered, often to their alarm, that companies like Sears and American Express are already heavily involved in CI—with retail banks as the targets.

■ The increasing presence of non-U.S.-based banks in the U.S. markets has sensitized some retail bankers to the importance of CI, because the foreign-based parent banks have used CI for years.

■ Retail bankers are finding that they must understand and provide a greater range of products than ever before. To understand those products—whether insurance, credit card enhancements, financial planning, or brokerage services— retail bankers have had to learn about companies that are structured differently from their banks, that operate differently from banks, and where the executives may not even "think like bankers."

The growing use of CI is not limited to major industrial or financial firms. Firms in other areas, such as *business services,* are finding that their use of CI is gradually increasing. Again, there are specific reasons for this growth.

■ Business services have become more important in our service-oriented economy.

■ Business services are becoming more competitive, particularly in terms of the number and variety of participants.

■ The influx of new sources of business services makes it critical to keep a broad competitive horizon under surveillance.

■ Business services are in a period of transition. In some areas, consolidation is emerging as a trend. In others, fragmentation and specialization seem to be developing. Those service firms most sensitive to the importance of trends in these sectors already realize that CI is vital to their survival.

Competitive Information Gathering Is Already Part of Your Business

Competitive intelligence is *not* an operation separate from your normal business management. To help you, CI should be an integral part of the way you handle business each day.

Table 1.1 lists survey results about the importance of competitor monitoring activities to managers today.

In many small ways, you probably use some aspects of CI informally now. If you are at a trade show, you may stop by a competitor's exhibit to take a look at a new product line. An effective CI system, however, might have alerted you well *before* the show about the likelihood of a new product line.

CI can answer a wide variety of key business questions—ones you may think can only be handled with "hunches" or through instinct:

■ Who *are* our competitors? Who are our *potential* competitors?

Table 1.1.

Importance to Top Management of Monitoring Competitors' Activities

Rating	Percentage of Managers
Very Important	59
Fairly Important	30
Slightly Important	11
Not At All Important	0

Source: The Conference Board, Inc., *Competitive Intelligence,*
Research Report No. 913, 1988, p. 6.

■   How do our competitors see themselves? How do they see us? What information are they using?

■   What are the track records of the key people at our competitors? What are their personalities? What difference do these people make in terms of our ability to predict how competitors will react to our competitive strategy?

■   What are the short-term and long-term trends in our industry? How have our competitors responded to them in the past? How are they likely to respond to them in the future?

■   What patents or technology have our competitors or potential competitors recently obtained? What do those innovations mean to us?

■   How and where are our competitors marketing their products and services? What is their rate of success? What new directions will they probably take?

■   What markets or geographic areas won't be tapped by our competitors?

■ Can the markets and geographic sectors respond to changes in pricing, delivery terms, or warranties? Will they?

■ What are our competitors' overall plans and goals for the next two to five years in the businesses where they currently compete with us? What are their plans and goals for their other businesses and how will those affect the way they run competing businesses?

Summary

Competitive intelligence is the use of public sources to develop information about your competition, competitors, and market. Public sources include not only news articles and government data but also the press releases and other communications your competitors prepare. You are probably using CI to some extent in your day-to-day business management. Effective use of CI can help your business withstand threats from competitors, maintain or enhance your market share, and create innovative products or services that anticipate customer needs.

CI ALERT: What does this tell you?

"In January 1989, John Deere will introduce the largest number of new agricultural products ever announced at one time in its 151-year history. These products include an all-new generation of combines; updated row-crop tractors over 100 horsepower, including John Deere's first 200-horsepower model; a cotton picker with variable row-width flexibility; round balers; and a new series of disk harrows to expand the line of tillage tools."

Source: Deere & Company, 1988 Annual Report.

13

Notes

1. The Conference Board, Inc., *Competitive Intelligence*, Research Report No. 913, 1988, p. 17. International Science & Technology Associates specializes in developing information on Japanese industry.

2. U.S. Congress, Office of Technology Assessment, *Science, Technology and the First Amendment—Special Report*, OTA-CIT-369 (Washington, D.C.: U.S. Government Printing Office, January 1988), p. 11.

3. U.S. Congress, Office of Technology Assessment, *Science, Technology and the First Amendment—Special Report*, OTA-CIT-369 (Washington, D.C.: U.S. Government Printing Office, January 1988), p. 14, n. 37.

4. The Conference Board, Inc., *Competitive Intelligence*, Research Report No. 913, 1988, p. 7. This book frequently refers to this report for several reasons. First, it is a relatively current report on CI. Second, it reflects a comprehensive survey, in contrast to other sources that are less comprehensive. Third, most of its case studies identify the company involved, whereas other studies tend to conceal the company and the industry involved.

5. The Conference Board, Inc., *Competitive Intelligence*, Research Report No. 913, 1988, p. 6.

6. Mark Robichaux, "'Competitor Intelligence': a Grapevine to Rivals' Secrets," *The Wall Street Journal*, April 12, 1989, p. B2.

Chapter 2

How CI Can Improve Your Business

CI as an Integral Part of Management

CI can fit almost anywhere in your business and should be used by almost everyone. Paraphrasing Machiavelli:

> Executives should never have out of their thoughts this subject of competition, and when there is no significant competition, they should addict themselves more to its

15

exercise than when there is direct competition. This they can do in two ways—by action and by study.

Regarding action, executives ought above all things to keep their personnel well organized and practiced, by which executives accustom themselves to hard work and learn something about the nature of their own markets and company. Such knowledge is useful in two ways. First, executives learn to know their own market and are better able to undertake its defense. Afterwards, building on the knowledge and observation of that market, executives understand with ease any other market it may be necessary to study, so that with a knowledge of the aspect of one corporation or market executives can easily gain knowledge of others. And executives who lack this, lack the essential skill so desirable for leaders to possess, for such market expertise teaches executives to surprise their adversary, to select defense positions, to direct personnel, to engage in competition, and to assault markets to advantage.

To exercise the intellect, executives should read case studies and study there the actions of successful executives to see how they have borne themselves in competition and to examine the causes of their victories and defeats, in order to avoid the latter and imitate the former.[2]

Although Machiavelli was discussing warfare and the defense of cities, his perspective on effective competition remains useful today in thinking about the less violent, but no less aggressive, subject of effective business competition.

Where Can You Use CI?

CI data *should* be integrated into competitive analysis information and used in programs that supplement planning, mergers and acquisitions, restructuring, marketing, pricing, advertising, and research and development activities:

■ Planning: CI can provide accurate and current data on the context in which your business plan will be executed. It keeps you from falling into the dangerous, but common, trap of assuming that your competitors see the market just as you see it and will react to changes in that market just as you would.

■ Mergers and acquisitions: CI can help you spot important facts, such as interlocking directorships and critical relationships between a potential target company and its important banks, lawyers, accountants, and customers. CI can also help you to understand why a target may be willing to be acquired.

■ Restructuring activities: CI can help your planning for restructuring by showing what has worked—and failed—for others. It can also help you price assets you will sell.

■ Marketing: CI can reveal why your competitors have succeeded or failed in their marketing efforts and can provide new product ideas. In fact, according to one source, the largest single source for new consumer product ideas is an analysis of the competition.[3]

■ Pricing: CI can keep you abreast of your competition's current list prices, its terms, and what it is *actually* charging. It can also help you determine your competitor's cost structure, so you can adjust your prices most effectively.

■ Advertising: CI can help you find out how your competitors will be advertising and how much it will cost them.

■ Research and development (R & D): CI can provide an insight into your competitors' current technology, types of ongoing research, and probable resulting new products.

Each of these is discussed further in this chapter.

The Big Picture
■ ■ ■

However, CI can also be used creatively in numerous other business areas. Think about using CI throughout your company by asking questions like these:

■ Human resources: What are your competitors' payroll and salary structures? Does a key competitor have better productivity or lower employee turnover? Why?

■ Engineering: Is it important for you to know how a competitor designs and makes a key product? Who does that for the competitor—employees or consultants?

■ Sales: Would it be useful to know that your competitor's sales force is much more aggressive in New England than it is in the South? Do you know who sets prices and how?

■ Manufacturing: How can you compete when you don't even know where your competition makes its products—or if it even makes them itself? How old are your competitor's plants? Are they being upgraded—or abandoned?

The Conference Board, Inc.'s, 1988 CI survey asked over 300 companies to indicate the "Best Examples of Business Decisions Relying on Monitoring Information."[4] The top four answers were

Pricing (16%)

Strategy (15%)

New products/services (11%)

Acquisitions (6%)

Planning

The following pages cite some specific instances of how CI can help improve the way a business is operated. We will also note cases where CI helped specific businesses operate better or where CI could have helped companies to operate better. These cases are called *success and failure models*. You can learn a lot from each of them.

What does planning mean here? *Planning* has no generally accepted meaning in business. The term can encompass every management technique that deals with any future event. Other managers consider its meaning closer to scheduling. For most businesses, its meaning lies somewhere in between. The following definition summarizes what *planning* means in terms of CI.

Planning: *A process by which the mission of a business is defined, its competitive strengths (including its resources and its liabilities) are evaluated, its goals are established, its alternative courses of action are identified, its courses of action are selected from among them, and the programs, projects, and tasks necessary to achieving those goals are established.*

Clearly, planning is a process. It involves both obtaining needed information and deciding on a course of action in part based on that information.

The single most important reason for planning is that it helps you avoid managing either by reaction or by inaction. Planning does not guarantee that your business can influence events or that it will be positioned to respond rapidly to changes in the marketplace. However, the absence of any planning virtually guarantees that your business will be reactive and unable to respond to market changes.

> *Do your plans assume that your competitors view the market the same way you do? If so, you need CI to inject their reality into your plans.*

In Corporate Business Plans

Unfortunately, many corporate business plans are based on limited (or no) information about competitors and the competitive environment. Even worse, many plans make one or more of the following erroneous (but common) assumptions:

- Your competitors will continue to act in the future as they have in the past.

- Every one of your competitors, in any given situation, will behave just as you would.

- Your competitors know everything you know, but they do not know anything more than that.

- All of your competitors see the market in the same way your firm views it.

These assumptions may keep you from considering some of the surprises that occur with increasing frequency in corporations today:

- Rapid technological, social, and political changes continually impact consumers' tastes, income levels, and spending habits.

■ Globalization of companies, products, and services often means constant penetration of new markets for your venture abroad—as well as the introduction of international competitors in the United States.

■ Your competitors here and abroad can use today's rapid media services (such as commercial databases) to find and capitalize on any weaknesses in your product or service's quality, pricing, or technology.

To manage these surprises, your business planning needs to integrate competitive intelligence features in many areas. The following list summarizes core elements of business planning. Those marked with * are elements in which CI is important, and those marked ** are ones for which CI is *critical*.

Identifying opportunities*
Selecting objectives
Establishing the business context**
Identifying options*
Evaluating those options*
Selecting or modifying your options
Establishing or modifying your supporting plans
Disseminating the plan
Initiating the plan
Implementing the plan
Evaluating the plan's progress**
Getting feedback and updating the plan*

What can happen if you plan without adequate CI?

According to research done at Yale University, when the major international oil companies planned moves into the uranium industry in the 1960s and 1970s, they based their planning on data little better than mere guesses.

A Yale researcher characterized the predictions of the oil companies in this area as "base[d] on data we'd be ashamed of." For example, one oil company based a "major and costly diversification on rumors about what" a specific competitor thought uranium prices were going to be as well as on that competing firm's recruiting goal for summer students. In part because each of the firms "believed one another's apparent optimism," most moved into uranium. And, as of 1982, "most [were] getting bombed."[5]

In New and Developing Businesses
Ways to incorporate CI into traditional management planning vary slightly between established businesses and new or developing businesses. Developing business may have additional needs for CI.

Using competitive intelligence may be necessary *before* you have a business. The conclusion of those who fund start-up businesses is clear: A key to acquiring venture capital is the possession of a solid, realistic, and understandable business plan. That plan must frankly assess both your own abilities to make the business succeed and the marketplace and competition you will face. Even if you are not going outside for money to start your business, you should know these same facts.

Always assume the worst—that your competition already knows everything you have labored to find out.

As sources providing funding to new and developing businesses have confirmed, one of the most frequent shortcomings of companies looking for financial help is the absence of a complete, realistic business plan. And one of the most common elements missing from the plans they do develop is sound, current information on the business's current and potential competitors. Lenders and investors are much more willing to provide equity capital to a business that understands its current competitive position and its future market environment.

Once you have started your business, CI is necessary to *retain* your competitive position and vital to help you *increase* market share. To gather pertinent CI data, you must continually collect and analyze facts and signals about your actual and potential competition, and about today's and tomorrow's markets. Part II of this book explores strategies, techniques, and resources for finding CI data.

Another issue facing your developing business is how to generate and manage rapid growth. A great concept can cause uncontrolled growth when your business is not ready for it. And how can you really be prepared for it if you do not understand your own market? For example, if your key product's sales growth depends on the increase in the sales of a certain kind of equipment, are you prepared for the growth in your sales that a radical cut in the price of that equipment will produce? You cannot possibly be ready if you don't suspect that such a price change is coming.

The same preparedness applies to the downside. Do you know whether the makers of this equipment are threatened by a substitute technology that does not use your product? Assessing these risks can help you avoid being blind-sided and put out of business before you really get going.

Mergers and Acquisitions
In this increasingly competitive world, your business must always be aware of new opportunities to expand its operations. These opportunities may include potential merger candidates or acquisition targets, both within and outside of your industry.

Planning Stage
In the first phase of a mergers and acquisitions program, planning, CI forces you to define exactly what type of enterprise you are targeting. This definition occurs because you must focus on

23

precisely what information is needed. On more than one occasion, a merger or acquisition plan has been revised due to a demand for a clear statement of objectives of the plan and a description of the desired characteristics of the targets.

> *Your mergers and acquisitions program has three phases: planning, implementation, and execution. In which phases are you using CI now?*

For example, a few years ago, a major chemicals company used database research in its merger and acquisition program to develop information on the profitability of firms in the pigment business. The company's proposed entry into that particular business ended when the research showed that the field was less profitable than the company had believed. However, a lukewarm interest in another area, reverse-osmosis membranes, heated up after database research showed a higher than expected growth potential.[6] Thus, the use of CI early on can not only define potential targets but might well redirect the thrust of the program itself.

Implementation Stage

In the next phase of a merger and acquisition program, implementation, CI has its greatest application, both in providing general background information and in providing specific information about a particular company. For example, some databases focus specifically on particular industries, allowing you to keep current on developments in that industry. Other databases cover all industries and may be better suited to tracking industries not covered elsewhere as well as to supplementing industry-specific research. Yet other databases can provide immediate access to many local newspaper and regional business publications that are a rich source of current information on local markets and firms. The more information you have in choosing between targets and in negotiating a particular deal, the more successful your program is likely to be.

Using CI can also help you acquire significant data you may need to focus on potential mergers or acquisitions without contacting the potential target or those associated with the target firm, such as accountants, lawyers, or bankers.

As you produce profiles of potential targets, CI provides information about

■ The target's overall business strategies, policies, objectives, and perceptions of itself.

■ All products and services offered by the target.

■ The target's current—and possibly future—pricing policies and marketing plans.

■ Current sales levels.

■ The target's current technology, research, and development programs.

■ The target's financial and legal position.

■ The target's competitors.

■ How the target is seen by its competitors and customers.

Execution Stage

CI is less vital in the final stage of a merger and acquisition program, the execution of the transaction, because this phase involves the execution and implementation of the agreed-on plan. By that point, CI has completed its mission of providing useful information.

25

The Big Picture
■ ■ ■

Learning About Suitors of Your Company
CI can fulfill another role in mergers and acquisitions, however. CI can provide meaningful data on companies that are considering a merger with your firm or an offer to acquire your company. Of course, you can expect to receive information from these suitors about their current activities and past track record, but you should remember what you are being told is what they want you to know—nothing more.

Consider using CI to find out the following:

■ The suitor's overall strategies, policies, and objectives for your market.

■ How the suitor is perceived by its current competitors and customers.

■ The suitor's current and past financial record, as well as that of its principal owners and investors.

■ The suitor's methods of handling acquisitions.

■ The suitor's track record on dealing with acquired businesses and their officers and owners.

Restructuring
As a concept, restructuring is very broad. In general, the goal of a restructuring is to improve the competitive position, profitability, and manageability of a business. This can be accomplished by one or more of the following:

■ Acquisitions
■ Divestitures
■ Internal reorganizations
■ Joint ventures
■ Management buyouts
■ Recapitalizations
■ Split-offs
■ Technology sharing

Before your company undertakes or even plans a restructuring, know about the strategies and practices of your competitors. These facts are vital to optimal restructuring. CI can be a source of critical information in any restructuring program.

If restructuring involves a merger or acquisition, the points covered in the previous discussion apply. In addition, you should use CI to obtain the following kinds of data:

■ The future size and shape of markets that you have designated as your core businesses, as well as how your competitors view the future of the markets in which you will be active. These two information spheres not only help you set a fair price on the assets you are shedding but also confirm that the decision to restructure is sound.

■ Whether any competitors are in the market for the assets you are divesting. CI can help you determine whether competitors are considering divesting similar assets or ones that might complement those you are retaining. This can impact the market price for your assets as well as tell you if any asset swap is possible and beneficial.

■ Ways that other firms have restructured and what results they have had. This background enables you to learn from their successes as well as from their mistakes.

■ Potential buyers for troubled or peripheral operations that may initially appear hard to sell. For example, reports indicate some non-U.S. firms have a history of buying up certain moribund "smokestack" companies seen by their U.S. owners as of dubious value. To the new owners, these firms represent a way to enter the U.S. market. In addition, to the new owners, the current low profit margins are acceptable.

CI can help in other restructuring areas as well. For example, one conglomerate wanted to establish the cost of capital to be allocated to a subsidiary. The firm used online databases to discover the cost of capital for companies in similar businesses. With this data, the firm concluded that its subsidiary, which operated in a high-risk business, did not have as high a rate of return on capital as its competitors had. As a result, the conglomerate sold the subsidiary.[7]

The goal of restructuring should be to get "lean and mean." That process is obviously enhanced by sound CI. Too many restructurings, both planned and preemptive, have actually been caused by a lack of good CI. The lack of knowledge about competitors and their intentions and capabilities was at the root of the problems of the troubled company in the first place. Redeploying assets without acquiring a sensitivity for the importance of CI often results in a stronger company, but one that is still operating in the dark.

Marketing

With CI you help your company's marketing efforts by learning from the experience of others—both their successes and their failures.

For example, the Bank Marketing Association (BMA) gives awards for excellence in marketing. Each applicant for the award submits a package describing the nominated program. You can get the materials from BMA directly. You can also access a lot of the information online through BMA's database, FINIS. These materials let you look at and learn from a successful marketing campaign.

You can always learn from failure. The FINIS database also indexes student papers dealing with marketing financial services. These can include startling information. For example, one paper analyzed a marginally successful direct mail campaign run by a large bank to sell lines of credit. The paper included the following information:

■ The identity of the bank and information, including its size and the number of consumer accounts.

■ The sources for the mailing lists it used, plus profiles of the types of names provided by each list.

■ An analysis of how the bank purged the lists of names of consumers who did not meet the bank's marketing profile. By outlining *what criteria* were used to purge the names, the paper indirectly disclosed the standards the bank used for preclearing the lines of credit it was offering.

■ Copies of all direct mail advertisements and supporting advertising from newspapers and radio, plus the name of the marketing firm on the project.

■ A description of the entire campaign as planned and executed. Data for the mailing included the anticipated response rate, the size, and the actual response rate. It also provided a detailed analysis of the business actually produced.

CI CLOSEUP: "Window Shopping"

Many Americans believe that the Japanese have become the most advanced nation in terms of management techniques and productivity, but the Japanese do not share that optimism. In fact, U.S. service businesses, such as department stores, are the focus of many visiting delegations from Japan. These visitors seek information on subjects ranging from "creative flair" to efficient distribution systems. Reportedly, one of the most frequent targets of on-site research is Bloomingdale's. According to a Bloomingdale's spokesperson, the Japanese "study the clothes. They study the displays. They study the windows. They are curious about our cash registers, our inventory control. I would say there is nothing about Bloomingdale's that they're not interested in."[8]

The Big Picture

Uses of CI in marketing are not limited to plans you develop for existing products. Next you will see how valuable CI can be in marketing new products.

New Product Development

The new product development process typically involves the following major stages:

1. Generating an idea or concept.

2. Isolating its most promising features.

3. Selecting new products from the promising concepts.

4. Developing and testing the product.

5. Determining production costs and approximate pricing.

6. Market testing.

7. Forecasting production needs and revenues.

8. Developing marketing strategies.

9. Introducing the product.

10. Monitoring the product's progress and competitor responses.

The product development process can be helped by good CI at almost every stage.

> *Did you know that one of the most important sources of new-product ideas today is an analysis of your competition's product line?*

For example, the potential importance of CI in developing new products can be seen in data collected about the origins of new-product ideas for both consumer and industrial products, the very first step. According to one report, the largest source of new-product ideas for consumer products was an analysis of the competition. This was true in 38 percent of the cases. Published information provided the new idea in 11.4 percent of the cases.[9]

For industrial products, the same survey showed that an analysis of the competition was the second most productive source of new product ideas, being cited in 27 percent of the cases. In addition, new-product ideas were gleaned from published information in 7.9 percent of the cases.

Product Design Data

You can, however, use CI for much more than merely identifying new-product ideas. You can provide information to product designers that has previously not been used in product development because people thought it was difficult or impossible to gather efficiently. Examples include

■ The status of key technology to produce or support the product.

■ The track record for similar products, including the reasons for those results.

■ Potential sources of competition in a new market.

■ The likely responses of major competitors to the new product introduction.

Pricing

A common use for CI is in determining pricing. Pricing has two elements: the book or list price offered and the actual price charged, which reflects concessions, discounts, and special terms.

To learn the list or book price, simply try calling your competitor. Also, check with your marketing personnel. Ask them if any of your distributors handle competitor products. If so, they may be able to provide you with a price list. Do not forget local and national trade shows. At these meetings, you may find suggested prices openly displayed, and price lists often are distributed on request.

To learn the actual price, including special terms, turn first to your marketing personnel. Interviews and regular monitoring of their efforts may help you collect fragmentary comments from customers and from lost sales opportunities. Piecing the comments together may help you to assemble a picture of the pricing policies and discounts used by your competitors.

In addition, you can also use CI to help determine your competitor's cost structure, which in turn enables you to estimate its pricing or profit structure. For example, you can find out whether your competitor has a state contract. Get a copy of the contract and the bid documents. Studying them should reveal what the competitor is being paid. Also, you should be able to determine exactly what deliverables and terms the competitor provided. Putting the data together should let you estimate the competition's costs, pricing structure, and perhaps even the profit margin.

Advertising

Advertising efforts can use CI in two main areas: determining what competitors are doing and learning how well they are doing it. Knowing about your competitors' advertising campaigns and successes enables you to

■ Determine whether a new advertising campaign is a test, a feint, or a major assault.

■ Anticipate the impact of a new campaign on your markets and customers in time to take defensive action.

■ Evaluate the success of a competitor's current marketing efforts to determine whether that competitor's market is actually vulnerable to your penetration efforts.

32

■ Decide whether your competitor's campaign may be too costly to be kept in place indefinitely; if so, you can wait it out and avoid unnecessary spending in response to it.

Discovering Competitors' Advertising Programs

How can you find out what your competitors are doing? If possible, consider becoming a "customer." Regular customers receive mailings and other advertising approaches, which give you direct means of tracking advertising as it is released.

Have you ever considered becoming one of your competitor's customers?

Another option is to clip the competitor's advertisements and any articles in local newspapers about the firm. That may mean subscribing to publications used by competitors to reach their customers as well as to newspapers and business publications covering your competitor's national or regional headquarters. Clipping is something you can do, hire a clipping service to do, or have your advertising or marketing agency do for you.

For larger competitors, follow announcements by advertising and marketing firms in advertising industry journals, in addition to those in your own trade press. There are several reasons for looking at the advertising/marketing press in addition to announcements in your own trade press:

■ The advertising/marketing press issues publications more frequently, so that the lead time between an event and its report is shorter than in the trade press.

■ The story in the advertising/marketing press may be based on materials and interviews from the agency rather than from the client. This gives you a different perspective on the event. Also, the agency may tell you more about the competitor and its overall advertising strategy, because the source is talking to his or her peers.

■ Articles from the advertising/marketing press are more likely to be captured in online databases than are trade press articles, making your research faster.

Uncovering the Results of Advertising Campaigns

How can you find out what works well for others in your industry? First, find out who your competitors are. Then, track their most successful marketing campaigns, analyze their most important deals, and study their activity in particularly important markets.

There are numerous ways to do this analysis. Asking your competitors is an option, of course, but you cannot count on being told the truth. Your competitors may not want to be open with you, but they may have been more open to others already. For that reason, surveying trade and local press is a good tactic. Also, find out whether any commercial services monitor aspects of the industry or transactions in which you are interested. For example, if your competitors are commercial lenders, you can check reports of commercial services that monitor larger loans. These reports typically include the terms and profitability of the loans, and they may be a good way to check how aggressive a competitor is in making loans.

Another alternative is to tap the expertise of trade associations. This source is not limited to trade associations that include you and your competitors. Rather, seek out trade associations that serve potential *customers and clients*. You may find that associate membership in such associations may be one way your competitors are now reaching a key client base. To reach that client base, competitors communicate with that group. Once you identify with whom they want to communicate, you can begin to capture and analyze those communications, such as advertisements, interviews, and even speeches. And, from there you can begin to deduce their advertising and marketing strategies.

Identifying New Markets and Customers

CI can be valuable in identifying potential new markets and advertising avenues. One basic, inexpensive way CI can assist is by identifying potential new customers once you isolate key facts about them. For example, using online business directory databases, you could quickly develop lists of the following specific markets:

- All chemical businesses with over $100 million in sales and with plants in Ohio.

- The names and locations of every hospital in rural counties in a five-state area.

- The address and telephone number of every law firm in Pennsylvania with more than one office.

- Each of the plants currently making consumer goods for a major manufacturer, as distinguished from its distribution centers.

- All health food stores in counties with fewer than 1 million people.

CI can produce substantially more sophisticated information to help you find new customers. For example, in many states, information on most major state contracts is public information. Use these records, some of which are in the form of databases, to discover new government customers by isolating state agencies that purchase the goods or services you can supply. This process can yield data for potential private-sector customers by locating companies that could use your product or service and that already have state contracts.

Another approach is to put yourself in the place of your potential customers and to think the way they do. Specifically, that means determining where and when they make public anything about themselves.

The Big Picture
■ ■ ■

With this technique you should bear in mind that, because your potential customers must advertise to reach their own markets, you can find your potential customers by identifying these end markets and working backward. A way to do this might be to check out publications that offer the products and services of *your* potential customers to *their* markets, by using a source such as the Standard Rate & Data Service Inc.'s *Print Media Editorial Calendars*. Stories and advertisements about new products and companies can generate profitable leads for you.

Another approach is to determine what data these potential customers release and who collects it. If you are selling a product that can be used by companies in a particular industry and you wish to focus on a specific geographic area, consider contacting the local industrial development agency serving that area. The agency may be able to provide you with a list of existing as well as new industrial or manufacturing businesses of the type you have targeted.

Research and Development
CI has particular relevance to R & D activities. Using CI techniques in areas of technology and research, you can determine the following:

■ Current manufacturing methods and processes in use in the United States and overseas.

■ Key patents and proprietary technology being used or acquired by competitors.

■ Your competitors' access to, use of, and dependence on outside technology, as well as their need for new technology.

■ The size and capabilities of competitors' research staff, including the names of key personnel.

■ Types and levels of research and development being conducted by competitors, as well as estimates of current and future expenditures for research and development.

CI CLIP

"You can spend years developing a technology, only to find someone else patented it three years ago."

Executive vice president, Enzo Biochem Inc.[10]

Among the sources to which you would look for data to help you determine CI opportunities for R & D are

- Papers presented at society meetings and technical journal articles.

- Professional and industry association meetings and seminars.

- Interviews with your own personnel who are in contact with competitors or competitors' suppliers and customers.

- Discussions with members of the academic research community.

- Public records, such as building permits or licenses from environmental agencies.

- Promotional materials and product specifications prepared by competitors.

- Reverse engineering of competitor products or services.

- Patent and trademark filings, both in the United States and elsewhere.

The Big Picture

Summary

This chapter explored specific applications of competitive intelligence in the areas of planning, mergers and acquisitions, restructuring, marketing, pricing, advertising, and R & D. All of these business areas can benefit from consistent use of good CI.

CI ALERT: What does this tell you?

"The Quaker Oats Co. will jump into database marketing starting in September with an initial budget in excess of $18 million.

"A three-wave mail campaign will total more than 54 million packages. It will be followed by a November mailing and then one in February 1991, according to Michael Bronner, chief executive officer, Bronner Slosberg Associates, the agency handling the account. . . .

"Each mailing will have a different promotional partner and circulation of more than 18 million packages."

Source: DM News, January 15, 1990.

Notes

1. Brian Dumaine, "Corporate Spies Snoop to Conquer," *Fortune*, November 7, 1988, pp. 68-69, 72, 76.

2. Based on Machiavelli, *The Prince*, trans. W. K. Marriott, Chapter 14, New York: Everyman's Library, 1958.

3. Suzanne Lainson, *Crash Course,* New York: Putnam Publishing Group, 1985.

4. The Conference Board, Inc., *Competitive Intelligence,* Research Report No. 913, 1988, p. 20.

5. Paul Solman and Thomas Friedman, *Life & Death on the Corporate Battlefield,* New York: Signet Books, 1984, pp. 146-49.

6. "Want a Peek at Your Competitors' Data Base?," *Philadelphia Inquirer,* May 4, 1986.

7. "Want a Peek at Your Competitors' Data Base?," *Philadelphia Inquirer,* May 4, 1986.

8. John Burgess, "Japanese Still Learning from U.S.," *The Sunday Call,* November 20, 1988, pp. D1, D6.

9. Suzanne Lainson, *Crash Course,* New York: Putnam Publishing Group, 1985.

10. Doreen Mangan, "None of Your Secrets Are Safe," *Venture,* February 1988, pp. 61-67.

Chapter 3

Ethical and Legal Issues

CI CLIP

"The difference between a moral man and a man of honor is that the latter regrets a discreditable act, even when it has worked and he has not been caught."

H. L. Mencken, Prejudices.

As the art (or science) of CI develops, it is becoming more complex, a more pervasive part of the corporate environment, more efficient and more effective. But with this maturity also come some difficult ethical questions.

The Big Picture
■ ■ ■

> ### *How would you answer the following:*
>
> ■ *Is it proper for you to contact your opposite number at a competitor?*
>
> ■ *What should you do if you come across data on a competitor that should not have been made public? Use it? Ignore it? Let your competitor know about it?*
>
> ■ *Should you produce and manage disinformation? Should you suggest that your company begin to do it?*
>
> ■ *If a defensive CI assignment reveals to you that your company may be doing something improper, what should you do?*
>
> ■ *Where do you draw the line between the privacy of your employees' communications with outsiders and the need to protect your firm against the CI efforts of competitors?*

You have to be very careful to avoid crossing either legal or ethical boundaries when you collect and develop CI. Keep in mind that there is a distinct, critical difference between industrial espionage and CI. Industrial espionage involves breaking the law to collect data. Such data ranges from stealing samples at trade shows to illegally accessing (or "hacking") computer files.

A gray area exists between industrial espionage and CI where you may consider taking actions that are not illegal but that are questionable or immoral. Typical of such actions are widely different activities such as going through a competitor's trash at the curb or giving a competitor's employee an employment interview only to glean product or company information.

42

At present, your CI research is not subject to any special legal controls, nor is CI controlled by a quasi-governmental peer review or licensing system, such as those that govern trading securities or lawyer-client relations. That does not mean that those involved in CI may not find themselves involved in a formal ethical or legal system in the future.

The legal and ethical issues that you face in collecting and using CI arise from one or more of the following three areas:

■ What kind of raw data you are trying to collect and eventually get.

■ How you got that data.

■ What you will be doing with that data.

If you look at any particular problem in these terms, you should be able to identify the major legal issues and ethical considerations involved. How you handle the legal issues depends on what the law requires and what is seen as a violation of the law. How you handle the ethical questions depends on your personal value system and the way you see your public and private obligations. The following discussions identify the problem, but you must ultimately come up with your own solution.

One word of caution: Do not be influenced by what you think your competitors are doing or would approve of doing. One study suggests that people involved in collecting CI generally view their competitors very negatively. They believe that a competitor will go to much greater, less ethical, lengths to collect CI than they or their employer would.[1]

What Kind of Data Should You Question?

It is important to sort raw CI data into facts that are public information (as discussed in Chapter 1) and facts or plans that may have come from classified or confidential sources. If you cannot trace the questionable data to legal sources, this section explains the risks and liabilities you may incur.

> *Insider trading and the use of insider information do not affect CI—yet. The former deals with how corporate executives use nonpublic information to make illegal profits on the stock market. The latter deals with how others—outsiders—get and use such information. The easiest ways to protect yourself from both pitfalls are not to use any CI for stock trading and not to give CI to anyone else who might be tempted to use such information illegally.*

When you have finished considering the legal and ethical problems involved with CI, do not despair. The key here is to use common sense. As has been said in other contexts, don't do anything you would not want to see mentioned in a newspaper headline, and you will be safe.

Classified Government Materials

Your CI program might yield government materials that are classified. The only way you can accurately tell this is to note whether the documents are marked, usually with a stamp, as "classified," "secret," and so on. Your obligation here, from both a legal and an ethical point, is pretty straightforward: Immediately contact a security officer for the relevant government agency and tell the officer what has happened. At the same time, make sure that the materials are secure, so that they are not distributed any further, and turn them over to the government authorities promptly.

You should also cooperate in any efforts to find out how such materials became public. Any other actions may place you in danger of violating U.S. laws on espionage and related crimes.

Convictions of violations of these laws can carry with them prison sentences, severe fines, and even a forfeiture of assets.

How do materials inadvertently become public? There are any number of ways, but the key is generally a combination of human error and technological ability:

■ Confidential materials are misfiled by transposing a file number.

■ Unrelated materials are accidentally clipped together before being handled.

■ Files marked for copying are mismarked.

■ Too many pages are copied and distributed.

■ A telephone number is mistranscribed, and materials are faxed to the wrong destination.

How can you tell whether something has accidentally become public? Here are a few hints.

■ Some part of the document carries government markings such as *confidential, classified, restricted access,* or *embargoed for release before. . . .*

■ The document includes notes such as *Copy #3 of 20 copies,* or *Copy for. . . only.*

■ The document is marked *Do not duplicate.*

■ Some parts of the document clearly do not relate to other pages, such as finding the text of a memo on audits of farm subsidies in a file dealing with changes in postal rates.

■ The materials are marked as *Confidential business materials* in a file obtained from a government agency.

■ The materials originate from an agency or bureau that does not usually release data, such as the Internal Revenue Service.

■ The materials deal with a subject about which data is not usually disclosed, such as a pending (but unapproved) patent.

If you locate a patent and then read it, you are not violating any laws by either getting it or having it. It is public information. (Of course, if you infringe it, you have crossed the line.)

However, if you receive information on a pending patent, you may be in trouble, depending on how you obtained it and from whom. For example, if you obtain information from the Patent Office's files, you may be dealing with a theft from a government agency. If you pay a former employee of your competitor to get it, knowing that he or she is bound by a contract barring such leaks, you could be facing a lawsuit for inducing a breach of contract, or even criminal charges for accessory to theft.

Confidential Materials/Trade Secrets

When you obtain data from a private source, legal and ethical questions can arise if the data is stolen or has been released by an employee or former employee in violation of a confidentiality agreement. In either case, you are dealing with what are known as *trade secrets* or *proprietary information*. In general, unless a trade secret has been patented, it is not a violation of law to possess it. The violation, if any, lies in how you got it:

■ If you obtained trade secrets by accident that were stolen by someone else, you could still face the criminal charge of receiving stolen property.

■ If the material was provided in violation of a confidentiality agreement, the person disclosing it faces a civil lawsuit for breach of contract.

■ If you aided in that breach of contract or sought to have the provider breach a contract, you could also face a lawsuit seeking damages for inducing the breach of contract.

■ If you received the data innocently, you still could face a lawsuit forcing you to return the data and preventing you from using it or distributing it.

Government materials may be confidential as well, even if they are not classified. For example, several years ago, some U.S. Department of Commerce employees were fired following investigations into the premature release of sensitive economic data. It turned out that these employees used inside knowledge about economic projections to buy bond futures and profit from a bond rally they expected to occur after the official information was released. Department sources indicated that, in at least one instance, this information was passed to an outsider, who also profited from it.[2]

How Might You Get Confidential Data?

The way in which you obtain CI data affects both your legal responsibilities and your ethical obligations.

Purposeful Search

Looking at the ways of obtaining your data that were just discussed, it is obvious that if you purposefully seek out the data, you might be committing a crime. For example, if the material you obtain is classified U.S. government data, the crime might be an espionage offense. If it is confidential U.S. government data, the crime may be aiding and abetting a federal employee to commit a crime. If the data is stolen from a private firm, the crimes might be theft or receiving stolen property.

Also, remember that obtaining any kind of data by theft is a crime, even if that data could have been obtained legally.

The Big Picture
■ ■ ■

CI CLOSEUP: "Competitors' Proposals"
One firm in the travel business was offered all of its competitors' proposals on a large, multiyear contract by a customer. The firm was advised to take them. The consultant who advised the firm to do this indicated that if this were a classified project such as an aerospace contract, "that would be a different story." He also noted that the firm "had to wonder what information [it] would give this customer in the future."[3]

Accidental Receipt
If you *accidentally* receive materials whose release involves or could involve a crime, such as confidential government materials or company plans that are clearly stolen, the fact that your participation is accidental is significant only in one instance—if you *immediately* return the materials to the proper source. Once you hold onto them, use them, or pass them on to others, you have the same exposure as if you had purposefully sought and obtained them.

Has a competitor used false pretenses to get critical CI from you?

False Pretenses
CI is sometimes developed by people who misrepresent who they are or exactly what they are doing. A famous case of this occurred in 1988 when a group of MBA students conducted some class

research sponsored by two heavy equipment dealers. The students contacted other heavy equipment dealers and identified themselves only as working on a class project. What these manufacturers did not know was that the results of the study would be provided to the study's sponsors—their competitors.

The firms surveyed by the students were quite cooperative in their responses. Some provided detailed, nonpublic data on inventory levels, sales volumes, advertising expenditures, and potential new products.

When questioned after the details of the project became public, one of the competitors who took part in the study stated that not all of the data the students collected could have been obtained through "normal channels," that is, the public channels its competitors would normally have access to. "I wouldn't have given out that type of stuff [such as data on inventory levels] if I knew it was going to someone other than students."[4]

Violating a Confidential Relationship

As banking and legal professionals become more intimately involved in business transactions, they gain access to more and more business information, much of which is competitively valuable. When bankers and attorneys are faced with a need for data to help a current client or with a request for data on a client from an outsider, they must resist the impulse to provide data given to them under attorney-client privilege.

The problem of the violation of a confidential relationship can arise in contexts other than conflicts of interest. For example, banks possess substantial amounts of raw and processed data on their clients, ranging from average account balances through financial statements to copies of tax returns. Yet, on many occasions, business researchers are told to contact a bank for raw data on a target competitor. It is not improper to ask for data from the bank. What may be improper is the bank's sharing some of the data that it has with a third party without the client's express consent.

49

CI CLOSEUP: "Confidentiality"

The facts of one case illustrate how important it is for clients and their lawyers to exercise great care in handling confidential data.

A major law firm (The Firm) represented an oil and barge company (Old Client). In 1987, The Firm dropped Old Client to represent seven of Old Client's competitors (New Clients). Before ending representation of Old Client, two of The Firm's partners discussed "confidential business stratagems" with Old Client on the eve of an expected labor strike facing New Clients. These two partners later disclosed information from that meeting to a third partner of The Firm, who represented New Clients.

A judge ruled that The Firm had breached the rules of professional conduct governing lawyers, violating the attorney-client privilege. The issue was not whether the competitors learned of Old Client's strategies; it was that the attorneys for Old Client disclosed "sensitive aspects" of Old Client's business strategy to the third partner, who was representing Old Client's competitors. There is no indication whether this data was actually disclosed to New Clients.[5]

How Might You Improperly Use Confidential Data?

Even if your competitive intelligence comes from nonclassified, nonconfidential data and you obtain it from public sources, the way you use the data may incur ethical or legal problems.

Unauthorized Disclosure

If you are covered by a contract with your employer containing a nondisclosure agreement, and you disclose data you have located or information you have generated while covered by that contract, you may have violated that agreement. Even if you do not have an agreement that includes that sort of clause, ethically you owe it to your employer to keep confidential any critical information you receive as part of your job.

Libel and Invasion of Privacy

Concepts of libel and invasion of privacy are a part of the tort law, the body of law that governs injuries to persons and their rights to damages.

Libel: *Something false that also defames another's reputation.*

Tort law holds that a person who publishes libelous material about another may be forced to pay damages for that action. Businesses as well as individuals can be libeled. In tort law you do not have to be the person who created the libel to be held responsible for defaming someone's reputation. Publication includes repeating the libel and circulating it to others, if the person repeating the libel knew or should have known that the information being circulated was defamatory.

51

The Big Picture
■ ■ ■

The significance of libel for CI activities is that you and your employer could face a libel action if you repeat or circulate defamatory materials about a person or business, even if you did not create the defamation.

> *How have you handled potentially defamatory data in the past?*

You can have a similar problem in cases involving potential invasions of privacy. Although CI research generally does not involve detailed inquiries into personal backgrounds such that you should automatically be concerned about invasions of privacy, you might become accidentally involved.

Your involvement may be a result of receiving and using data that is later found in a lawsuit to have constituted an invasion of an individual's privacy. For example, you might prepare a CI report that contains substantial personal data released in a local magazine's investigation of a company's owners. At some later date, in a lawsuit, a court might find that the article constituted an invasion of privacy. What are your liabilities for having used and relied on that article? Unfortunately, no one knows.

Anticompetitive Actions

In some cases managers express concern that CI somehow violates our antitrust laws, particularly when it involves matters related to pricing. In fact, what is important in deciding whether your CI violates the antitrust acts is not necessarily the specific data you collected, but rather the purpose for which you collected it.

If you obtain data on a competitor's pricing to fix prices or divide up the market in concert with a competitor, then antitrust issues apply. On the other hand, if you are collecting the same data with intent to use it to compete more effectively and aggressively, you probably do not have an antitrust problem.

Sample Ethics Policy

As an example of some of the current thinking about handling CI ethical issues, Exhibit 3.1 shows a draft set of standards adapted from standards published by *The Information Advisor* to provoke your thinking. This ethics policy is not offered as a solution but merely to help you focus on the real-world problems you will face in determining the legality and morality of your CI data.

Summary

The primary ethical and legal concerns in competitive intelligence involve the types of data you obtain, the methods used to obtain them, and the ways that you put the data to work. Kinds of CI data that can cause ethical and legal problems encompass classified government materials and private companies' confidential materials such as trade secrets.

Methods of obtaining your CI should avoid purposeful searches for confidential or classified information, obtaining such information under false pretenses, and leaking confidential information among professionals such as bankers or lawyers.

Unethical or illegal ways that data can be used include unauthorized disclosure of information covered by a nondisclosure agreement, libelous material or information obtained by interfering with a person's privacy, and violating antitrust laws by using CI to fix prices or collude with competitors in pricing.

A Competitive Intelligence Ethics Policy

I. What Is Ethical Behavior?

Ethics is not easy to define. However, one might apply the golden rule of "do unto others" as a guideline. For this particular issue, we can state the golden rule as, "If you were the recipient of the information-gathering activity you are considering, would you feel wronged or done an injustice?" Another, simpler question to ask is, "Would I have any problem reading about my activity in tomorrow's newspaper?" With these guidelines in mind, the following research activities, we think, can be classified as ethical/appropriate or unethical/inappropriate.

II. What Is Ethical and Appropriate Data-Gathering?

- *Gathering information by consulting publicly available information (such as trade magazines, association reports, brokerage reports, and online databases.*
- *Gathering information by conducting interviews with knowledgeable sources, if those sources are informed of the following facts:*
  - *the name and affiliation of the researcher.*
  - *the fact that the research is being conducted for a client. This is done so that if the source decides to proceed, it will be with informed consent, fully aware of the action he or she is taking.*

Extra care in following these guidelines should be taken when the source is a direct competitor.

NOTE: We do not believe it is necessary or proper to identify the name of the client for whom the research is being conducted; however, the source should be aware that the research is being done for a specific client, as opposed to, say, an industry-wide market study. This *is* relevant. We will ask for permission at the end of the conversation to identify the firm and provide the information collected directly to our client. If the client does not wish his or her firm to be directly identified, we will explore more general methods of identification (for example, using terms such as *a local pharmaceutical firm* or *a Fortune 100 health care facility*).

Exhibit 3.1: Typical CI Ethics Policy

III. What Is Unethical and Inappropriate Data Gathering?

■ *Pressing for any proprietary information the source is uncomfortable in discussing or revealing.*

■ *Misrepresenting the identity of the researcher or the purpose of the research project by*

- *outright deception, lying, or telling of untrue statements.*

- *by deliberately omitting relevant facts or by stating half-truths in order to cloud the fact that the data is being gathered for competitive purposes. The following are examples:*

  —hiring a student to perform research in order to say, "I'm a student doing research."

  —describing a competitive analysis as a "national survey," "nationwide study," and so on to deceive the source into thinking his or her information will be used only in aggregate in a national study.

  —using any other phrase or combination of words that, although conceivably accurate on its face, actually works as a whole to paint a misleading picture of the research project.

NOTE: It is acceptable to call a direct competitor to ask for a publicly available document, such as an annual report without identifying the purpose of the research up front. The reason is that the firm, by creating and offering to disseminate these documents upon request, has implicitly given its permission that this information will be made available. We will not knowingly take advantage of lower-level employees to disclose information they might not have known would harm their firm. Therefore, we will make an effort to contact someone at the manager level or above.

The common denominator that differentiates ethical data-gathering actions from unethical ones is that the ethical activities do not involve any deliberate deception. The use of deception creates a situation where the interviewee might unwittingly take an action harming his or her interests, and such an action would likely not have been taken had the true reasons for the research project been known.

Source: The Information Advisor, *copyright 1989 by the Winters Group, New York. Reprinted with permission. All rights reserved.*

Exhibit 3.1: *(continued)*

CI ALERT: What does this tell you?

"A business newsletter, ordered . . . to halt publication of an article containing confidential information about a major accounting firm [Ernst & Young], sent out a special edition Friday with the story.

"The move came one day after a . . . state appellate judge ruled that the information, already published by The New York Times, could not be kept sealed by a lower court. . . .

"Ernst & Young contended that the information in the articles was proprietary, and the firm's lawyers compared it with Coca-Cola's secret formula. . . .

"Among other things, the articles said Ernst & Whinney partners take home roughly 65 percent of profits earned jointly with Arthur Young for the next three years, while Arthur Young's partners share the rest."

Source: The Associated Press, January 19, 1990.

Notes

1. William Cohen and Helena Czepiec, "The Role of Ethics in Gathering Corporate Intelligence," *Journal of Business Ethics* 7, 1988, pp. 199-203.

2. "Leaks of Economic Data Punished by Commerce," *The Morning Call*, August 21, 1986, p. B8.

3. Craig Mellow, "The Best Source of Competitive Intelligence," *Sales & Marketing Management*, December 1989, p. 28.

4. Clare Ansberry, "For These M.B.A.s, Class Became Exercise in Corporate Espionage," *The Wall Street Journal*, March 22, 1988, p. 1.

5. Milo Geyelin, "Pepper Hamilton Is Cited by Judge in Ethics Violation," *The Wall Street Journal*, April 24, 1989, p. B4.

Part II

Finding Information
About Your Competitors

Chapter 4
An Overview of the CI Process

Chapter 5
What Do You Need to Know?

Chapter 6
Finding the Information You Need

Chapter 7
Developing Research Strategies and Techniques

Chapter 8
Specific CI Techniques

Chapter 4

An Overview of the CI Process

CI CLIP

"The sales force has current information [on the competition]. What's available on a secondary basis is history, which is sometimes ancient history."

Director of Intelligence Operations, Educational Testing Service.[1]

The CI Process

The CI process can be divided into four basic phases and one overriding process. Exhibit 4.1 provides a checklist for the CI process.

The CI Process: A Checklist

Phase I. Establishing Your CI Needs

1. *Identify your targets.*

2. *Determine what specific information you need.*

3. *Establish who will get and use the finished CI.*

4. *Decide which of several assignments are most important and which must be done first.*

5. *Decide when you need the CI for it to still be useful.*

6. *Review what you think your CI needs are in light of results of the other three phases.*

Phase II. Collecting the Raw Data You Need

1. *Identify the most likely sources for that raw data.*

2. *Develop research strategies and techniques.*

3. *Arrange to get the raw data, either on a regular basis or on a one-time basis.*

4. *Review your data collection efforts in light of results of the other three phases.*

Phase III. Evaluating and Analyzing the Raw Data

1. *Establish the reliability of the sources of the raw data you obtained.*

Exhibit 4.1: Summary of Phases in the CI Process

60

2. *Estimate the accuracy of the raw data you have.*

3. *Make sure the data is relevant to your CI needs.*

4. *Analyze the raw data.*

   a. Identify and deal with misinformation.

   b. Identify and deal with disinformation.

   c. Anticipate how your competitor thinks, based on what it has done.

   d. Draw conclusions.

5. *Conduct supplemental data collection efforts, if necessary.*

6. *Review your evaluation and analysis in light of results from the other three phases.*

Phase IV. Preparing, Presenting, and Using Your Resulting CI

1 *Format the results so the CI is readable, understandable, and useful.*

2. *Integrate the CI into your business decision making.*

3. *Make sure the CI is kept secure.*

4. *Review the way you prepare and use the CI in light of results in operations from the other three phases.*

Exhibit 4.1: *(continued)*

Finding Information About Your Competitors
■ ■ ■

1. *Establishing your CI needs.* This means that you both recognize the need for CI and define what CI you need. It also means considering what type of issue (strategic or tactical) is motivating the project, what you want to answer with the CI, who else may be using it, and how it will ultimately be used.

2. *Collecting the raw data you need.* You may have to decide who should be performing the CI (you, a CI professional, the person who will be using the CI, or some combination of people). You should by this point have a realistic understanding of any constraints you face in carrying out this assignment (such as time, financial, organizational, informational, and legal), to identify the specific competitors or markets you are checking on. Identify the data sources that are most likely to produce reliable, useful data.

3. *Evaluating and analyzing the raw data.* In this phase, the data you collected is evaluated and analyzed and is transformed into CI. This might involve comparing the data you found with data from other sources, integrating your conclusions from the data with other CI, or measuring the results of your CI against predetermined benchmarks.

4. *Preparing, presenting, and using the results.* The CI may have to be distributed to those who asked for it and, in some cases, to others who might profit from having it. The final form of the CI, plus its security, are important considerations.

We will cover each of these phases in the chapters that follow. However, there is one additional element that runs through and really connects all of the four phases of CI. That is the need to continually monitor what you have done and how you have done it. Your goal is to provide feedback to every other phase of the process and thus to improve both the product of an individual assignment as well as the entire CI process as you use it. Feedback to and from each phase is essential. For example, a change in your job description or in that of those to whom you are giving

62

the CI could mean that you have to change the kind of data you are collecting or the way in which you are presenting your results. Difficulty in collecting important data, if identified in time, may mean that you have to reconsider the type of data you are seeking or even reconsider the specific targets, despite the fact you may be in the middle of a project.

If you find out, for example, that regular updates of a CI report you are preparing might be wanted, you should think about changing the way you are collecting data now, so that you leave lines of contact in place for the future. This may mean making sure you spot sources of data that might have key data in the future, even if they do not now have anything you can use.

Another topic is related to the CI process in operation: defending against your competitors' CI efforts directed at you. What you learn to do in your own CI activities will help sensitize you to what your competitors are or might be doing to you. This topic is covered fully in Chapter 15, so you will have already become familiar with CI in operation before you explore this topic.

Summary

The initial phase of competitive intelligence information seeking is to establish your information needs. Decide at this point who the targets are, what intelligence you require, to whom information should be distributed in your company, which priorities are greatest, and what the timetable is. These steps are covered in more detail in Chapter 5.

The next phase involves preparing for and performing the actual intelligence gathering. You select sources for CI data, devise the strategies and techniques you will use, and make the arrangements for the data to be delivered. Chapter 6 covers ways to find the information you need.

Next, you convert the raw data into information through evaluation and analysis. Spend time analyzing only the data that proves relevant to your CI needs. The analysis weeds out misin-

63

formation and disinformation, then synthesizes fact-based perceptions about your competitor. By the end of this phase, you can draw conclusions based on the information you have gleaned. See Chapter 7 for more information.

The final phase ensures that your information reaches the right people at the right time. Format the information so it is clear, concise, and usable. Present it in time to be used during critical business decision-making efforts. Arrange for secure storage of the valuable information. Chapter 8 covers these procedures.

CI ALERT: What does this tell you?

"Lilly and The Dow Chemical Company have made significant progress in the formation of the proposed Dow Elanco joint venture. . . .

"Dow Elanco will include the plant science businesses of both Dow and Elanco Products Company, the agricultural division of Lilly, as well as Dow's industrial pest-control businesses. . . .

"[T]he joint venture's worldwide corporate and research headquarters would be located in Indianapolis on a 325-acre site near two major Dow facilities. The 800,000-square-foot complex will cost approximately $100 million. . . .

"The joint venture's business is expected to be evenly split between North America and the rest of the world."

Source: Eli Lilly and Company, Third Quarter Report 1989.

Notes

1. Craig Mellow, "The Best Source of Competitive Intelligence," *Sales & Marketing Management*, December 1989, p. 26.

Chapter 5

What Do You Need to Know?

CI CLIP

"It's become clear that managers not only need up-to-date information about their competitors' activities but also have to make strategic use of that information."

Senior Research Associate, The Conference Board.[1]

Before you start any project, it helps to know exactly where you are and what resources you currently have; otherwise, you are operating at a disadvantage. You may be duplicating work that has already been done. One way to know what you already have is to conduct a CI audit.

CI Audit

A review of your current operations to determine what you actually know about your current competitors and about their operations. A CI audit also helps you focus on what kind of CI you currently need.

This chapter discusses the five steps included in performing a CI audit and four methods that will help you define your information needs.

Reasons You Should Perform a CI Audit

To be most effective, your CI audit should

■ Involve the operations of each of your departments.

■ Be undertaken by persons who understand CI.

■ Be conducted on an ongoing, regular basis.

One example of how to run a CI audit can be seen in the audit conducted by Ford Motor Company in the mid-1980s.[2] Ford's management believed that millions of dollars was being spent for information but that the output was "incomplete, fragmented, and rarely effectively shared." To correct this, Ford decided to create an in-house data-sharing service, which it called the Corporate Technical Information System (CTIS).

Ford decided it needed an audit before establishing CTIS. During that audit, Ford personnel were sent around to determine the information needs of each of Ford's major business and technical groups.

This audit disclosed two types of CI needs for the automaker:

- *Access:* Some employees "knew" data was available, but that data was seen as hard to retrieve; other employees were "uncertain" about the availability of information and were unsure whether any retrieval method existed.

- *Distribution:* As a company, Ford was "addressing virtually every need," but little information was being shared between units. In addition, many activities at Ford were suffering from a form of "information overload."

To handle these problems, CTIS was established in 1985 on a small scale. At that point, the system had about 50 users and about 6 files. But as the system was used and the users reviewed what they needed and how they were using this system, the system grew rapidly. Within two years, it had expanded to over 1000 users. By the end of 1989, it had almost 4000 users.

Although Ford has been close-mouthed about the specific, tangible results of CTIS to date, outsiders have evidently seen changes in Ford, some potentially attributable to this process. For example, Stanford Business School Professor Richard Pascale has labeled Ford's CEO as an executive with "a vision of organization and how they might perform beyond the ordinary. . . . He tries to squeeze more out of it by fine-tuning it."[3]

Excuses Not to Perform a CI Audit

If you try to conduct a CI audit at your firm, be prepared to find others in your company who do not want to participate in it. You may well hear one or more of the following reasons why a CI audit, or CI in general, is not needed—at least by them. Listen for these reasons; their existence should be danger signals to you.

- "Don't worry, we've been in this business for 10 (or 20) years. We know what's going on."

■ "We have new (or established) technology, so we really do not have *any* competition."

■ "We don't have enough time/money to do this."

■ "All of our competitors are privately held so there is no data out there."

■ "This business (industry) is so highly competitive that no one can find out anything."

■ "Our competition is very diffuse (or very concentrated), so there is no way we can get any good data."

■ "We don't really know who our competition is or our customers are."

■ "None of our competitors do CI, and they don't seem to have any problems."

None of these excuses are valid reasons for not conducting a CI audit. In fact, except in rare instances, many of these statements are generally *just not true.*

Steps in Performing a CI Audit

Your CI audit can lay the groundwork for your competitive intelligence program by assessing both the knowledge you already have and the information you currently need. Next, we will show you how to proceed with the audit.

Step 1: Defining Your Competition
Just who *is* your competition? You probably think you know, but your perceptions may be incomplete. The best thing to do is to start from scratch with no preconceptions, at least once.

First, how do you identify your competitors? That's where thinking in CI terms is critical. One way to reveal hidden competitors is to visualize all of your competitors as those companies that have been or are going after your current or future clients or customers. From that perspective, ask the following questions:

■ Do you know who got the clients or customers you have lost?

■ Have you ever checked to see who else your clients and customers dealt with before they came to you?

These are but two of the myriad questions you should be asking. And, as with many other types of CI, some of the answers may be found within your own company. To answer them, ask your sales force, your marketing group, your customer relations personnel, and, last but not least, ask your customers.

CI CLOSEUP: "Check It Out"
At the Chicago Tribune, *each member of the sales research staff "shadows" a competitor. Matters such as advertising rates, marketing and sales are all monitored. Whenever anyone finds out about a rival publication's changes in matters such as rates, the information is passed "immediately" to managers.[4]*

There are other ways to approach competitor identification. To be effective in generating useful CI, you must identify *all* of the businesses you are now in. If you have not already done this kind of analysis in connection with strategic planning or developing a marketing strategy, it is important to do it at least once in connection with developing a CI audit.

Finding Information About Your Competitors
■ ■ ■

Deciding What Business You Are In: Your Direct Competitors
One way to approach this is to define what business you are in. This is not as easy as it sounds. Take, for example, a company that makes copper pipe fittings. What business *is* it in? One could say, the business of making copper pipe fittings. An alternative is that it is in the business of making pipe fittings, removing the limitations of "copper." What is the difference?

If the company limits its types of fittings to copper, managers may view their competitors as only those companies that also make copper pipe fittings. Taking the wider view that includes all types of pipe fittings, however, managers can add to this list companies that use any material for pipe fittings, including iron and PVC. This is a broader, more diverse group.

You have to decide the scope of your competition, not from your own perspective, but from the perspective of your customers. In this case, do your customers see one industry—pipe fittings—or several separate and competing industries?

Another approach is to look at your business from its end use, not its end product. Again, taking the example of a company making copper pipe fittings, the business could be considered as making plumbing supplies or as making plumbing construction supplies for new buildings, for renovations, or for repairs.

> *How do you decide in what business you are operating? If you sell a product, go to the retail outlet selling your products. Check on what else is stocked near them. If you are selling a service, where do you find your business classified in a business directory? For both services and products, what SIC code do you put on your tax return?*

70

The answer is that it depends, again, on where your product is sold, to whom, and what choices your customers *see* that they have at the time they make the purchase decision. This approach tends to help you see more completely just who your *direct* competitors are.

Conducting a Product-by-Product (or Service-by-Service) Evaluation: Your Indirect Competitors

An alternative approach for assessing the competitive field is to narrow your focus, not broaden it. This is especially helpful if you offer many different products or services. To use this avenue, you break your operations down to the basic product or service level. Take, for example, a law firm, which is a classic service business.

What services does any typical law firm offer? It may have trial lawyers, able to bring civil cases for damages due to product defects. It may also have, however, a divorce or family relations practice. Whereas that practice is one of the recognized legal specialities, such a practice may also involve counseling family members as a part of the process of representing them. That means, to a limited extent, a family practice lawyer is also involved in the family relations/counseling business, in competition with social service agencies, private marriage counselors, and so on.

A further complexity to this business is the firm's tax lawyer. That lawyer is likely to also be a provider of financial planning services. In both of those areas, the lawyers are competing, to a greater or lesser degree, against such varied professionals as certified public accountants, licensed tax return preparers, financial planners, and even insurance agents. In cases like this, the product-by-product or service-by-service approach helps to identify *indirect* competitors.

After you have done this, step back and think about competitors that are not yet there—the emerging company. Smaller businesses are particularly adept at finding and exploiting niche opportunities. Put yourself in their position and try to see what they see.

Finding Information About Your Competitors
■ ■ ■

Step 2: Pinpointing Your CI Needs

Many devices exist to help you structure your thinking and develop your plans for CI. We will explore several popular devices here: use of internal resources, a competitor analysis needs worksheet, the plain paper process, and the competitor analysis checklist. Use whichever device(s) you feel most comfortable with.

Using Internal Resources to Determine Information Needs

At this point, you can begin to see that the small steps in the CI process can tend to blur together. It is best, however, if you keep the steps separate in your mind, even if they blend together in practice.

Before you even start to gather any data, you *must* ask the right questions. Your answers will be more useful and comprehensive if you make your questions specific rather than just asking for "some information on. . . ."

> *A better question produces a better answer.*

Motorola Inc. provides a good example in the process it used to establish a corporatewide intelligence system. At the beginning, Motorola's director of corporate analytical research established the company's overall CI needs by a frontal assault. He met with 15 top vice presidents and general managers who were responsible for the corporation's operational divisions, as well as those responsible for its staff functions, such as personnel, international, and finance.

He asked each one "What are the five most important things you need to know about the external world?"

The answers varied a lot, from "I want to know about a particular competitor who's really eating our lunch" and "I

72

want to know who my competitors are going to be in China," to "I need to know more about a new technology that will affect the way we build our microprocessors."

From those discussions, I drew up a list of about 35 key intelligence topics and assigned each a priority. That exercise produced the table of contents for our program, which, in turn, determined the kind of talent we needed on [our] staff and the kind of information to collect.[5]

A similar approach to determining both what you know and what you need to know is to sit down with the key personnel in your business. In a smaller business, you may want to use your staff, colleagues, and advisors such as your accountant or lawyer. Have everyone contribute to a list of assumptions they all have about the competition. Be very careful to be noncritical in compiling the list, however, to encourage everyone to contribute assumptions freely. Chapter 17 includes a sample form for recording the responses.

Then organize that list, combining similar assumptions. If possible, reword the assumptions so that it is not easy for anyone to identify the source for each assumption. This will make those participating feel more comfortable.

At that point, without attributing any single assumption to any particular person or department, have each participant identify those assumptions on your list for which they see little or even no supporting data that they can *specifically* point to. You may be surprised how many there are. If it seems that all of the assumptions are likely to be supported by the participants, just reverse the process. That means you should have each person give one brief example of a fact he or she believes to offer support of each assumption. Those assumptions with few or no supporting facts will quickly stand out.

Now, regardless of which way it was compiled, you will have a list of supported assumptions, as well as a group of partially or even unsupported assumptions. From the group of partially and unsupported assumptions, you should isolate those that appear to be the most important to the way you operate and the way that you make decisions about your market and your competitors. Those assumptions are the ones that should be reviewed, challenged, supported, or supplanted by good CI first.

Using a Competitor Analysis Needs Worksheet

Another approach to pinpointing your information needs is provided in Exhibit 5.1, the competitor analysis needs checklist. By answering the questions and prompts in this worksheet you can help establish exactly the kinds of CI you need.

> *What types of CI about your competitors are usually most important? According to The Conference Board, 90% of the corporations it surveyed indicated that they regarded CI on the following topics as either "very useful" or "fairly useful"[6]:*
>
> | | |
> |---|---|
> | *Pricing (97%)* | *Sales statistics (94%)* |
> | *Strategic plans (93%)* | *Market share changes (93%)* |
> | *Key customers (91%)* | *New product programs (91%)* |
> | *Expansion plans (91%)* | |

Using the Plain Paper Process

Another good approach for structuring the audit process is the "blank page" or "plain paper" system. In a nutshell, it involves visualizing a blank page in front of you. Then you visualize filling it with what you envision the final report to be. What points are critical for you to make? What data do you need to make those points? How specific and current does that data have to be?

Competitor Analysis Needs Worksheet

What information about your competitors do you think you need? (You may want to list different information needs for different competitors.) _____

_____

_____

Why do you think you need that specific information? __

_____

How would you or your organization use that information?

_____

For each competitor and for the market at large, restate your CI needs in the form of a few questions that you would like to have answered. _____

_____

_____

Now begin to narrow these broader questions into specific, detailed questions. For example, can you restate a general issue, such as "What are my competitors' current marketing plans?" to the narrower question, "Is a specific competitor preparing to introduce any new consumer products in the next three months?"

_____

_____

For each question, determine how important and valuable the answers would be.

Very ____   Mildly ____   Not at All ____

What do you risk if you do not have the answer to these questions? _____

How much might a lack of good CI cost you? _____

_____

Exhibit 5.1: Sample of a Competitor Analysis Needs Worksheet

How much can you spend on good CI? _____
_____

*The importance of the information (in terms of both oppor-
tunities and risks) should determine the effort and resources that should be devoted to answering these questions, as well as how, specifically, your questions must be
answered.*

For each issue or set of questions, also determine

How often will you need this data?
   On a regular basis ____   Only once ____

*When do you need this CI? The timeframe within which
you have to operate may dictate the depth of your avenues of research.*_____

*What kind of data will best help you to answer your
specific questions? For example, do you need direct evidence of your competitor's marketing intentions (say, an
announcement that the target has hired a new advertising agency for a particular product)? Will indirect evidence do (such as a report in local business newspaper of
recent promotions that hint at the development of a new
marketing campaign)?* _____
_____

What type of data do you need?
   Macro level (general)___ Micro level (specific) ___

Will the data have to be
   Current ____ Historical ____ Both ____

*Look at previously unused or underused resources inside
your own firm. Talk with employees who have just come
back from trade shows, with sales personnel who have
been hearing rumors from their customers. What data do
you already have on this subject?* _____
_____

Exhibit 5.1: *(continued)*

76

It is best to start with your ideal solution, and, if necessary, compromise at some later point. Given your ultimate goal, you then work backward to decide what kinds of data you will need to enable you to reach your conclusions. It may be seen as research turned on its head: Instead of seeing what is available and working from that, you decide what you need and then you go look for it.

This approach forces you to start at the end—the goal—rather than the beginning. This way you avoid being influenced by any preconceptions about what you may expect to find. Instead, you set as your goal the data you need and then work backward to locate that data. Exhibit 5.2 summarizes how to establish the goal and locate all pertinent data.

Using the Competitor Analysis Checklist

The competitor analysis checklist can also help you establish your CI needs, by identifying the specific targets and the relevant data you will seek. Are you seeking data on specific direct (or indirect) competitors? Which ones? Are you seeking data on designated lines of business? What lines? What types of data are you seeking—micro level or macro level?

> *Know both what you want to find out—and why.*

Very few reports will cover all of the topics listed here. This checklist, however, provides one way to make sure you are not omitting anything critical. You can use this sample or develop a checklist customized for your own business.

Again, though, it is important to start at what some may view as the end of the process—the questions to be answered—and then

Phase 1

To develop your goal, outline the first page of a possible report on your project. Make sure that outline shows a possible recommended course of action, for example:

> *"Our company should begin to use expert systems in its manufacturing activities."*

Phase 2

Following the action statement, list the key finding(s) that might support your recommendation:

> *"Our competition has and will continue to have substantially lower costs than we do for manufacturing the same product."*

> *"Existing expert systems are sufficiently developed to be able to support our manufacturing needs."*

> *"The experience of manufacturers in other industries illustrates that expert systems can be successfully adapted to our manufacturing operations within a short period of time, providing important cost savings."*

Phase 3

Now, convert these statements into questions. First, rephrase the conclusion you drew in Phase 1:

> *"Should our company begin to use expert systems in its manufacturing activities?"*

Exhibit 5.2: Phases of the Plain Paper Process

This is the goal of your CI research. Knowing the goal is crucial. It enables you to focus the data gathering that needs to be done. Also, once you know the goal of the assignment, you will be more likely to identify any data of potential interest to you, even if it does not go into your final report. For example, here, if your research disclosed that a major consulting firm has just created an expert systems consulting practice, you might want to save that information for future reference, because you may well be seeking such expertise after the project is over.

Phase 4

Now, repeat the conversion process from Phase 3 for all your key findings you developed in Phase 2:

> *"Does our competition have substantially lower costs than we do for manufacturing? If they do, will that continue?"*

> *"Are existing expert systems sufficiently developed to be able to support our manufacturing techniques?"*

> *"What has been the experience of manufacturing firms in other industries with expert systems? Specifically, can it be successfully adapted to our manufacturing operations within a short period of time, and will it provide cost savings?"*

These are now the questions you have to answer.

Exhibit 5.2: *(continued)*

79

move to the beginning, to find the data needed. Exhibit 5.3 is a sample checklist for competitor analysis reports.

Summary: Pinpointing Your Information Needs
The goal of any of these methods is to help you to define your information needs. Whether you start with the worksheet or develop assumptions from meetings with other company members, you will begin to discern knowledge gaps that have important implications for your company.

The information areas you choose to focus on should be well defined. By defining your information needs up front, you can now make up a list of specific questions that will provide the focus for your CI efforts.

Step 3: Assessing What You Already Know
Your questions can now provide almost an interviewing questionnaire for determining the information you currently have available. Develop an outline—the form of this outline may well serve as the structure of your final report. Now use your outline to talk with your salespeople, your distributors, and your internal staff. What do they already know or believe they know that bears on your questions? Go through your internal documents, any clippings you may have saved, and your past business and marketing plans. Fill in the information you already have. Make sure you differentiate between the hard facts you have on hand (your quarterly sales figures, for example) and facts that require additional verification.

Keep track of all the data you obtain. You can use the checklist in Exhibit 5.3 as a data organizer. Some of the data you have may have direct bearing on the questions you've outlined. Some may have little or no immediate use. Nonetheless, keep track of everything you already believe you know, because the scope and direction of questions may change as you continue your investigation.

COMPETITOR ANALYSIS CHECKLIST

Use one checklist form for each competitor, although the industry information may not change from competitor to competitor unless the competitors are in different fields. Place a check in the blank to the left of each item that you have identified or can identify in your CI audit.

Industry Information

■ *What is the competitive environment?*
_____ Industry structure.
_____ Number of competitors, their product lines (or range of services), and locations.
_____ Market shares, gross sales, and net profitability of competitors.
_____ Expansion potentialities of competitors.
_____ Important differences among competitors.
_____ Industry marketing, distribution, and pricing practices.
_____ Need for new technology.
_____ Barriers to entry and exit.
_____ Regulatory constraints.
_____ Potential entrants and future competitors.
_____ Attitude toward likelihood of new competition.
_____ Indirect competition.

Individual Competitor Information

■ *Who are the owners and managers?*
_____ Major shareholders/partners.
_____ Directors and officers, their backgrounds and other business relationships.
_____ Corporate and management organization: formal or informal.
_____ How decisions are made and who makes them.
_____ Management styles, abilities, and emphases.
_____ Depth, capabilities, and weaknesses of management in key functional areas.
_____ New personnel and recent restructuring.
_____ Corporate politics.

Exhibit 5.3: Sample of a Competitor Analysis Checklist

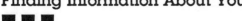
■ *What products and services are offered?*
_____ *Product lines and services currently offered.*
_____ *Current and future applications of products and services.*
_____ *Depth and breadth of products and services offered today.*
_____ *Analysis of new products and services, including impact on the market and on competition.*
_____ *Customer service policies and performance.*
_____ *History of key products and services.*
_____ *Products or services likely to be introduced or eliminated in the near future.*
_____ *Channels of distribution, including their strengths and weaknesses.*
_____ *Possible changes in distribution channels.*

■ *What are the sales and pricing policies?*
_____ *Commercial, nonprofit, and government sales.*
_____ *Domestic versus foreign sales.*
_____ *Seasonal and cyclical problems.*
_____ *Pricing strategy: who prices products and services and how.*
_____ *Price levels and flexibility.*
_____ *Credit, discounts, incentives, consignments, any other special pricing policies.*

■ *Who is the sales force and who are the customers?*
_____ *Type of sales force: in-house versus independent sales agents.*
_____ *Organization of sales force: by product line, by geographic market, or by end-user.*
_____ *Training, capability, and compensation of sales force.*
_____ *Number of customers.*
_____ *Distribution and concentration of customers.*
_____ *Analysis of largest or most important customers.*

■ *How is marketing being handled?*
_____ *Market shares by product line, by geographic area, and by industry segment.*

Exhibit 5.3: *(continued)*

_____ *Marketing approaches and their current effectiveness.*

_____ *Samples of advertising, product literature, and other promotional materials.*

_____ *Probable future changes in marketing direction and timing.*

_____ *History of any questionable marketing practices.*

■ *What are the financial and legal positions?*

_____ *Short- and long-term borrowing capacities and ability to raise equity financing.*

_____ *Sources of financing, including duration and strength of the relationship.*

_____ *Sales margin, return on assets, and return on equity.*

_____ *Profitability of key divisions, products, or services.*

_____ *Projections of financial position over next two to five years.*

_____ *Comparison of profitability, cash flow, and other key ratios with those of major competitors.*

_____ *Liabilities.*

_____ *Major lawsuits and regulatory actions: probable impacts on company.*

■ *What is being done with technology, research, and development?*

_____ *Current manufacturing methods and processes.*

_____ *Key patents and proprietary technology.*

_____ *Access to, use of, and dependence on outside technology.*

_____ *Need for new technology.*

_____ *Potential changes in manufacturing methods and processes.*

_____ *Size and capabilities of research staff.*

_____ *The rate of technological change in this industry niche.*

_____ *The usual lead time between a research and development breakthrough and the delivery of a product to market.*

_____ *Types and levels of research and development, including current and future expenditures.*

Exhibit 5.3: *(continued)*

83

Finding Information About Your Competitors
■ ■ ■

■   *What personnel, resources, and facilities are available?*
     _____ *Labor force: cost, availability, turnover, and quality.*
     _____ *Raw materials: sources and availability.*
     _____ *Quality control programs in place or planned.*
     _____ *Level and consistency of quality control.*
     _____ *Manufacturing and operating costs.*
     _____ *Facilities: locations, current performance, and potential.*
     _____ *Planned improvements to existing facilities or new facilities.*
     _____ *Facilities closings or divestitures planned.*
     _____ *Productivity programs.*
     _____ *Joint ventures, minority interests, and other investments or ownership interests.*
     _____ *Make/buy policies.*

■   *What are the competitor's strategies, objectives, and perception of itself?*
     _____ *Business philosophy and corporate strategy.*
     _____ *How strategy is made and implemented.*
     _____ *Targeted markets and market shares.*
     _____ *Target growth rates and other financial objectives.*
     _____ *Technological trends and objectives.*
     _____ *How the company sees itself.*

■   *What are the competitor's perceptions of its competitors and customers?*
     _____ *Quality of product or service.*
     _____ *Pricing.*
     _____ *Marketing and service capabilities and reliability.*
     _____ *Management and organization.*
     _____ *Technological base and capabilities.*

Exhibit 5.3: *(continued)*

> *If you don't know where a fact fits—don't just throw it away.*

This step in the process will point out some important knowledge gaps. For example, you may not have a complete list of competitive products. Or you may be lacking pricing, discounting, or distribution information for key competitive products. Again, by starting with analyzing your information needs, you can discern the relative importance of these different knowledge gaps. From there you can produce a list of the data that has the greatest immediate bearing.

Step 4: Specifying Your Data Needs

Steps 2 and 3 can help you assess what you need to know and what you already know. To clarify where you will obtain the data, your next move is to pinpoint the type of data you are looking for.

Types of Data Sought

Determine whether your CI program will need qualitative data (narrative responses), quantitative data (numbers and statistics), or both. For example, if you are trying to determine how your competitors see you and your marketing activities, you are probably looking for qualitative, rather than quantitative, data. The types of questions you are trying to answer in part determine the type of data you seek.

"Soft" CI

Not all CI that you get will be "hard" data, that is, numbers and specific facts. Don't assume that you should only be looking for hard data for your CI. In some cases, you may find that all that is available is "soft," that is, nonquantifiable or opinion, data. In other cases, the best CI is "soft." For example, in discussing the problems of keeping up with Japanese research and development activities, four scientists at the Battelle Pacific Northwest Laboratories observed:

Finding Information About Your Competitors
■ ■ ■

> [W]e have found that scientific and technological advances in Japan are often first communicated by word of mouth within the Japanese scientific community. . . . It is also important to recognize that many significant technical developments in Japan do not appear directly as experimental results or as business news. . . . Thus technical journals and databases are helpful but only supplementary. Closer contact between our countries' specialists is the primary way to supply the necessary details and overall insights.[7]

In deciding to accept soft CI, don't overlook one of the best, but often least obvious, sources of soft CI: your own competitors. Consider the following practical advice given to radio station managers on how to compete in selling their advertising:

> [C]all every TV station, newspaper, shopper [publication], billboard company, speciality advertising company, and magazine in your market. Call the *Yellow Pages* representative. Set up a meeting. Ask each to bring information on his or her medium, including rates. In a short time you will have media kits on file for all the media in town. . . . This kind of intelligence gathering should help you.

> You may find an idea for promoting your station on another medium.

> You will have important information on how to counter the competition's claims and you will know what your clients are being told.

> Another important source of monitoring is direct mail. It is a good idea to give stamped, self-addressed envelopes to a media buyer or key advertiser so he or she can drop information into the mail that is mailed to [the buyer or advertiser]. For example, a special package or station newsletter could provide you with intelligence that will help you make better decisions and set more workable strategies.[8]

> ### CI CLIP
> "The reasons for statistical abuse range from ignorance to arrogance. Sharing the blame is the 'give me any numbers you have' mentality of some statistics users who are willing to sacrifice accuracy for immediacy. When quality is questionable, however, any numbers are not superior to no numbers."
>
> Former director of the Census Bureau.[9]

The Customer's Perspective

One type of critical information is the perspective of your clients and potential customers. This data may often be "soft" CI, for example, opinions, attitudes, or stories.

Specifically, what can the client/customer perspective tell you? A lot. Look at your business from the perspective of how clients and potential customers see you. One factor is how they see the quality of your products and services. This is not the same as evaluating the results of your own internal quality control (QC) program and the way your products and services conform to your own specifications. The QC is really linked to manufacturing productivity. Rather, the focus here is the relative perceived quality of your products or services. In this context, quality includes all of the nonprice attributes that influence your customer's decision to buy, including both the primary product (or service) as well as any associated products and services.

In the area of products, such a profile might seek to determine how your product compares, in the eyes of your customers, in terms of product characteristics such as the following:

Finding Information About Your Competitors
■ ■ ■

- appearance
- conformity to specifications and expectations
- durability
- ease of assembly and use
- packaging
- performance
- price
- workmanship and quality

For service businesses, the service characteristics may be the following:

- conformity to specifications and expectations
- performance or expertise
- price and value
- overall quality

You might also evaluate the product in terms of the comparative quality of associated services, such as

- credit and terms
- delivery and scheduling
- parts and service support
- responsiveness to customer inquiries and complaints
- warranty

This type of analysis can help you understand the following:

- Why customers in each market segment buy from one supplier rather than from another.

- What unsatisfied customer needs exist.

- What competitive threats you face and what competitive opportunities are present in the marketplace.

- Where your perceptions differ from those of your customers or potential customers.

In essence, the marketplace is defined by your customers and potential customers. Understanding how they perceive your products or services, as well as those of your competitors, can provide a framework for assessing both opportunities and potential threats.

Step 5: Establishing a Timeframe
When you are ready to start a CI project, be honest with yourself about your time limits. To do that, answer these questions:

■ Just how much time do you have for the project in total?

■ Of that period of time, how long do you have to collect the raw data? How long will it take you to collect the kind of data you think you need? Are these the same?

■ How much time do you think you will need to analyze the raw data you expect to get?

■ Exactly when do you have to have an answer to the question or a report prepared?

■ What percentage of your time can you spend on this project between the time you start and when it is due?

The answers to these questions will greatly influence what CI you will look for and how you go about collecting it.

Choosing the Cutoff for Research
In particular, make sure that you honestly set the timeframe for making your report or for finishing the project. Unlike pure academic research, when you are doing CI research, there comes a point when you must finish the research and write the report. The point is not to collect data, but rather to provide information for making decisions. You probably will not have the luxury of finishing your research when everything possible has been researched. With new developments, products, speeches, announcements, and situations occurring every day, you might never "finish" the research. At some point, you just have to choose an end for it.

The "Half Life" of CI

Become sensitive to the critical need to keep to a schedule to produce finished CI. CI does not age well. When you (or someone else) needs it, you usually need it by a certain time, *not* a day or two later. On the other hand, the data on which your final analysis is based should be as current as possible. You may be tempted to wait "just a little bit longer" for that one key piece of data you need to complete your analysis. Unfortunately, no matter how good your CI is or how critical it may be in decision making, if it comes the day after a crucial decision had to be made, it is no good at all.

This conflict is just one example of the fact that CI has a short "half life." Here this term means the period of time for which the data you have collected retains at least 50 percent of its accuracy and relevance. In general, the more detailed (micro level) the CI, the shorter the period of time for which it is valid or useful.

In the case of raw data collected for CI, the half lives are typically like those described in Table 5.1.

The concept of half life also applies to any analysis you develop or any report that you present to others. Try to caution those who are using the CI you have developed to be conscious of its short shelf life. CI users should not store the information and then drag it out a year later, expecting it still to be accurate. The conclusion you draw or the report you present is completely valid *only* as of the date you completed it.

Summary

The five steps involved in producing a CI audit are defining your competition, pinpointing your CI needs, assessing what you already know, specifying your data needs, and establishing a timeframe. As we've underlined throughout this chapter, the most important step involves determining your information needs specifically and understanding the importance of different information needs.

Table 5.1

Half Lives of CI Data

Type of Data	Range of Half Life	Example
Micro Level/Current	As short as a day; probably no more than 3 months	Interest rates offered on accounts payable by competitor
Macro Level/Current	From 1 month to 6 months	Increases in consumer demand for your product
Micro Level/ Historic	From 2 to 12 months	Average turnaround time on service proposals of competitor
Macro Level/ Historic	From 3 months to 2 years	Investment patterns of all competitors over past two years

CI ALERT: What does this tell you?

"Travel Management at General Foods:

Annual Travel Volume:	*$31.0 million*
Air Expenses:	*15.5 million*
Hotel Expenses:	*4.8 million*
Car Expenses:	*1.2 million*
Ground Expenses:	*0.8 million*
Meal Expenses:	*2.0 million*
Miscellaneous Expenses:	*6.6 million"*

Source: Business Travel News, *January 15, 1990.*

Notes

1. "Corporate Cloak and Dagger," *Agenda—Supplement to Chrysler Corporation Times,* January 1989, p. 3.

2. F. C. Linder, "Ford's Corporate Technical Information System," *Information Times,* April 1989, p. S/1.

3. "The Q&A/Richard Pascale," *Business Month,* February 1990, p. 70.

4. Howard Sutton, "Keeping Tabs on the Competition," *Marketing Communications,* January 1989, p. 43.

5. The Conference Board, Inc., *Competitive Intelligence,* Research Report No. 913, 1988, p. 12.

6. The Conference Board, Inc., *Competitive Intelligence,* Research Report No. 913, 1988, p. 16. The totals do not add to 100 percent because each company that was surveyed characterized many potential uses of CI.

7. "Getting to the Heart of Japanese R&D," *High Technology,* February 1987, p. 7.

8. Chris Lytle, "Attacking Newspapers," *Radio Only,* April 1986, pp. 15-16, 20.

9. John G. Keane, "Questionable Statistics," *American Demographics,* June 1985, pp. 19-21, 48.

Chapter 6

Finding the Information You Need

CI CLIP

"You don't have to do anything illegal to get the appropriate information. There's more information around than you can handle."

Vice President, General Development, W. R. Grace & Co.[1]

The sources listed in this chapter represent a starting point for obtaining CI data. Note the tips on the importance of CI for smaller and emerging companies. The chapters in Part III of the book contain additional resources such as online databases and international organizations. You can also refer to Appendix B for a list of specific resources for various types of CI information.

Treating Data as a Commodity

One approach to collecting information that often has been successful is to think of the data you are seeking as a commodity—a tangible product. When you do, the following questions arise:

■ Who produces the data I want?

■ Who collects the data I want?

■ Where is the data that I want transferred, and why?

■ Who uses the data I want?

■ Who accumulates the data I want?

■ Who else has an interest in the data I want?

Now take these one at a time, exploring some specific examples of what each question means. When you ask these questions, remember that, in many cases, some of the answers will overlap. That is to be expected.

Who Produces the Data I Want?

In most cases, the raw data that you seek is company-level or even divisional-level data. That means that the targeted competitor actually produces it. But you have to inquire further. Specifically, who at the competitor is likely to produce this data? For example, is marketing strategy determined by the marketing department, dictated by a strategic plan prepared by the planning department, or the result of a compromise by both? If the answer is that the strategy is a blend of marketing and planning department information, when you are, for example, interviewing personnel formerly with a target firm, make sure you get people from the appropriate department involved in the process.

Who Collects the Data I Want?

The person or department you identify may not be the same person who actually produces the data. The key concept here is transmission. When data is transmitted, it is assembled and sometimes analyzed, but always moved. One key to locating raw data is to determine where the data is moving so you can try to intercept it, in a figurative sense only. That is why the next question becomes important.

Where Is the Data That I Want Transferred, and Why?

Assume that for any number of reasons, your firm wants detailed but apparently unavailable data on the performance of the U.S. gambling operations of a casino owned by a competitor in Atlantic City. Perhaps you want to determine whether the casino is so profitable that your competitor can expand into other lines or is losing so much money that the competitor will have to delay expansion plans in the areas in which it competes with you.

You should check with the New Jersey Casino Control Commission. This is because, as a regulator, the commission has an interest in that same subject—the profitability of the casino. Because it is a public agency, the data the commission requires the casinos to provide to it may be public, and therefore available to you. By calling the New Jersey Casino Control Board, you can access the monthly records of the activity of each casino in the state, by type of game. The state requires this data to be filed so the state can estimate expected tax revenue. For you, however, these records are important raw material from which to develop CI.

Who Uses the Data I Want?

To determine who uses the kind of data you want, you seek out persons, such as securities analysts, who want data from public companies to generate company and industry forecasts. For you, what the analyst has to offer is, first of all, his or her analysis and conclusions. However, of potentially greater importance may be the raw data—whether numeric or narrative—provided by the target competitor. That data may, in turn, be disclosed in the analyst's reports, or you may be able to get it by direct contact with the analyst.

Who Accumulates the Data I Want?

To reach the handiest repository of accumulated data, contact government regulatory bodies and, in the case of publicly traded companies, investment analysts and trade associations. Each of these sources has data of differing types and quality. The type and quality of that data depend on why each collected the data in the first place. For example, investment analysts are often privy to information that differs from that made available to the press, including the financial press.

> *Understanding why a source does not provide useful data is one key to finding a source that does.*

Organizations such as the U.S. Census Bureau and trade associations generally (but not always) work with aggregated data, as opposed to data at the company level. Using disaggregation may enable you to isolate significant data that you and the providers of the data both assume to be masked by the aggregation efforts of those providing the data. Just how to disaggregate is covered later, in Chapter 12.

Who Else Has an Interest in the Data I Want?

To learn what other organizations and people may have done this data collection, your attention should be drawn to a wide range of potential resources, ranging from the advertising departments of trade publications to academics. The advertising departments of trade publications may collect or even generate data similar to that you are seeking in an effort to show that their publication represents the audience an advertiser wants to reach. To that end, the advertising department may choose to educate potential advertisers about the industry and about its key participants.

Academics are an interesting resource, because their access to data is sometimes much freer than that of trade associations and the like. This may be because the companies they interview and deal with make an implicit assumption that giving academic researchers the data is "harmless" in a competitive sense. Of course, some firms are wise enough to insist that the academics who have access to data do not release any of the data, except in the aggregate. Even if the academic is operating under such a limit, in talking with him or her, you may be able to discern some of the conclusions drawn by someone who has already studied your target industry or company. In that case, the interview may give you valuable indirect data.

Differentiating Between Who Creates Data and Where You Find It

As you focus on where the data you need might be located and accessed, keep in mind that where you get the data is not necessarily the ultimate source of that data. This distinction is an important one. First, this means that you may be able to access the data you want without having to contact the data's original source. This also means that you must ensure that you know whether a source of data actually produces the data or merely transmits it. Confusing the producer of data with the provider of that data can have important consequences.

> *Did the place you are getting data from actually generate that data?*

Two cases illustrate the danger of confusing the provider of the data with the source of the data. In the first case, in 1986 and 1987 a 27-year-old Pennsylvania man allegedly obtained "almost unlimited credit" from five banks using a Dun & Bradstreet rating based on false information about himself and his business. He had himself supplied this information to Dun & Bradstreet. According to federal officials, his company was reported as being worth over $40 million when in fact it was never even an operating company and never had any "legitimate income."

Finding Information About Your Competitors
■ ■ ■

A local newspaper report detailed the consequences of not paying attention to the difference between the source of data and the provider of the data:

> "In defense of Dun & Bradstreet," said Paul Gray, assistant U.S. attorney assigned as prosecutor, "the investigation states that Dun & Bradstreet does not check the accuracy of the information supplied to it. It only reported the information came from [the defendant] himself."

> But apparently for banks and credit rating services, the Dun & Bradstreet rating that valued [the defendant] at more than $50 million was sufficient.[2]

In the second case, federal prosecutors indicted eight people and charged them with operating five fraudulent businesses that bilked at least 300 companies of an estimated $1.5 million. The scheme involved ordering merchandise from manufacturers, distributors, and suppliers on credit with no intention of paying for the shipment, then reselling that merchandise.

According to the indictment, "To establish satisfactory credit ratings, the defendants submitted false information to Dun & Bradstreet about the background of each of the fraudulent companies and its principals, its financial stability and its assets."[3]

In addition, the defendants were charged with using other fraudulent companies and companies associated with or controlled by the defendants as credit references.

This same source/provider distinction applies to data other than credit ratings as well. For example, just because information is available through a database does not make it correct. Cross-checking past estimates in a trade publication that prints market predictions about an industry with the industry's actual performance may disclose that this publication is often incorrect in its predictions. And, if you find that such information in a particular

98

trade publication is consistently wrong, you may decide you cannot rely on that publication for accurate information about your competitors' plans.

Likely Sources of Raw Data

What do businesses that already collect CI see as the most useful sources of CI about their competitors? According to The Conference Board, over 70 percent of the 300 corporations it surveyed in 1987 through 1988 on CI activities rated the following sources of CI about competitors (shown here in descending order of importance) as either "very important" or "fairly important":

Own Sales Force
Customers
Industry Periodicals
Target's Promotional Materials
Own Marketing Research Staff
Analysis of Target's Products
Target's Annual Reports
Meetings, Trade Shows
Distributors[4]

As you can see, these sources are a widely disparate group. We have divided the most often used potential sources of raw data into four basic categories:

■ Government
■ Specialized Interests
■ Private Sector
■ Media

This grouping not only gives you an analytical tool but, as you will see, the sources within each category tend to have common characteristics.

Finding Information About Your Competitors
■ ■ ■

In each case, knowing what characteristics the data sources have in common becomes important when you must analyze and evaluate the data they provide.

In each discussion of the source groups, you will see an exhibit listing typical sources you can start with. Of course, no such list can be complete; it is only an aid to get you thinking in the right direction.

Government

Government sources generally are characterized as providing only indirect assistance. That is, the data that they can release may be aggregated, or the governmental unit may only provide data already collected by another provider, such as a commercial directory. However, governmental units do receive some data through channels other than data collection, such as licensing, regulation, and litigation files. This data tends to be more company specific than aggregated. Exhibit 6.1 lists common government sources.

Federal Government

Among the resources available to you at the federal government level are the files of numerous regulatory agencies, such as the Environmental Protection Agency. Records of patents and trademarks granted to businesses are also open to the public. In addition, personnel at many offices of these agencies and departments—in particular the U.S. Department of Commerce—are often "wired into" various industries. These offices can provide you with leads to trade publications and trade associations.

> *Data easily obtained is not necessarily worth less than data that is hard to get.*

- Federal Government
  Regulatory Agencies
  Trade Promotion Offices
  Congressional Hearings
  Court Cases and Records
  Patents
  Trademarks
  One-time Studies
  Regular Publications

- Foreign Governments
  Regulatory Agencies
  Trade Promotion Offices
  Quasi-government Bodies
  Regular Publications
  Patents
  Commercial Attaches

- State Governments
  Regulatory Agencies
  Court Cases and Records
  Environmental Permits and Other Filings
  Trademarks

- Local Governments
  Zoning and Building Permits and Other Filings
  Court Cases and Records
  Industrial Development Authorities

Exhibit 6.1: Typical Government Data Sources

Finding Information About Your Competitors
■ ■ ■

As an example, assume that you are interested in estimating the quality and design problems a truck manufacturer is having. One way to do that would be to study the defects and related data already available in Washington:

At the U.S. Department of Transportation, the National Highway Transportation Safety Administration (NHTSA) maintains a database of safety information about automobiles and trucks manufactured during the past 10 years.

NHTSA can search that database by make, model, year, or even specific equipment (such as brakes). A search will identify any publicly accessible data held by the NHTSA. This may include crash test results, repairability and damage statistics, safety recall information, defect investigation/engineering analyses, insurance and accident costs, technical service bulletins (memos from manufacturers to dealers on problems, repairs, and modifications), consumer complaints filed with NHTSA, used vehicle information, and tire tread wear and skid resistance data.

NHTSA will run searches of that database without charge. Requests are placed initially by calling a hotline and leaving a message, describing the request and giving a mailing address for the results. Simple requests are often handled without anything more than a call and message to this number. Requests for more complex research as well as for specific materials identified in a search may have to be placed through the NHTSA's Public Affairs Office.

Almost any analysis of a competitor whose stock is publicly traded should begin with a review of the corporation's annual report filed with the U.S. Securities and Exchange Commission (SEC). This document is often confused with the Form 10-K Report. In general, it is a summary document, prepared for shareholders and others. It may contain a letter from the company's chairman or president discussing the past year, management's analysis of the previous year, or a report on public issues of importance to the corporation's future. The level of detail in these sections varies widely. Compare the Spartan approach of CNA Financial Corporation's 1988 Annual Report, featuring a 2-page letter to shareholders, employees, and agents, with the 16 pages in Mobil Corporation's 1988 annual report that detailed its corporate strategy and the activities of its various divisions. Substantial operating details are scattered throughout ITT Corporation's 1988 Annual Report. In some cases, management may combine the annual report and Form 10-K into one document.

Many people, however, stop with the annual report, which should be just the beginning. Numerous other documents can provide even more information than that in the annual report. Consider, for example, the following, which are in the SEC's files:

■ *Form 10-K:* This annual document must contain detailed financial statements covering a period of five years (including data by major business segment). In addition, it must contain background information on senior management and on the corporation's competition, corporate assets, research and development plans, regulatory problems, and any other issues that affect the corporation's overall operations, and thus the price of its stock. It may incorporate by reference many detailed contracts and other documents, dealing with subjects ranging from officers' compensation packages to agreements to acquire other corporations. All of these documents must be filed with the SEC. The result is a report and associated filings that can be quite detailed and revealing.

■ *Notice of annual meeting and proxy statement:* For the annual meeting, these documents contain basic information on the backgrounds of all directors, plus information on the compensation of top officers. When a proxy statement has been issued in connection with a merger or acquisition, it contains very detailed information on the proposal the stockholders are to vote on.

■ *Interim reports:* There are various kinds of specialized reports required by the SEC, covering financial matters as well as significant changes affecting the corporation. Some corporations distribute the quarterly reports to stockholders with no other materials. Others use the distribution of the quarterly reports as an occasion to communicate with stockholders and with the investment community by including such things as news notes.

■ *Annual meeting summary:* Some corporations distribute a summary of the proceedings of the annual meeting of stockholders to all stockholders and the investment community. In addition to recording the results of votes, they may also summarize questions from and answers to stockholders and even reprint addresses by corporate management to stockholders. A recent typical example was that of the Sara Lee Corporation, which combined its first quarter report in 1989 with a report on its annual meeting. The report featured a summary of remarks made by several corporate officers, the results of votes of the shareholders, and "significant" questions asked by stockholders and answered by Sara Lee's chief executive officer. In addition, the summary featured a full-page report on the corporation's marketing efforts and strategy in one of its major consumer goods markets.

Information on contracts a key competitor has with the U.S. government may enable you to determine where that competitor's research and development program is going.

Many other sources of direct and indirect data originate at the federal level. For example, assume that your firm is seeking information on a competitor's current research and development efforts in an information technologies field. One solution may be to identify any federal government contracts that have been awarded to the target firm. Then you can get copies of the contracts and study both the specifications for the contract and the contractor's reports on its progress, most of which should be obtainable under the Freedom of Information Act. This data reveals just how far the competitor's research and development has progressed, as indicated by the kinds of technology it needs to perform under the contracts.

The Freedom of Information Act (FOIA) requires U.S. government agencies to provide information to the public on written request. The way this operates varies from agency to agency. Some agencies produce information requested under the FOIA at no charge. Others may charge for the time involved as well as the cost of copying the files. Not every federal government record is subject to public disclosure under the FOIA. Important exceptions from disclosure include classified information, personnel files, and some material that is confidential or proprietary from private persons and companies.

Getting documents under the FOIA can be time-consuming and occasionally frustrating. In spite of strict time limits in the FOIA, it may take several months for an agency to produce the documents you have asked for. And, even when you receive them, you may find that some sections of the documents have been blacked out on the basis that the material in those sections is exempted from disclosure.

In spite of these problems, the FOIA can be a useful way to dip into federal government records.

Finding Information About Your Competitors
■ ■ ■

The U.S. government can also be a major source of aggregated data, usually developed as a part of the ongoing census process. Although this data is typically somewhat dated (three to six years old), it can serve to help you determine the overall structure of an industry and some of the major trends affecting it. Among such resources are the following:

■ *U.S. Industrial Outlook:* This annual provides manufacturers shipments' values over a five-year period; it gives annual and long-term projections for the industry. Not all industries are updated every year, and it does not contain reports on all industries.

■ *U.S. Economic Censuses:* These reports, published every five years, give sales volumes at the U.S. and state levels by four-digit SIC code, as long as there are a number of establishments covered by each report, so that individual data is masked. There are separate reports for the retail trade, wholesale trade, service industries, transportation, and construction industries. The censuses do not include all types of firms. Among the most significant omissions are agricultural businesses, real estate, finance, and public utilities, as well as firms with no payrolls. One word of caution: An "establishment" is not the same as a company. The census counts each location of a firm with multiple sites in an area as separate establishments.

■ *U.S. Annual Survey of Manufactures:* This report provides dollar values of shipments for manufacturing SIC codes. It also provides some information on total wages and number of employees by SIC codes. The data, based on U.S. Commerce Department estimates, is given at the national and state levels. A similar report, the U.S. Service Industry Annual Surveys, provides similar data on the service SIC codes.

■ *U.S. County Business Patterns:* This survey is published annually and details the number of establishments per SIC code at the national, state, and county levels. Unlike the censuses, which are based on direct counts of establishments, this report derives its data from social security records, so that there are inconsistencies with economic censuses covering the same areas and industries.

SIC code: *The code assigned by the Standard Industrial Classification System. This is a major statistical classification system used to promote the comparability of statistical data describing the U.S. economy and U.S. businesses.*

Do not overlook Congressional hearings and court records, which often contain data that might not otherwise be made public.

How to Find Out About Congressional Hearings

Basic information about congressional hearings and the witnesses who have appeared there is available from several sources:

■ *The committee or subcommittee that held the hearings, if you know its name and the date of the hearings.*

■ *Commercial and trade association hard-copy services that track the operations of the Congress. (See Appendix B for a listing.)*

■ *Articles in trade publications, as well as in* The Washington Post.

■ *If the hearings have been printed, the U.S. Government Printing Office's indexes, both hard-copy and online, detail the publication information.*

Finally, ways you can tap foreign government data sources, such as regulatory agencies and trade promotion offices, are described in more detail in Chapter 10.

State and Local Governments
State and local governments can also provide useful data. What is defined as public can vary from state to state. Despite that, a lot of data is available to the public.

For example, in most states, the zoning and building files of local governments (such as townships) are open to the public. Examining the file dealing with a building under construction by a competitor can be instructive. For example, the plans and permits may show that the building will have 16 parking spaces for employees and 25,000 square feet of space. These facts tell you about the size of the facility. The file may also disclose that the building is to be used for light manufacturing. However, a cross-check with the local zoning ordinance may reveal that a commercial building in this area must have 1 parking space for every 1.5 full-time employees. That, together with the plans, should lead you to conclude that your target does not intend to have more than 24 full-time employees in the beginning at the new plant.

Specialized Interests
This group is composed of sources who collect data to advance their own "interests." That interest may be professional or may be what the group's members see as a "public" or "industry" interest. Exhibit 6.2 lists common specialized interests that serve as good data sources.

These sources, the specialized interests, all collect and provide data for a reason—to advance what they each see as their own best interests.

For example, academics may seek funding support for research in which they are interested, advancement of their professional careers, or consulting assignments, in addition to their own research interests. In these efforts the professors and researchers

Court Records

Finding out about any pending court cases you should review is not always easy. If your target firm's Form 10-K refers to a case, that helps you to find it. Another way is to check local newspapers for stories about cases that have been filed.

To find out about closed cases is somewhat easier. At a law library, have a librarian check for cases involving your competitor or its staffperson on one of the legal databases. That search produces a reference to a reported case. In turn, the case history will tell you where the court records are located.

In any event, you have to contact the clerk of the court in which the case is or was being handled. Ask the clerk whether the records are available, where they are, and when you can examine them. In some cases, if a case has been appealed, you will find that all or a portion of the record has been transferred to another court.

One useful item to obtain is a copy of the clerk's docket or the entry docket. This lists all the filings made with that court for the case file you are seeking to examine. In some courts, however, it is only a list of all of the actions the court took, not of the contents of the file. Usually you can obtain a copy for a small fee from the clerk's office.

What is available to you from a court record varies widely from state to state and case to case. Typically, you can see the final opinion of the judge (if there is one), and a transcript of the trial, copies of documents put into evidence, and copies of all motions made by the parties. Attached to these motions may well be documents and affidavits containing data important to you.

On the other hand, you probably cannot access most of the "discovery" the parties provided. The discovery comprises answers to written questions; documents provided for review; and transcripts of depositions, if that material was never introduced into evidence. In addition, if the case has been settled, the terms of that settlement may be withheld from the public record if the parties have agreed to do so and the judge handling the case approved it.

■ Academics and Academic Resources
  Faculty
  Regular Publications
  Special and One-time Studies
  Industry Research Centers
  Specialized Libraries
  Teaching Materials

■ Consumer and Advocacy Groups
  Product Tests and Comparisons
  Regular Publications
  One-time Studies
  Position Papers

■ Experts
  Consultants
  Expert Witnesses
  Security Analysts

■ Trade Associations
  Regular Publications
  Membership Directories
  Special Studies and Reports
  Meetings
  Reprints of Speeches
  Statistical Abstracts

Exhibit 6.2: Typical Specialized Interest Group Sources

may provide you with such useful input as publications, special detailed studies, and access to research centers for collecting important historical data.

Here is a specific example. Many companies give interviews and other materials to the Harvard Business School to assist its professors in preparing case materials for use in MBA courses. The Harvard Business School sells these case materials at a low price to other schools for their business programs. Private companies can also buy the case materials, however. Although the material tends to be a little dated, the studies can be quite revealing. A case note prepared in 1983 on Canon, the giant Japanese copier manufacturer, profiled the firm's long-term strategy for penetrating the copier markets both in the United States and throughout the world. Given the conservative nature of the Japanese corporation, that material is almost as accurate today as it was when it was first published.

> *Have you considered whether a business school case study may help you understand a market or large competitor?*

Consumer and other advocacy groups have an "ax to grind." That is usually the advancement of the public good as they perceive it. However, they may well be spending significant time and funds to collect data, publish reports, bring lawsuits, or test products and services, all of which can provide raw data for you.

"Experts" can include consultants, expert witnesses, and security analysts. Their work reflects a common goal: to advance the individual's career, whether it is by obtaining assignments, by helping an employer sell stock, or by some other means. One subgroup, investment analysts, often is privy to information that differs both in detail and currency from that made available to the general press or even the business press. For example, analysts may receive financial and marketing strategy briefings that the business press never sees.

The issue is, then, how you can access the data analysts receive. There are at least four ways:

■ Obtain copies of the reports and studies these analysts prepare. You can identify the reports as well as the individuals preparing them by using sources such as InvesText®, a database (see Chapter 8), or specialized directories of such research reports, both in hard copy and online.

■ Contact the company involved and ask for a copy of any briefing it has given to analysts. Some corporations will cheerfully provide these; others will have little or nothing to provide.

■ Check both online and offline sources, such as the Wall Street Transcript, which provides summaries or even the full text of such briefings.

■ Interview the investment analyst directly.

Trade associations exist for the "good of their industry." In some industries, trade associations are unwilling or even unable to share data with nonassociation members. This may be due to association rules to protect the members or just due to limited resources. In other industries, the trade associations are important, but little known, research and resource centers whose data is available to all outsiders.

In addition, a trade association can serve as a means of accessing employees of the competitor. For instance, purchasing a trade association's membership directory may enable you to find out who at a competitor is responsible for the area in which you have a particular interest. Similarly, attending a trade show may give you access not only to products and promotional materials but also to people. Finally, trade association committees can be good places for collecting raw data. For example, you may be able to find out important facts about your target company simply by finding out what committees the company is represented on. Beyond that, you can also use the directory to identify your own employees (or others) who are on key committees and who might be willing to discuss what they have heard or inferred about the target competitor from meetings of the committee.

Private Sector

The private sector includes persons and organizations whose business involves the data you seek. For some, providing the data *is* their business. Others come across data you may need as a part of their own business. Exhibit 6.3 lists common private sector sources of data.

The private sector makes up the most eclectic of the four groups of information sources. Business information services include firms such as Dun & Bradstreet and Standard & Poor's that provide a wide range of business data, as well as firms that provide credit reports. However, in dealing with these sources in particular, avoid confusing the package with its contents.

To be specific, assume that you have just received a TRW Credit Report on a competitor and are reviewing the data it provides on the firm's size, employees, sales, and so on. To verify the data, you compare it with data obtained from another business information source, such as Dun & Bradstreet. The facts appear to be similar or even identical. Such confirmation from another business information source does not mean, however, that you can assume that the data is necessarily correct.

You see, TRW *buys* the data you were just reviewing. So if it looks the same as data from another business source, that may be because it is the same. It may have actually come from the source with which you are comparing it. That does not mean it is correct. This is known as *false confirmation*, which we discuss in Chapter 12. It is also related to the issue of confusing the source with the provider, as discussed earlier.

■ Business Information Services
Dun & Bradstreet
Standard & Poor's
Credit Reports

■ Chambers of Commerce
Domestic
Foreign Chambers in the United States
U.S. Chambers Abroad

■ Your Own Employees
Sales
Market Research
Planning
Engineering
Purchasing
Former Employees of the Target Company

■ Target Company
Employees
Catalogs and Price Lists
In-house Publications
Press Releases and Speeches
Advertisements and Promotional Materials
Products
Annual Reports and Other Regulatory Filings
Former Employees
Competitors
Customers
Suppliers
Retailers, Distributors, and Agents
Ad Agencies
Consultants
Investment and Commercial Banks

Exhibit 6.3: Typical Private Sector Sources

Skipping to another example of private sector data sources, look at your own firm. Internal data sources can be particularly valuable. Where should you be looking for data that your firm might already have? Consider the following:

■   Your own sales staff. Salespeople deal daily with your customers; thus salespeople can be getting a lot of feedback about your competitors.

■   Your market research department. This group may be wired into resources, such as your own advertising agencies, that can provide critical data. For example, your market researchers may already be collecting sample advertising by a competitor just to serve as a model for their own efforts.

■   Your planning, engineering, and purchasing personnel. All of these people may be dealing with their counterparts at the targeted competitor. These relations may be through formal channels, such as associations; through indirect mechanisms, such as through common providers of goods and services; or through networks, such as common contacts within firms for which they worked before.

■   Your employees who formerly worked for the target firm. They may be hard to find, but what they have to say, if it is fairly current, may be very enlightening.

> *One of the best sources of information on a competitor is the competitor.*

The last data source is the target company itself. Consider the following potential sources of raw data, all prepared and released by your competitor:

115

Finding Information About Your Competitors
■ ■ ■

- ■ Annual reports
- ■ Catalogs
- ■ In-house publications
- ■ Press releases
- ■ Price lists
- ■ Promotional packages
- ■ Regulatory filings
- ■ Samples of products
- ■ Speeches by executives

Companies are often more than willing to discuss what they are doing. For example, many non-U.S.-based corporations have concluded that they must develop an image of openness in order to do business in the United States. The result is the production of corporate information brochures, such as one produced by Siemens Corporate Research and Support, Inc., "Siemens Manufacturing—A U.S. Perspective." This eight-page report outlines the scope of the U.S. operations and the nature of the U.S. facilities owned by a German multinational parent doing over $25 billion in business each year.

Substantially more detail is provided in NEC Corporation's corporate profile, "NEC: A Growing Commitment to America." This 12-page presentation, first printed as an advertisement in *Fortune* magazine, provides plant-level details about the Japanese telecommunications company's numerous U.S. facilities.

Media
These sources generate and collect data for a specific audience. To fully understand both the data you may find and how to analyze it, you must understand from whom the media collects it, how, and why. Exhibit 6.4 summarizes common media data sources.

The media, in the broadest sense, can be one of the most fruitful resources. In particular, always remember that many publications exist to serve a particular industry or market. Thus they are, or should be, positioned to help you locate important data and develop leads for additional data.

■ Business Newspapers and Magazines
Advertisements
Want Ads
Articles
Reporters

■ Wire Services
Articles
Reporters

■ Directories and Reference Aids

■ Local and National Newspapers
Advertisements
Want Ads
Articles
Reporters
Obituaries

■ Technical Journals
Articles
Authors

■ Trade Papers and Journals
Advertisements
Want Ads
Articles
Reporters
Marketing Studies and Media Kits
Special Issues
Related Publications

■ Financial Periodicals

■ Security Analysts' Reports
Company Reports
Industry Profiles

Exhibit 6.4:   Typical Media Sources

117

Finding Information About Your Competitors
■ ■ ■

How do you locate the important publications? There are several ways:

1. Ask someone who knows about the industry, such as an industry desk officer at the U.S. Department of Commerce.

2. Check with the relevant trade association; it may print one of the publications in which you should be interested.

3. Check an advertiser-oriented publication, such as those issued by Standard Rate & Data Service, Inc. (SRDS). Such publications divide periodicals of all kinds by industry and, for each field, indicate the subject matters covered, audience served, and frequency of publication. The goals of the SRDS publications are to enable advertisers to place their message most effectively. They can serve to help you find that message.

> *Have you ever checked a trade publication's media kit as a data source about your competitors?*

What kind of help can you expect from trade and industry media resources?

■   They carry stories, announcements, annual industry reviews, interviews, and advertisements. In short, some print the raw data you are seeking.

■   They can provide leads—to experts, to studies and reports, to court cases, and the like.

■ They can give you information on the industry that they cover. For example, advertising departments need to show that their publication is a good advertising buy. To do that, they usually develop a media kit. In addition to specific information about the publication, its advertising rates, and schedules of special issues (themselves an important resource), the kit may contain special studies commissioned by or paid for by the publication.

For example, to promote itself as the best magazine in which to advertise trucks, *Southern Motor Cargo*'s advertising department commissions a study each year on new registrations of all kinds of cars and trucks, by manufacturer and model year, and distributes the results to its potential advertisers. That data is national and regional. The goal is to show you, as a potential advertiser, that this publication reaches most of the audience you want to reach—buyers of new trucks. If you need data on truck production by company, this report data might be a good substitute for an estimate of the production by specific model by each of the companies.

To take another example, one firm was very interested in plant-level data on a particular factory owned by a major international petrochemical corporation. A careful survey of the trade press disclosed general information about the plant's initial and ultimate potential capacity. This was important, but it did not indicate what the plant now produced or at what stage in its expansion it stood. But other sources were used to produce the missing data. The key data was provided by a local newspaper and the chamber of commerce.

A local newspaper had run several stories on the plant because it was the town's largest employer. The stories included information on the current number of employees, where the latest new construction stood (with pictures), and even on the specific products currently being produced. A call to the local Chamber of Commerce produced a four-color glossy booklet promoting doing business in the area. Featured in the booklet was a full-page

---

CI CLOSEUP: "Using the Press"

In recent years, the increase in takeover activity has resulted in the growth of so-called rumor wires. They were created by major news services to cash in on professional investors' thirst for the latest gossip about companies and stocks. Sometimes these rumor wires are targets of manipulation, however. In one case, a reporter was called by a corporate raider who wanted to tell the reporter that a rumor being spread about the raider and a particular company was true.

The problem was that the reporter had not even heard the rumor. What the raider really wanted to do was to make sure that the reporter heard the gossip, so that it would be put on the newswire. The story, even labeled as a rumor, would then spread more quickly and could, the raider hoped, put pressure on the company mentioned in the rumor.[5]

---

advertising spread by the plant. That ad included color photos of the plant, taken from an airplane, as well as many interior shots showing equipment and finished products. The photos, the clippings from the local paper, and the data on the plant's expansion potential provided raw materials for the detailed CI being sought.

Summary

If you treat the CI data you are seeking as a commodity, you can find the most likely public sources for the facts you need. You may even be able to tap information already collected by others, such as government regulatory bodies or academic researchers.

Always distinguish between where you obtain CI facts and who ultimately originated that information. Avoid confusing the provider of the data with its source.

Likely sources of raw data include all levels of government, from the local building department to federal files; specialized interest groups, including academics and analysts; private sector resources at services such as Dun & Bradstreet including those within your firm or at the competitor; and the media.

CI ALERT: What does this tell you?

"Alliance Research Corporation, an electronics supply company, has relocated to its new headquarters at 9410 Owensmouth St., Chatsworth, CA 91311.

"The 80,000-square-foot building also will serve as the national warehouse for all divisions of ARC, including ORA Electronics, DATA SPEC, and STUDIO SPEC."

Source: Announcement, Telecommunications Equipment Retailer, August 1989.

Notes

1. The Conference Board, Inc., *Competitive Intelligence*, Research Report No. 913, 1988, p. 5.

2. JoAnna Poncavage, "Paper Tycoon Faked Credit, U.S. Says," *The Morning Call*, April 17, 1987, pp. B1, B5.

3. John Clark, "L.V. Men Among 8 Indicted in $1.5 Million Fraud Case," *The Morning Call*, March 17, 1989, pp. A1-A2.

4. The Conference Board, Inc., *Competitive Intelligence*, Research Report No. 913, 1988, p. 19.

5. John Crudele, "Takeover Artists Adept at Using the Press," *The Sunday Call*, January 1, 1989, p. D3.

Chapter 7

Developing Research Strategies and Techniques

CI CLIP

"We always have to ask: What do you really want to know? What are you going to do with the information? How will it affect your decisions?"

Director of Marketing Information, Kraft, Inc.[1]

The success of your CI efforts depends on how well you recognize the constraints you are subject to, how well you structure the data-gathering process, and how practical your decisions are about the trade-offs of your CI sources.

Basic Guidelines

If there is any rule to follow in conducting your CI research, it is "Be realistic but optimistic. If you can determine what you need, the data is almost always somewhere to be found."

To locate the raw data you may need for your CI, remember the guideline from Chapter 6: Reason out who else has an interest in that data and why they have an interest. Each person or organization you have identified in this way is a potential source for your raw data. For example, if you are interested in the sales of certain departments in chain drugstores, using these criteria could lead you to trade associations, corporate annual reports, and trade publications.

Do not limit yourself. If you have identified a trade publication of potential interest, check whether that publication has a special annual issue that covers major financial or marketing issues including those that concern you.

Constraints

Your CI research and collection strategy must reflect the unique CI needs of each assignment. Among the critical points to take into account in developing a research and collection strategy are the following:

- Time constraints
- Financial restrictions
- Staffing limitations
- Self-imposed constraints
- Likelihood of obtaining the data
- Relative priorities of data
- Sequencing of raw data

Time

Time is one of the most critical elements in CI. The key factor here is for you to determine when the information is needed, then work backward. For instance, if you have three weeks to develop data on the market plans for new products of key competitors, planning to go to a trade show that will be held in four weeks is not a viable option.

CI CLOSEUP: "The New Inside Information"

A new business is developing in Washington, D.C.—a service that jumps on documents as soon as they are filed with the U.S. Securities and Exchange Commission, the Federal Trade Commission, and other agencies. The mission of this business is to identify and then transmit, quickly and accurately, to their Wall Street clients parts of documents filed and released by these agencies. The services are looking for data that can affect stock prices. To their clients, "getting information one minute ahead of everyone else can mean millions of dollars in profits."[2]

However, knowing about the trade show may cause you to change the nature of your assignment and try to get an extension on its due date. For example, you might want to spend the time before the trade show learning about marketing strategies, then attend the trade show or review the trade press coverage of the show. Such a plan provides you with specific details on new products, which you can integrate with the general data you have already developed on strategies in order to present a complete picture of your competitors' marketing plans for their new products.

Money

Financial restrictions drive more CI decisions than most people realize. For example, should you plan to interview key executives in person or over the telephone? Interviews are likely to produce more raw data but cost considerably more.

Similarly, if you monitor a competitor over a prolonged period of time, using a clipping service may be a cost-effective way to collect articles about the firm. However, if the analysis of the same competitor is just a one-time project, you might do better using online commercial databases, even if their costs average $250 an hour. Such services provide you the data you need virtually immediately and permit you to go back in time, whereas a clipping service generally only allows you to go forward.

Staffing

The amount and timing of staff resources that you can put on a project can be a very important constraint. Other types of staffing limitations include considerations such as how many people are available, what they can do, and when. Typically—if there is a typical case—a CI assignment requires fewer personnel during the planning and early collection phases than it does in the middle, when the data collection and review work begins to pile up. And, at the end, bottlenecks develop as stacks of unsynthesized information accumulate.

You probably can use very few people to help you analyze the raw data and present it, but the process of analysis may consume most of the time of those involved. This means that these people (including you) may not be available to handle the collection of necessary supplementary data. You may need to plan for quick access to a few people familiar with the earlier stages for assistance in supplemental research at the end.

Self-Imposed Constraints

Self-imposed constraints vary widely. You may be comfortable with contacting your competitors directly. However, you may also find that you cannot do this due to company policy. This may force you to approach the project from a different angle.

Another constraint may be a limit on what you tell your competitors. For example, although a survey of your competitors might appear to be a useful data-gathering device, you may find that you do not want to share *any* of the results of the survey with those surveyed. That means that you should probably not use a survey as a data collection tool.

Yet another constraint may be a concern about too many employees learning about a project within your own company. In some cases, you may not want your employees to be involved with the assignment at all, for example, in cases involving a potential acquisition. This constraint may mean either abandoning the project entirely or turning it over to outside CI specialists.

How Likely Are You to Get What You Want?

Make a preliminary determination of the likelihood of your obtaining good data from each target source you have identified. Assume that you have concluded that a particular trade association may be a good source for the raw data you need. What is the likelihood that the association will have exactly what you want, that it will provide it to you, *and* that this will happen within your time and cost limitations? Similarly, if your project involves reviewing the back issues of a local newspaper for want ads placed by a target competitor in 1985 and 1986, is it likely that you can access a complete set of issues for the years 1985–1986? If not, before you start, try to identify alternative approaches or sources of data that may satisfy your CI needs.

What Do You Need First?

Throughout your CI research, maintain a clear idea of the relative importance of the data you are seeking and of the data sources you are trying to locate. Do not waste time tracking down minor pieces of data to produce a picture-perfect product. CI is not academic research; it is a commercial activity—one in which the final product ages rapidly. CI that is not delivered on time loses substantial portions of its value, and may quickly become worthless.

> *Remember, CI is time sensitive. Getting a good answer on time is usually more important than getting a great answer sometime in the future.*

In setting your CI research and data collection needs, your progress may depend on collecting certain data first. For example, if you are going to interview key personnel at a competitor's distributors, you must first identify the distributors, then identify the key people at each one.

Also, some data arrives more slowly, even when you have located it. To understand the trade-offs involved in timeliness, compare the following potential ways of obtaining the contents of documents filed by a target competitor with the U.S. Securities and Exchange Commission:

■ You can ask the target firm for copies of them (slow but cheap, *if* the firm responds).

■ You can get summaries of key documents online through a database (faster, more expensive, but *sometimes* incomplete).

■ You can hire a commercial service to copy the documents directly from the SEC's files and air ship or fax them directly to you (more costly but complete and swift).

> *Often in your CI work, you will face a trade-off between time and money.*

Similar choices are involved with almost any documents in which you may be interested. If, for example, you have identified a potentially helpful report available through the National Technical Information Service of the U.S. Department of Commerce, you can call up and order that report. However, it can take two to six weeks for a regular telephone order to be filled. Although this is slow, the service is quite reasonably priced. A rush order is handled much faster, often overnight, but it carries a substantial additional charge for *each* document ordered, plus express shipping charges. Again, that option is faster but much more expensive.

In addition to deciding what you need first, consider two other related concepts: tiering your research, and exploring and exploiting linkages in your research.

Tiering CI Research

Often, you may not be able to find the exact data you think you need either quickly or easily. This is particularly problematic when your time, money, or personnel resources are limited. When a project turns out to be excessively demanding, divide your assignment into tiers, or levels, of research.

Attack the most general level first and go after the most easily obtained data from public sources, which can then be reviewed quickly. Next, analyze that data in terms of what it tells you about additional, more specific data you need to complete your task, and where that data may be. Then, move to the next tier, collect and analyze the results, and continue until you are done. By doing this, you can often save both time and money, because you focus your resources on locating the most critical bits of more specific data in the second and following tiers.

Linkages in Research

When you look for raw data, do not restrict your search. Not only can one source provide several important types of data but multiple sources should be checked to generate data on the same point. For example, do not rely only on either online databases or hard-copy sources alone for data.

Finding Information About Your Competitors
■ ■ ■

To illustrate how and where data obtained from online databases can be linked with data from other sources of CI, Exhibit 7.1 summarizes the sources of raw data actually used in a CI project conducted by a major aerospace contractor. The company sought information about the technological capabilities of one of its competitors in a particular market.[3] That report was based on some data from each of the listed sources. The sources marked * can be searched and reprinted, in whole or substantial part through commercial online databases.

The aerospace company identified the specific data sources that made the most significant contributions to portions of the final report as follows:

1. *Overview and History of the Competitor:* Magazine and news articles, competitor's product brochures, business school case studies.

2. *Organization and Product Lines:* Financial directory data.

3. *Financial Data:* Annual reports, 10-K and quarterly reports, investment bank reports.

4. *Corporate Strategy:* Annual report, magazine and news articles, investment bank reports.

5. *Company Relationships:* Interviews.

6. *Marketing Strategies:* Interviews, advertisements.

7. *Research and Development Strategies:* Annual report, presentations at technical conferences, interviews.

8. *Defense Contracts:* Contracts awarded by the federal government.

10-K and Quarterly Reports Filed with the SEC by the Competitor*

Advertisements Placed by the Competitor

Annual Reports to Shareholders Distributed by the Competitor*

Case Studies of the Competitor Prepared by Business Schools

Competitor's Briefing Packages for Investment Analysts

Competitor's In-house Directories

Competitor's Product Brochures

Contracts Awarded by the Federal Government to the Competitor*

Financial Directory Data on the Competitor*

Interviews with the Competitor and with Other Mutual Competitors

Interviews with Customers of the Competitor

Interviews with Former Employees of the Competitor

Interviews with the Corporation's Own Management, Marketing Personnel, Program Managers, Engineers, and Scientists

Investment Analyst Reports on the Competitor's Performance and Its Plans*

Magazine and Newspaper Articles About the Competitor*

Organizational Charts of the Competitor

Presentations by the Competitor's Employees at Technical and Professional Conferences*

Proxy Statements of the Competitor

The Final Report on the Competitor covered eight major topics:
1. Overview and History of the Competitor
2. Organization and Product Lines
3. Financial Data
4. Corporate Strategy
5. Company Relationships
6. Marketing Strategies
7. Research and Development Strategies
8. Defense Contracts

Exhibit 7.1:   CI Data Sources Used by an Aerospace Company

Finish It

> ### *CI CLIP*
> *"Nearly every project could logically be extended into a lifetime study if you consider everything that bears on it directly or indirectly."*
> *Former military intelligence officer.*[4]

In planning and executing your research strategy, be thorough, but do not be obsessive. In economics there is a concept called "satisfysing," a term that evokes a combination of satisfactory and satisfied. In the context of CI, satisfysing is important. To you, it means accepting something that is less than perfect but that accomplishes almost the same desired end. In other words, many times you have to say "close enough"!

> *You are done when your research has taken you back to where you started.*

How do you know when you are done? In some cases, unfortunately, you will not know until you get there. There is an informal test we have found useful. It is called "tail-chasing" or, more elegantly, "closing the loop." This occurs when new sources of raw data continually give you leads that take you back to previously exploited sources. At that point, you are usually near the end of your basic research.

Developing CI Strategies
for a Smaller or Emerging Company

Too often, people assume that CI works well only against public companies. That is not always true. In fact, it may never be true. CI can work against almost any type of business of almost any size.

One way for the small, independent business to develop CI is to look inward and think about its own experiences. Try listing the following:

■ Every place you have sent documents of any type.

■ Every government agency, at every level, with which you have dealt or will deal.

■ Every marketing channel into which you have sent information on your company, its products, and its services.

■ Every directory or business information service inquiry you have answered.

■ Every part of the media that has expressed an interest in what you do, as well as every part of the media you have tried, perhaps in vain, to interest in your venture.

Notice that you should include in your list anyplace you sent information on a confidential basis. The reason for that is that confidential information does not always stay put. When it moves, it may lose its confidentiality.

If you are thorough, you will find you have generated an impressive list of places to start checking on your own competition.

Some information is relatively easy to find and can provide a good starting place for small business CI. Following is a list of key areas for small business CI that are generally easier to develop data about.

Finding Information About Your Competitors
■ ■ ■

■ Ownership: major shareholders, partners, and investors.

■ Special relationships with larger corporations: exclusive licensing agreements, joint ventures, sale of minority interests or other investments by major corporations in the competitor.

■ Number of direct competitors, their product (or services), and locations.

■ Industry marketing, distribution, and pricing practices.

■ Regulatory constraints.

■ Competing product lines and services currently offered.

■ Customer service policies and performance.

■ Channels of distribution, including their strengths and weaknesses, as well as possible changes in distribution channels.

■ Credit, discounts, incentives, consignments, and other special pricing policies.

■ Type of sales force: in-house versus independent sales agents.

■ Marketing approaches and their current effectiveness.

■ Samples of advertising literature and other promotional materials.

■ History of any questionable marketing practices.

■ Major lawsuits and regulatory actions; probable impacts on company.

■ Current manufacturing methods and processes.

■ Key patents and proprietary technology.

■ Facilities: locations, current performance, and potential.

■ How the company sees itself.

Summary

As you develop strategies for your CI program, analyze the constraints that are inherent in your efforts—time, money, and staffing—as well as constraints you place on yourself.

Determine what data you need first, then try methods like the tiered approach or linkages to save time and money. Finally, learn to know when to accept the limits of what you have gathered and synthesize your results. Because CI data is so time sensitive, your highest priority usually is to get the information to the people who need it, so it can be used for effective decision making when it's needed.

CI ALERT: What does this tell you?

"In other regions of the United States, we are developing our operations based on the characteristics of each region. . . . In the Midwest, centered on Chicago with its important capital market serving many of the largest U.S. corporations, we are concentrating on corporate banking and on building our corporate client base. In the South, we are promoting futures and options trading and corporate business with Japanese and U.S. companies, especially in the Atlanta area, where many Japanese companies are located."

Source: The Dai-Ichi Kangyo Bank, Limited, Annual Report 1989.

Notes

1. The Conference Board, Inc., *Competitive Intelligence*, Research Report No. 913, 1988, p. 25.

2. John Crudele, "Companies Bloom to Watch SEC Actions," *The Sunday Call*, May 7, 1989, p. D3.

3. David Conley, "Competitive Analysis Case Study A," SCIP Annual Business Meeting and Workshop, March 19, 1987.

4. Washington Platt, *Strategic Intelligence Production*, New York: Frederick A. Praeger, 1957, p. 13.

Chapter 8

Specific CI Techniques

CI CLIP

"Without the application of competitor intelligence, a utility simply has to accept the word of its customers concerning the competitive standards it must meet."

Manager of Regulatory Finance, Portland General Electric Company.[1]

Now that you have the basic principles of gathering raw data in mind, we can show you just how to use them. In this chapter we cover a number of specific techniques. In Chapter 9 we expand on one of them—the use of online databases.

Finding Information About Your Competitors
■ ■ ■

Using Government Sources and Resources

As Chapter 6 showed, the U.S. government can be a veritable gold mine of business and economic information, much of which should be useful to you in your CI research. If you have ever tried to obtain some of that data, however, you may have given up in frustration.

Based on experience in dealing with the federal government, we can offer you some hints. Although the tips apply to getting information directly from the federal government in Washington, D.C., the same principles apply when you deal indirectly with the federal government through its regional offices. In addition, we have found the hints to be just as worthwhile in contacting many state, county, and municipal offices.

In general, writing for the information you want can take too long, or it may be impossible to do. Often you may not know *exactly* what you want or who has it, so you are guessing about both the subject of the study or the data collection efforts you want and the identity of the office or person who has it. Remember these caveats:

■ If your written inquiry for data is not directed to precisely the correct person or office, you may never get a reply.

■ If the written inquiry does not specify what you are seeking in terms that are familiar to the agency to which you are writing, it can take weeks before your request gets to the proper person or office, if it ever gets there.

> *When you want something from the federal government, the best way to get it is probably to use the telephone.*

That means, in most cases, you use the telephone to reach the right agency, office, and person. Before you call, be ready to make notes so you can retrace your steps to your final contact person.

Know What You Are Looking For
Before you begin making calls, jot down what you want in a single sentence. You will have to be able to elaborate on your request and eventually explain why the data you are seeking is important, but you do not have to start with that. If you do not know exactly what you want, get as close as possible. In your single sentence, try to use key words like *data, reports, studies*, and *expert*.

The key to successful government telephone inquiries is to keep the statement of your search very short but to include all of the most important concepts. Your first words in the request are the ones on which the representative you speak to will take action.

Try the reporter's technique of expressing the most important concepts in the first few sentences and placing key words first in your sentences. The words that are important vary from agency to agency. For example, if you call the Department of Agriculture about the price of sugar, stress *price* and *sugar* together. Merely asking for data about crop prices will not get you very far, because there are many persons and offices within the U.S. Department of Agriculture concerned with some aspect of crop prices.

On the other hand, at International Trade Administration (ITA), the key words probably should be *crops*, not *sugar*, followed by *price*. This is because the ITA deals with crops, raw materials, and manufactured goods, so focusing your inquiry on crops is important.

Where Do You Start?
To learn what office to call, refer to books like Congressional Quarterly's *Washington Information Directory* or another of the directories listed in Appendix B. Do not stop there; solicit suggestions from your co-workers or from a trade association to which your company belongs.

139

Finding Information About Your Competitors
■ ■ ■

> *There is no such thing as a fact without a context.*

If those do not give you a good idea of where to start, contact either the public information office of a likely agency or the office of the secretary or administrator of that agency. From that point, you can work your way through the agency.

Avoid any referral by directory assistance or any reference book to a federal information operator, because you only get a telephone number from such a source. Those numbers are almost always indexed by the name of the person to whom you wish to speak, rather than by the name of the unit you are trying to reach. Also, if you call that number for help, you cannot then be transferred to another federal number.

A further complication is that almost every source of information on federal agencies and their telephone numbers is usually a little out of date. Telephone numbers, personnel, particular assignments, and even agencies change too rapidly for anyone to keep up with everything. In fact, even the federal information operator is likely to be as wrong as any other source of government telephone numbers.

When Should You Call?
If you have a choice about when you solicit the data,

■ Avoid calling government offices on Monday or after a three-day weekend.

■ Avoid calling on a Friday afternoon during the summer months. Just as with private businesses, there is always a lot of catching up on that day.

■ Call before 3:00 P.M. in the agency's time zone.

■ Avoid the period just around lunch time.

What Etiquette Should You Follow
in Government Calls?

These tips should minimize frustration for you and the government representative you speak with:

■ Make certain you will not be interrupted when you make your calls. Locating the data you want could take some time, so allow enough "search" time.

■ After you identify yourself, confirm where the representative works and his or her extension.

■ Explain why you want the data as well as what you want, so the representative can determine where the data you want might be.

■ Try to note buzzwords used by the representative. They may turn out to be your key to getting data. Revise your target question to incorporate or avoid some of the important buzzwords.

■ If what the representative says does *not* apply or is not covered by an agency or unit of a department, take note. That way you will not get transferred back to that office by someone else.

■ Get suggestions about where you can acquire new leads, but don't rush off to call immediately. When you get the data from the representative, ask him or her for other suggestions about where to call, particularly other government agencies but also perhaps academics, consultants, experts, or trade associations. Even if these outsiders lack specific information, they may be able to direct you back to another part of the same agency or a different agency that can also help you.

■ Ask for a name you can call for more help. Ask whether you can use the name of the person you are speaking to in contacting the names you are given. A referral like that can save time and speed up return telephone calls.

141

How Should You Handle Transfers and Referrals?

You will probably have to be transferred at least once when you call government offices. Before you are transferred, make sure you have the direct dial number (with area code for federal offices, because Washington, D.C., offices cover three area codes), as well as the name and office of the person to whom you are being transferred. Even if you are just referred to someone else, but not transferred on the telephone, you will need this.

When someone tells you he or she will transfer you, make sure you know the number you are being transferred to—and the number you are being transferred from.

Of course, if you are stuck in one of the increasingly popular computerized transfer systems (the ones in which the recording prompts, "Press 1 if you want this office. . ."), you can face even more difficulties. How do *you* know which office or service you need? One suggestion is to select the one that sounds best. Once you have located a real person, resist being transferred back into the system; firmly ask for a name, extension, and department if you have to talk with an operator.

Sometimes you can get stuck in an endless loop: Representative A transfers you to B, B transfers you to C, and C tries to send you back to A. Simply say, "I've already spoken with A. He (or she) suggested you could help." Get help in breaking out of a loop. Sometimes just knowing where you have been, without success, may help a federal employee know where you should try.

How Can You Get Documents and Materials Easily?

When you have finished with your conversation, ask if there are any documents that can be sent to you. If so, how long will it take to get them out? Remember, at some agencies, copying may involve a long wait. If you are referred to a publication for the information, get the *full* name and *all identifying numbers* of that document before you hang up. Shorthand titles or incomplete names are of little or no use when you go to the library or order a document from the U.S. Government Printing Office.

When you are sure what documents to order, have ready a clear and simple address where the materials can be sent. Be patient. They take a while to get to you.

Make a note if someone is sending you literature so you can follow up if you do not get it. But allow a week before you do follow up. Even though U.S. government official materials are supposed to go by first class mail, experience shows that they take longer than you might expect for first class.

Overnight Express Shipments
If you need the materials quickly, you can ask if the person can have it sent by overnight air freight and charged to your account. Some agencies can and will do this. If you intend to ask for this service, prepare in advance of calling with the account number, job number, and any other data the representative will enter on the freight bill. A federal employee can *only* do this if it is being charged to your account.

Faxing Materials
Sending data via facsimile machines is an increasingly popular option among businesses. Its popularity among government agencies varies. Some willingly fax materials; others have a limit—informal or formal—on the number of pages they can fax. If this is the case, respect the limit.

Still other government agencies can only fax materials at the end of the day (or later) to save on telephone charges. If that is the case, make sure you leave your fax on its automatic setting and ensure that it has enough paper.

You may even find that some agencies, for cost reasons, do not fax any materials. If someone says he or she cannot use the fax, you might want to offer to absorb the charges by having the call made collect.

Congressional Materials

Capitol Hill is a special case. For example, you generally get information from a Congressional committee staffperson. To request documents, you are transferred to the same committee's document clerk. Get the title, date, and committee print number for each document you want from the staffperson before you are transferred to the clerk.

However, if you are getting committee reports that summarize the bills being considered and hearings held or a copy of a bill or public law, you generally contact the clerk of the House or Senate or the House or Senate Document room. For these offices, ensure that you have the document number, which begins with the number of the Congress—that is, H. Rep. 100–1101 or P.L. 99–51. Such offices (and some committees) do not send out materials based on a phone request. You must write and enclose a self-addressed label or envelope for them to use. Call first, however, to confirm they have copies in stock before you write and to make sure you are writing to the correct office. Some, but not all, of them will hold the materials aside while they wait for your request and label.

Another tip is to ask the sender to enclose a card or a note containing his or her name so that you can call again if you have any questions about the materials.

If you are referred to a report printed either by the United States Government Printing Office (USGPO) or the National Technical Information Service (NTIS), U.S. Department of Commerce, it is critical for you to get the full title, date, and most importantly the full access number before you hang up. You need this information when you order and pay for copies of documents. Documents from these agencies take an especially long time to be delivered. In the case of NTIS, you can pay for expedited handling.

Government agencies provide valuable data for your CI program, but often the lead time required to obtain government documents is excessive. A much faster—although more costly—method for finding competitive information is the online database.

Using Online Databases

> **Online database:** *A collection of information on a particular topic, such as stock prices or company profiles, or from a predetermined set of sources, such as the Associated Press wire service. It is assembled so it can be stored in a large computer and accessed electronically.*
>
> **Commercial database:** *An online database accessible by computer over telephone lines that is offered to members or the public for an access fee.*

To use a commercial database, you must first arrange for permission to use it and to pay for it. Usually, you are given a password so you can access the database from your computer using telephone lines. Once you access the central computer storing the databases (called "signing on"), you can search databases using key index terms, codes, or identification numbers inserted by the company preparing the database, or by searching for any word or words you select.

Sometimes individual databases are provided directly by the firms that create them, such as the legal research database WESTLAW®, available directly from the West Publishing Company. However, more often you will be going to an intermediary, known as an *online service vendor* or simply a vendor. Vendors load individual databases onto their own computers and make them available online by subscription. They are like wholesalers. To contact one, check the listing of popular business database vendors, such as DIALOG® and BRS, in Appendix B.

> *There are two basic types of databases: biblio-graphic and full text.*

The two basic types of databases are bibliographic and full text. Understanding what data each contains and how it is arranged will help you understand how to design a search, how to execute that search, and how to use the results.

What Do Databases Contain?

Commercial databases contain vast amounts of information on virtually every subject. Although there is no definitive source of information on what is in every database, one way to check on these is to use another database, the Database of Databases, available through Dialog Information Services, Inc.

For businesses in the private sector, surprising amounts of information can be available through databases. Filings with the U.S. Securities and Exchange Commission—searchable on several databases—can disclose critical competitive information. For example, a filing may contain your competitor's forecasts for market growth over the next several years, as well as an overview of its research and development efforts, which can help you to respond with your own strategies. The Disclosure® database, available through DIALOG among other services, is an example of a database you can use for searching government filings.

146

CI CLOSEUP: "Commercial Databases"

"Unclassified technical documents from all countries—including engineering analyses and research results—are targeted by Soviet intelligence and other collectors because of their value to Soviet engineers seeking creative designs and alternative engineering approaches. . . . The individual abstracts or references in government and commercial databases are unclassified, but some of the information, taken in the aggregate, may reveal sensitive information concerning U.S. strategic capabilities and vulnerabilities. Numerous unclassified U.S. Department of Defense and contractor documents are sought by the Soviets from the Commerce Department's National Technical Information Service. Documents dealing with design, evaluation, and testing of U.S. weapon systems . . . are in the [NTIS] database."

U.S. Department of Defense.[2]

What Do Databases *Not* Contain?

The only information not potentially available through a commercial database is information that has restrictions on its release, such as classified government documents or individual credit records. Note in particular that you cannot directly find out any information that has not been released to the public in some form at some time, such as the income of an officer of a privately held business. And, of course, you cannot find information that has not yet been collected.

147

Finding Information About Your Competitors
■ ■ ■

Bibliographic Databases
Bibliographic databases were the earliest of the commercial databases. As the name implies, they were basically lists, or bibliographies, of books and magazine articles organized by title, author, and subject. These have grown over the years in number and scope.

Today's bibliographic database usually provides all of the following information with each entry:

■ The title of the book, article, paper, report, hearing, or lawsuit. In most cases, a subtitle is included if available. That subtitle can be very helpful, particularly when you are dealing with publications whose titles are designed to catch the eye and not to alert researchers to the full scope of the underlying article.

■ The author of the work. Unfortunately, you do not always find the author's *full* name. Some databases, however, include identifying information, such as the author's professional credentials and affiliation at the time the article was published.

■ The name of the publication where the article was published or the organization before which a paper was presented. The name of the publication or group can be an important tip-off about the contents of the work. For example, you would expect differing types of information on selling insurance to senior citizens to appear in *Marketing Communications*, in *Life Insurance Selling*, and in *Modern Maturity*.

■ The date of the work. For a book, this is the year in which it was published, not when it was actually written. For an article, this is the cover date of the issue in which it appeared, which is not the actual date of publication. For a news story, it is the date of the newspaper in which it was printed or the date it first appeared on a wire service. The

148

dateline may also include the pages in the publication on which the article appeared.

■ An abstract of the piece. This is a summary of the document's contents, often prepared by someone other than the author.

■ Indexing terms. Instead of, or in addition to, an abstract, you may find the article has been labeled with some key words by the company that prepared the database. These terms may be the names of people, places, or businesses mentioned in the work, as well as codes. All of these are means of classifying the work according to a system developed by the database's creator.

■ Miscellaneous data. Other facts may include the language of the work, if other than English; length of the work; its availability from the database vendor; or the type of piece being indexed, such as a book review or an editorial.

One variation of the bibliographic database is the *reference database*. It directs you where to go to obtain the actual information you seek. For example, one database, FINDEX, identifies over 12,000 industry and market research reports commercially available from U.S. and non-U.S. publishers. This can be contrasted with InvesText, described next, which contains the full text of about 100,000 industry and company reports generated by financial analysts of leading research organizations.

Full-Text Databases
Full-text databases, once rare, are becoming increasingly available. They make all of the contents from a specified source, such as articles in *Business Week*, available online. With a full-text database, you get immediate access to a complete article in which you are interested, instead of an abstract and a citation to help you decide whether to read the original, and if so, where to find it. You can also run a search of all the text material in the article, instead of being limited to searching only what is contained in the abstract, the title, and indexing terms.

149

Finding Information About Your Competitors
■ ■ ■

Searching the full text of an article can be very useful when you are researching a subject or person whose mention in an article was not considered significant enough to be identified either in an abstract or in any indexing terms.

Getting Copies of the Articles and Searches
Once you find what you want, you will probably want a copy of the article. There are three ways to do this—and not every option is available with every database:

■ You can save your search results while you are running the search on your computer. This is "downloading." Then you can reprint it, either through a word processing program or directly.

■ You can instruct the database vendor that you want certain search results printed out while you are online.

■ You can order reprints of the articles you select from the database vendor (or other suppliers) while you are still online or after you sign off.

Understand what options are available—and at what cost—before you go online.

Copyright Issues for Online Information
The contents of databases are almost always copyrighted. For example, the title (and body) of an article may be copyrighted by the author or the periodical, whereas the abstract and indexing terms might be copyrighted in the name of the producer of the database. The scope of the copyright law and its impact on the production, distribution, and use of online databases is the subject of much study and some controversy, which are well beyond the scope of this book. Simply remember that the text you buy from a database search is owned by someone. Treat the data as you would any other copyrighted information: Don't plagiarize; give credit for information by using citations; and don't store it permanently or resell it as your own.

Using Databases for Developing Data
on Publicly Traded Companies

With the exception of the materials filed with the U.S. Securities and Exchange Commission, not all of the materials described here are necessarily available for all publicly traded companies.

> *A full-text database can help you track a publicly traded competitor.*

Filings with the U.S. Securities and Exchange Commission. Filings for SEC include annual reports to shareholders, proxy statements, and forms such as 10-K and 8-Q. They can be obtained directly from the corporations themselves if you are a shareholder. In some cases, even a nonshareholder can arrange to be put on the mailing list for some or all of the reports. Unless you are a shareholder or potential shareholder, however, the corporation is not obligated to provide these documents. Some corporations exercise the right not to provide these documents on demand. Some corporations distribute these reports widely when they are first released but do not reproduce them once they have run out of stock. That means you cannot always count on getting all of the reports from the corporations themselves.

For these reasons, commercial services have moved to take up the slack. For example, one of these services provides online abstracts of what it deems to be critical materials found in annual reports. Other online services index the documents actually filed with the SEC. Still others, some online and some not, can provide you with copies of all documents actually filed with the SEC.

Investment Community Analyses of Corporate Operations. The largest single source of reports prepared by investment analysts on publicly traded companies is the InvesText online database. It currently includes over 125,000 reports on publicly traded companies. These reports are prepared by a large number of participating investment banks and brokerage firms and are provided to subscribers to the database in full text. This database does not contain all of the company reports prepared by Wall Street analysts. However, it usually provides a good starting point for this type of information.

InvesText has several limitations:

■ The firms providing the reports to InvesText are allowed to embargo their release to InvesText for up to 30 days. This allows the firms to provide the reports first to their own customers.

■ InvesText takes about a week to load these reports onto its database.

■ Some of these investment analysts' reports are little more than rehashes of quarterly corporate releases, such as 8-Qs.

■ The number of analyst reports you can actually search online depends on how and where you access InvesText. For example, if you access it directly through InvesText, you can search all reports. Going through Dow Jones News/Retrieval®, however, only accesses the most current of these reports, typically about 20 percent of the total.

Other online databases index investment analyses, together with other materials, such as magazine articles or commercially prepared reports, which are available on microfiche or microfilm from the sources indicated in the database entry. As with the entries in InvesText, they may be somewhat dated. However, you can use these databases to identify investment analysts who follow the target company. A call to their offices may disclose the availability of a more current, as yet unindexed, analysis. Even these reports, however, may be embargoed until they have been distributed to clients.

Nondatabase Options

There are, of course, other ways to get these materials. First and foremost, you can call the target firms and ask for the data. When the materials arrive, you can review them. However, there are other types of data that are not widely available from databases.

Data generated by the corporations themselves includes speeches at annual meetings, as well as interviews given to members of the investment community.

Transcripts of speeches given at annual meetings may be available (sometimes for a fee) directly from the corporate communications or shareholders services office of the corporation. Some corporations routinely abstract these speeches and distribute them to those on their mailing lists, either separately or as a part of a quarterly report to shareholders. In addition, some corporations also distribute copies of other key speeches or approved corporate profiles. These may provide some insights into the corporation, its senior management, and its strategies. Of course, it is not likely that all of your direct competitors will knowingly forward such material directly to you, a competitor.

Interviews given to members of the investment community may be available from several sources:

■ *From the corporation itself. Some corporations, such as Heinz and Citicorp, routinely reprint annual interviews with senior management and make them available both to shareholders and to the general public.*

■ *From investment community sources. Two of the most prominent such sources are* NYSSA *Analyst Reports and the* Wall Street Transcript. *The former sells reprints of interviews, typically given by senior management to members of the New York investment community. The reprints run about $10 to $20 each. The latter regularly publishes full-text interviews.*

■ *From publications. An alternative is to seek out profiles or interviews in financial industry publications, such as* Institutional Investor, *or in more general publications, such as* Business Week. *A search for them can usually be conducted using online databases.*

The decision to use or to avoid databases should not be made lightly. First, make sure you know what using the database will cost. Typically you pay a connect charge for the telephone for every minute you are online; you pay a separate charge for every minute you use the database, and you may pay a charge for each item you see (such as $0.75 for an abstract or $9 for the full text of an article).

Now, weigh that against the costs of your own time to locate and review likely leads, then make a decision.

For more help on using databases effectively, see Chapter 9.

Using Databases—A Case Study

Assume that you want to track, on a regular basis, several publicly traded firms in your industry. You want to be aware of any early signs that one or more of these companies is getting ready for some major change. That is, you want a kind of early warning system, but you are not precisely sure what you are looking for.

There is no information without supporting data; there is only opinion.

One way to do this is to start with a regular (even daily) check for stories on the targets in current, full-text print sources, such as *The Wall Street Journal, Business Week,* or the Associated Press. All of these are available through online database in full text. In addition, you could also periodically search, online, the major local newspapers in cities where the targets have their corporate headquarters, as well as papers covering communities where their major regional operations or subsidiaries are located.

This type of coverage should help you learn what is happening with competitors. In addition, you can monitor new filings by the targets with the U.S. Securities and Exchange Commission, to see if any of the targets has made any significant filing. Your option would be to monitor press announcements made by the target corporations themselves, as well as industry specific newsletters.

Finding Information About Your Competitors
■ ■ ■

Each one of these steps can be done, at least in part, using an online database, covering full-text sources.

Handling Interviews and Surveys

When you are considering conducting a CI project, think of what people already know as a potential resource. To get at this type of data may require that you conduct a survey or interviews.

Keep in mind here you are not conducting a typical market survey. You are seeking answers to specific questions that will often give you a "feel," not abstracted data. Also, here you may want to call on everyone who has data; a market survey usually settles for a small sample and uses it to draw broad conclusions.

Surveys
Unlike the well-known polls conducted for a political candidate, your survey will tend to be tightly focused and aimed at extracting a narrow spectrum of data of immediate use to you. The goal of your survey will tend to be very specific and is not for tracking broad trends.

For example, you may want to survey your own customers or distributors to determine why they selected your firm's products. You may want to survey customers and distributors of your competitors, to find out why they selected the competitors' products. Or you may want to do both.

Surveys can provide a good source of information for any size business. You may want to just start out surveying your own customers. How did they hear about your business? What alternatives did they consider? Did they find everything they wanted? A short questionnaire at the checkout counter or at the time you make the sale can provide interesting insights, as well as potential marketing opportunities. You can also expand from that to more systematic approaches to surveying.

> *Before you start a survey, remember that the selection of those being surveyed can largely influence the answers you get.*

Regardless of what you want to learn, careful surveying can contribute significantly to your own CI. Properly done, a survey can be relatively inexpensive. The key is to observe the following rules:

■ Clarify what you want the survey to accomplish. Specifically, what types of data do you expect the survey to contribute?

■ Select the target group you wish to survey. Decide whether to survey the whole group or just a sample. If you use a sample, how will you select that sample: by size, location, age, or at random? The way you select a sample influences the results of the survey.

■ Be frank about any limitations you face with the survey. For example, do you have to complete it in a very short time? Might the interviewees tend to be uncooperative?

■ Keep the survey as short as possible. Every additional question you ask adds to the length and tends to decrease the number of responses.

■ Check the questions to make sure that they are not ambiguous. Review them to make sure they are not biased in any way and that they do not have any "obvious" answer.

■ Make the questions easy to answer. You are better off having several short questions that are easy to answer than one longer question that may be hard to understand or answer.

- Make the answers you are seeking simple. You may want to provide multiple-choice answers so you can tabulate a large number of responses. However, sometimes you may want to record the interviewee's specific response and may prefer a more open-ended format.

- If the survey is short, consider doing it over the telephone. Your response rate will be higher than mailing it. If you are doing it by mail, prepare yourself for a very low response rate, possibly less than 5 percent. To improve that rate, prepay the postage for the reply.

- Consider sending potential interviewees a letter before you call, so they expect the survey and will be more willing to respond.

- When you approach people, be honest about the length of the survey. Do not promise them the survey takes 5 minutes to complete when it will take 15 minutes. Also, be honest about the survey's purpose. If you are using it to generate specific sales leads, don't tell people "this is not a sales call."

- Give people a reason to participate. If the survey is internal or for long-time customers, you may want to appeal to company loyalty or to participants' desire to enhance company services. Consider offering everyone who participates a *summary* of the results.

- If you have time, test the survey on a small group to see how they respond and with what questions they have problems.

- Set your own deadline for completing the survey and receiving responses. Stick to it. If you are mailing the survey, tell the respondents that there is a deadline and what it is.

- Be polite. If you try to survey someone, thank them for their time, even if they do not participate. Remember, no one *has* to participate in your survey.

Our goal here is not to provide a manual of surveying techniques, but rather to point out that important additional information can be provided through surveys. Surveys can be an easy and relatively affordable source of information for almost any size business.

Interviews

Interviewing individuals for CI data is similar to surveying them. One major difference is that with an interview you are trying to develop a significant amount of data from a few people, whereas in a survey, you are trying to develop a lot of data from a larger population, with a little coming from each participant.

When you interview someone, you may have to hear many comments you do not view as important or useful. Be patient. A well-conducted interview with the right type of person can produce valuable data as well as personal estimates.

For example, you may have the problem of developing background data on an industry with which you are unfamiliar. One way to gain familiarity might be to talk with sales representatives of magazines serving the industry you are trying to study. Magazine sales representatives ("reps") are one of the major ways that magazines—particularly consumer and trade magazines—reach potential advertisers. Reps make themselves available to media planners and buyers to present the benefits of using the publications they represent. However, magazine sales reps can provide additional important CI if you are willing to wait through the sales pitch. As one publication put it, "A sales rep can be the source of key facts about magazines (their own *and* the competition's), about a particular industry, and maybe even about your own client [or company]."[3]

Following are a few hints for interviewing:

■   Be clear in your own mind what you want to accomplish in the interview. Specifically, what types of data do you expect the interview to contribute?

Finding Information About Your Competitors
■ ■ ■

■ Carefully identify the specific people you want to interview. What do they do? What can they provide—data, leads, perspectives?

■ Be frank about any limitations you face with your interviews. For example, do you have to complete them in a very short time? Do you expect the interviewees to be easy to reach and cooperative?

■ Keep your questions as short as possible. Decide whether you want to ask very focused questions or very broad-ranging ones. The former provide more specific, statistically usable data, but people feel more comfortable dealing with broad, open-ended questions—especially if their answers draw on personal experience.

■ If you have a lot of interviews to conduct, do them over the telephone. Although a face-to-face interview may provide more data, they are harder to schedule and require travel time.

■ Consider sending potential interviewees letters before you call, so that people expect your call and are better prepared to talk with you.

■ When you do interview people, be honest about the length of the interview. Also, be honest about its purpose.

■ Give your interviewee some reason to participate. For example, if you are going to interview a newspaper reporter, you may want to offer the reporter copies of *public* information you have already developed on the target company in exchange for the reporter's assistance.

■ Set your own deadline for conducting interviews and stick to it. You can unknowingly but quickly get enmeshed in an endless round of interviews that provide decreasing amounts of useful data.

What You Can Learn on the Road

One of the best ways to keep tabs on your competition is to do it in person. CI uses concepts such as reverse engineering and benchmarking to help you "take apart" your competitor's goods and services (both are discussed in Chapter 14), so that you understand them better. You can and should be doing the same with respect to your competitor's regular operations.

CI CLOSEUP: "Sleep-In"

In 1986, Marriott Corporation had an intelligence team spend six months traveling throughout the United States, gathering information on the economy hotel business. This was a business Marriott wanted to enter.

The team's work included staying at competing hotels. While there, the team's members checked on numerous details, such as how well the customers were taken care of; how soundproof the rooms were; and even the brands of soap, shampoo, and towels provided with the room.

With the data the team gathered, Marriott designed an economy hotel chain it felt could beat the competition. Evidently, Marriott was right. Marriott's Courtyard chain, launched in 1987, reportedly has an occupancy rate about 10 percentage points higher than the rest of the industry.[4]

Finding Information About Your Competitors

Drive-Bys and On-Site Observations

Do you live near a competitor's plant or headquarters? If so, try to arrange to drive past that facility on a regular basis. After a while, you will begin to notice how full the parking lot is around the building. If there are more empty parking spaces at the same time of day, that could mean there are fewer people on each shift. In turn, that may tell you that you should be checking whether that competitor has experienced slowdowns, has changed its shifts, or has just improved its productivity and is now more efficient.

If you can't determine whether production is down or up, check out the trash. That does not mean going through your competitor's trash bins. Rather, figure out when trash from the plant is hauled away. Then, monitor how many trucks come to pick it up now, as compared with several months ago, or how full they appear in comparison with prior months. More trash probably means more production.

Keep an eye on external activities. Note when you drive past the plant whether a sign announces newly open positions. If you see signs of new construction at the headquarters, perhaps you should check the local building inspector's office to learn what permits have been issued, for what, and when.

The same applies to checking your competitors' dealings with their customers. You can go to a competitor's outlet and actually study how the store or outlet is laid out, what products and services are available to customers, and how the customers are treated. A few visits, or even photographs from the outside, may tell you a lot.

To determine a competitor's volume of business, watch the place of business over time. How many cars come up and during what hours? Is that volume and pattern the same as at your company's place of business? How many trucks make deliveries and pick-ups? Can you determine who owns them? That may alert you to new suppliers or customers.

Checking out things firsthand is useful not only for direct comparison of products or services or to develop company-level or plant-level estimates of data, such as production or employment. It is also used as the basis of highly sophisticated estimates. For example, in 1989, *Business Week* reported on an economist at a major international bank in New York City who forecasts the balance-of-payment deficit. He does not use the traditional method, a macroeconomic model of the economy. Instead, he prepares forecasts by asking the people who "actually handle the imports and the exports." The economist surveys about 30 of the largest seaports and air cargo companies, asking how much export and import traffic they expect over the next three months. "Putting together their responses gives him a good picture of near-term trade trends."[5]

Drawbacks and Limitations
of Getting On-Site Information
A few words of caution are in order. First, remember to respect the law in doing any of this hands-on work. If the competitor's parking lot is off-limits to nonemployees, then it should be off-limits to you as well. You can learn a lot merely by watching from across the street.

Second, bear in mind to make your observations casual so nobody calls the police to check on the "suspicious character" seen hanging around.

Third, make detailed notes. Much of what you glean from first-hand observations is based on comparisons, on comparing factors that have changed over time. Note what you saw and when you saw it to enhance your comparisons and evaluations.

Fourth, avoid jumping to conclusions and always confirm your facts with a second source. You may notice a change that doesn't prove to be significant. For example, when you observe a drop in the number of cars in a parking lot you may initially conclude that a major layoff has occurred, when the lack of cars really reflects employee observance of a religious or company holiday.

Case Study of Specific CI Techniques

As you saw in Chapter 7, one of the keys to developing CI is to treat the data you seek as a commodity. That means that you identify exactly what data you need to answer your questions and then begin to look for that particular data. In turn, this means that you must be clear about what you seek and why. A lack of clarity in the needs analysis phase causes problems in the collection phase.

We will now take you through a very abbreviated review of a portion of a CI assignment. After stating the goal of the assignment, we will show you how to apply some of the data-collection techniques just covered.

The Assignment

This assignment is to study the extent of existing competition in a particular market before you decide whether to enter this market. You have already concluded that you need to determine the extent of competition in the financial-planning software industry. In our example, we will take one part of this, identifying the companies providing these products, but we will not try to determine the actual or potential demand for the product.

In this assignment, by financial-planning software, you have decided that you mean both of the following:

■ Commercially available software, sold for use on personal computers by persons doing individual financial planning, either for themselves or for clients.

■ Commercially available expert systems, sold for use on either personal computers or mainframe computers, to be used by persons and businesses selling financial-planning services.

To keep things simple, just call both of these financial-planning software. In terms of defining your CI needs, assume that you have already eliminated software that a business uses for its own financial planning.

The Potential Data Sources

Applying one of the precepts of CI—treating data as a commodity—you now ask who already has an interest in collecting data on such products and companies. For purposes of this case study, you can artificially limit the research to using the media. There are at least two segments of the media you should consider as potential sources:

■ Media targeted at potential customers for the PC software. That market group includes customers buying it for their own use; customers seeking to use the software to sell their own financial-planning services (independent financial planners and accountants); and those seeking to sell financial services products by offering financial planning services, such as insurance agents and stockbrokers.

■ Media targeted at the customers for the expert systems. That market group includes businesses buying an expert system in order to sell financial-planning services; and those seeking to sell financial services products by offering financial planning services, such as banks, insurance companies, and stock brokerage firms.

As you start this project, you find that expert systems and artificial intelligence are closely related concepts. That means you have to add artificial intelligence sources to your research plan after you have begun.

You can learn a lot about your competitors by checking out their advertisements and the publications in which they advertise.

Finding Information About Your Competitors
■ ■ ■

Once you determine that you are seeking leads from a narrow portion of the media, to what sources can you now turn for assistance in finding the relevant media? Experience shows that the following may be potentially useful sources in identifying the particular publications in which you are interested:

- Academic groups
- Business newspapers
- Chambers of commerce
- Databases
- Directories
- Experts
- Federal government
- Trade associations
- Trade papers and journals

Again, for the sake of this case study, limit yourself to only one of these—directories. In fact, you could start with almost any one of them, and you should be able to develop much of the raw data and leads you would develop starting with the directories.

A major reason to look to the media is for their advertising, so it makes sense to try and find a directory created to sell advertising. A number of such directories exist, among them ones published by the Standard Rate & Data Service, Inc. (SRDS). Each SRDS publication lists different types of publications, such as magazines, business publications, and newspapers. There you will find a list of current publications organized by target market. For each publication, you can find an entry featuring basic data on the topics featured in each issue, special issues, circulation, target audience, advertising deadlines and rates, and publisher.

For purpose of this case study, one you should check is *Business Publications Rates and Data,* a monthly directory. It contains entries on many potentially relevant publications. Following are major entries on those publications dealing with the following topics or markets:

- Artificial intelligence
- Banking
- Business computing
- Business software
- Expert systems
- Financial planning
- Financial services
- Insurance
- Marketing
- Personal computers
- Securities

From those entries, you identify the following publications as potentially important leads:

American Banker   *High Technology*
Bank Marketing   *InfoWorld*
Banking Software Review   *Insurance Software Review*
Best's Review   *Insurance Times*
Business Software   *Life Association News*
Computerworld   *PC Week*
Financial Planning   *Wall Street Computer Review*
Financial Services Week

These publications cover both ends of the spectrum—those who are making and selling the software as well as those who are or might be using it. Not all of these publications will be helpful, and a publication that is helpful in one way—say by featuring a certain type of article—may not contain other data, such as data on specific products. In fact, several journals, including *Financial Services Week, Insurance Times,* and *Wall Street Computer Review,* prove to be no direct assistance in this assignment, even though their SRDS profile indicated they might be useful.

Using the Data Sources
One way to use these publications is to review their recent back issues. This review can produce sample advertisements for finan-

cial-planning software, an important source of raw data about who is doing what, or at least who is selling what. In this case, such ads are found in *Financial Planning, Insurance Software Review*, and *Best's Review*.

From your check of online databases that index these and other publications, you obtain citations to articles on the subject. In this case, the number is limited, but the quality is good. Two of the best are "Financial Adviser Goes Online" in *Computerworld* and "Technology Today and Tomorrow: Electronic Field Support for Financial Planners" in *Best's Review*.

Going back to the entry in the SRDS, you also consider exploiting the identification of the publishers of the listed magazines provided. Interviews with editorial and marketing personnel at these publications might generate leads to related annual publications or to special annual issues such as "Directory of Financial Marketing Services," published each summer by *Bank Marketing*, and "ICP Software Directory: Mainframe & Minicomputer Series: Banking, Insurance & Finance," published each autumn by International Computer Programs, Inc.

The former lists companies currently selling expert systems for financial planning to banks. The latter would be of little or no use, because it lists financial planning software used for a company's own internal planning, which is not a part of this project.

In this case, the articles highlighted two specialized groups that appeared to be studying various aspects of this issue. One was the College for Financial Planning, a trade organization referred to in an advertisement as having reviewed and rated a particular piece of financial-planning software. That group turned out to be of little real assistance, because it had terminated its program of reviewing financial-planning software several years before the date of this study.

Several other articles referred to a proprietary report, "Expert Systems in the Insurance Industry," prepared by the accounting and consulting firm of Coopers & Lybrand. Although the report

168

was over two years old, reviewing that study might provide an idea of which firms in the insurance industry were using or considering using financial-planning software. That might, in turn, give you targets for telephone interviews. In addition, you might also identify some of the persons at Coopers & Lybrand who worked on this report. Knowing who they are and where they went after the report was released could help identify firms that might be preparing to enter this market in the near future.

Of course, each of these data sources can help you develop additional leads to more data and persons. Just to give one example, remember that often a good source of data on who competitors are is someone already in the business. In addition, the media may also be able to help if and when you need to develop data on the demand for this software. This means that a publication that seems to be heavily used to sell this particular product may, in its media kit, provide some data on the size of the market for these very products.

Summary

This chapter discussed the ins and outs of using government data sources and contacting agency representatives. The advantage of using such sources is their low cost. For faster turnaround, however, online databases may be the preferred choice for your CI data.

Surveys can yield lots of statistically usable data about products and competitors, whereas interviews give you more in-depth perspectives from a limited sampling of people.

You can learn much about your competitors' activities from on-site observations.

You saw how a typical CI data search is conducted using a variety of data sources. Later chapters show how to integrate the raw facts gleaned from searches like this one to create the kind of CI program that can give you a competitive edge.

CI ALERT: What does this tell you?

"Struthers-Dunn and Hi-G, two producers of military/aerospace relays, said their merger . . . is virtually complete. . . .

"The merger calls for the consolidation of Hi-G's two previous production facilities in South Windsor and Hartford, Conn., at the 50,000-square-foot South Windsor plant. In addition, plans call for an upgrading of manufacturing capabilities at both the South Windsor plant and the 100,000-square-foot plant in Pitman."

Source: Announcement, Focus, January 17, 1990.

Notes

1. Robert McCullough and Lincoln Wolverton, "The Competitor Intelligence Concept Applied to Power Marketing," *Public Utilities Fortnightly*, September 18, 1986, p. 11.

2. U.S. Department of Defense, *Soviet Acquisition of Militarily Significant Western Technology: An Update*, September 1985, p. 17.

3. "Space Sales Representatives: What They Can Teach Media Professionals," *The SRDS Report*, April 1989, p. 6.

4. Brian Dumaine, "Corporate Spies Snoop to Conquer," *Fortune*, November 7, 1988, pp. 68-69, 72, 76.

5. "If You Want to Know About Trade Flow, Ask a Stevedore," *Business Week*, May 1, 1989, p. 20.

Chapter 9

Using Online Databases Efficiently

> ## CI CLIP
>
> *"People won't pay for quality of information, because the valuing is retroactive, but they will pay for quality of source, because the constancy (reliability) of source makes value somewhat predictable."*
>
> Stewart Brand[1]

In the past, the decision whether to use databases for CI was fairly simple. The contents of the few databases you could use were at least as dated as their hard-copy indexing equivalents, which could be as much as 6 to 12 months old by the time they were printed. Most of these databases typically gave you citations to articles without providing any text, or even an abstract. This meant these databases were just another way to do what you could already do by hand, that is, look for preindexed articles.

Today's databases are increasingly current. Some provide access to information that is not indexed elsewhere, and in some cases, databases contain reports and newsletters not published elsewhere. Many allow access to some news sources almost as fast as the data is available on wire services to the press. Increasingly, today's databases give access to the full text of article and reports, as described in Chapter 8. As a result, databases often are an effective first source for CI in areas of interest to your business.

Advantages of Databases Compared with Indexes

There are several advantages to using online databases to check materials that may be abstracted in other places. First, the databases are updated more frequently than are the hard-copy indexes. Second, you can usually search the databases without having to subscribe to the corresponding hard-copy index. Third, using the online search you can scan every word in every abstract.

Checking Related Industries

Assume for a moment that you are interested in tracking technical developments affecting the manufacture of cars and other vehicles. Many databases deal with various aspects of engineering, which might be helpful.

The following online sources (in addition to the numerous databases dealing with U.S. and international patents and patent claims) may be of interest from time to time:

■ Ceramic Abstracts: This covers all scientific, engineering, and commercial literature pertaining to ceramics and related materials. It is equivalent to the publication *Ceramic Abstracts.*

■ Compendex Plus: This is the online version of the *Engineering Index.* It indexes about 4500 journals, as well as selected government reports and books. It also covers the published proceedings of engineering and technical conferences.

■ Corrosion: This contains data on the effects of over 600 agents on the most widely used metals, plastics, nonmetallics, and rubbers over a wide temperature range. It corresponds to *Corrosion Resistance Tables—Metals, Plastics, Nonmetallics, and Rubbers.*

■ Current Technology Index: This indexes current periodicals from all fields of modern technology. Although it indexes only journals published in the United Kingdom, its scope is worldwide.

■ Engineered Materials Abstracts: This corresponds to the publication of the same name. It provides access to published materials from around the world dealing with both the science and practices of materials science and engineering related to polymers, ceramics, and composite materials.

■ Metadex: This covers international literature on the science and practice of metallurgy. It includes about 30,000 citations each year from about 1100 primary journal sources.

■ SAE Global Mobility: This accesses technical papers presented at Society of Automotive Engineers (SAE) meetings and conferences, as well as papers from the International Federation of Automobile Engineering Societies (FISTA), transportation-related papers from the Institution of Mechanical Engineers, and the International Technical Conference on Experimental Safety Vehicles. It contains over 26,000 records.

■ Standards Search: This covers standards, specifications, test procedures, recommended practices, and proposed standards developed by SAE and the American Society for Testing and Materials (ASTM).

> ### CI CLOSEUP: "Local Angles"
>
> An investigative reporter in Toledo, Ohio, has adopted some CI techniques to help him do his job better. In one case, the reporter suspected that local developers were about to sell a large piece of property to an individual with a questionable background. The reporter cut short his field investigation by using a database search to check the stories in the hometown newspapers of the potential buyer. The reporter found no evidence there to substantiate his suspicions. The 15-minute search "saved days of investigation."

How to Use Databases

The balance of this chapter is aimed at helping you use online databases more effectively. If you use them or are thinking of using them yourself, this discussion can help you do a better job. If you do not actually use databases, this chapter is still important, for the more you know about how to use them, the easier it will be for you to have someone else help you with their use.

Getting Familiar

The more you use databases for CI, the better you will get. If you use a limited number of databases on a regular basis, you soon become familiar with their peculiar quirks. Knowing that, you can be more effective in narrowing the focus of your research, which, in turn, means you can keep costs down. On the other hand, the less frequently you use databases, the more it will cost you each time you get online.

One way to increase your experience is practice. Database vendors and producers have a number of ways to help the novice or the occasional researcher acquire and improve search skills, without substantial expenditures:

■ Some vendors offer practice databases, which you can use at sharply discounted rates.

■ Database producers and vendors sometimes offer users free or discounted time to be used during a particular limited time period (say, a few days or a month) on a particular database. The goal is to convince you that the particular database should be used more frequently. These promotions can provide a good opportunity for you to learn how to use a particular database or to sharpen your skills.

■ Some producers publish newsletters, articles, and even books illustrating specific search strategies and the results they produce. Although this is not the same as doing it yourself, reviewing them can make you feel more comfortable.

■ Many database vendors and producers offer seminars to train you on specific databases. Some of them are free. The sponsors generally include some free time for those taking the seminar to try out the selected databases. Often free time on the database is given to you after the session.

Know What You Want

Effective use of databases requires you to be able to state clearly and precisely exactly what you need. One way to prepare for this is to use the plain paper approach. Put a blank sheet of paper in front of you, then write out exactly what you want as a report or as an answer to your question(s). Emphasize key words, concepts, numbers, and dates as you go.

Focusing on Your Objective

By doing this, you may make your focus clearer as you define exactly the kind of data you will collect. If you start an online search with a specific objective, you are more likely to get the specific data you need for your CI project at the lowest cost.

Special Challenges

After you have written out your target answers, try to narrow your focus. Consider the timeframe during which the data you are seeking would have been released, as well as potential sources for that data. For example, are you seeking only the most current information, or is it desirable to have a historical perspective? Consider what sources you want to scan for your data and, just as importantly, what sources you do not want searched. Every source you can exclude at the start should help make your ultimate search faster and less expensive.

Hints for Designing Your Search
The checklist in Exhibit 9.1 should help you make sure that you have thought through your database search before you start it. This is true whether you do the search yourself or have someone else do it.

The next sections elaborate on the checklist's important points.

Can You Get the Data Without Using a Database?
Although this question may sound a little sarcastic in this context, it is in fact important. It challenges you to review the description of exactly what you need and who might have it. If you can identify an organization that has some of the data you are looking for, you might be able to refine your search without an online service. And finally, the source you contact for the data may be able to tell you that the data you are seeking is not where you thought but rather is in a database you did not include in your initial search design.

Know What the Database Contains—And Doesn't
Some databases are updated every day; others may go for 6 to 12 months between updates. But you cannot simply check whether a particular database has been updated recently. You must find out the age of the material used.

Always check on the overall coverage of any database. The same database accessed from two different services may have differing coverages. For example, if you sign on to InvesText directly from

- *Know what you want before you go online. Keep your search focused.*

- *Select the right databases.*

- *Find out whether you can get the information you want without using a database.*

- *Know what each database contains. Check on how current its contents are.*

- *Review specialized search aids such as prewritten search strategies, manuals, newsletters, and brochures dealing with the database you are considering.*

- *Ask for help from the database supplier or producer. Many will help you over the telephone; some have toll-free numbers.*

- *After you have selected the best databases, find out whether you can search all of them together. For example, DIALOG uses a technique, called OneSearch*^sm^*, to allow searching of several files at once.*

- *Learn whether the database has its own special vocabulary, search codes, or key words—and use them.*

- *Write out your search strategy before going online.*

- *Practice your search strategy on a low-cost base, if you can. If you cannot do that, try out your search strategy by running a small part of it first.*

- *Monitor your results as you proceed until you are sure that your search strategy works.*

Exhibit 9.1: Online Database Checklist

its producer, the base you search is historically complete. That is, it contains every investment analyst report InvesText has put into its database. However, on Dow Jones News/Retrieval, that same database contains only the most current series of investment analysts' reports. That is because Dow Jones sees its prime market as made up of investors, who evidently are seen as being most interested in current, rather than historical, data.

Exhibit 9.2 shows a simple matrix design for organizing comparative information about multiple databases.

Database Name	TOPIC			
	XXX Industry	*YYY Industry*	*ZZZ Industry*	*Marketing*
123	b/h,c	b/h,c	b/h,c	b/h,c
456	b/h,c	b/h,c	b/h,c	b/h,c
789		d/c		
121	b/c	b/c	b/c	b/c
314	b/c	b/c	d/c	

Key:
Coverage:
    b   Broader, but shallower, coverage of the topic.
    d   Deeper, but narrower, coverage of the topic.
Currency:
    h   Better for historical information.
    c   Better for current information.

**Exhibit 9.2: Organizing Information About
Databases You Use Often**

Learn to Speak the Database's Language

Following are a few techniques for optimizing your time on the online services.

Check Specialized Search Aids

Many database vendors publish magazines or newsletters filled with information and helpful tips on using their databases. With some vendors, you can also use an electronic bulletin board to ask other subscribers how they handle research problems. In addition, the vendors can often direct you to special search aids, such as manuals, sample searches, bibliographies, and the like, available from the firms which produce the individual databases. These can be very helpful.

Learn the Database's Technical Vocabulary

When you use a database, you get *exactly* what you ask for, whether or not it is what you *intended* to get. Because of this, you must identify and deal with the problem of synonyms and confusingly similar terms in a search.

For example, say you are seeking information on Ford Financial, one of the major business groups owned by the Ford Motor Company. You are looking for this in two different types of full-text databases—one that reports business news and another containing publications of broad, general interest. Searching for the terms *Ford Financial* will identify the stories about it, but it will turn up even more sources than you want. In the business news database, it will turn up stories containing a reference to "Ford Financial reports" for the first quarter, meaning those of the Ford Motor Company. In the general-interest publication database, this search concept may lead you directly to articles analyzing the current financial situation of former President Gerald Ford or of actor Harrison Ford! Remember, you only asked for references where both of these words appeared—that is *exactly* what you got.

Special Challenges

Use Special Search Codes

Special search codes and key words typically have their origins as indexing aids to hard-copy sources of information. These codes may be quite comprehensive, allowing you to design a search statement without resorting to anything else. On the other hand, they may be quite limited and only assist you in dividing large amounts of data into several gross classifications. In that case, they must be used in connection with other search statements to produce a meaningful result.

Increasing numbers of databases containing data on many businesses are using some variation of Standard Industrial Classification (SIC) codes in their indexing. SIC codes are developed by the U.S. government as a tool for classification of industrial and business activity. Usually you can search by either a two-digit or a four-digit SIC code.

When you use SIC codes as a method of locating data, remember that they change from time to time. The latest version, the 1972 Edition, was revised in 1977 and again in 1987.

Using Databases Creatively

The creative use of databases can produce unexpected results. As is always the case with CI, you should think of information as a commodity and determine who produces it, who collects it, and why. This step helps you put databases to more effective use. The key to the creative use of databases is to understand their contents and to think of them in broader terms than their creators do.

Checking Your Competitors' Moves

For example, assume that you are designing some software to help small and medium-sized businesses in managing their investments and other liquid assets. If you need CI on current and potential users of this software, with an eye toward identifying customers so you can get financing, you might want to use some online databases to help you spot these companies.

To begin with, you should check the recent entries in marketing and new-product databases, such as PTS Marketing & Advertising Reference or New Product Announcements. Remember to check publications serving your target market, the small and medium-sized businesses, for articles supporting your assertion that there is a need for such software.

In addition, check computer industry and software publications for any product announcements by companies that already sell software to this market. Some databases are set up to help sell software. You can use them to see whether any software listed directly or indirectly competes with your design.

Finding New Customers

Continue to think about using a database for purposes other than those for which it was created. For example, if you are identifying potential new customers for your business, which will soon be producing a basic raw material, how could you go about it? You should seek out data on companies in industries you have already identified as consumers of this product. But this works only after you have already identified industries that now use the material. Thus, you might want to start with the Thomas Register Online. This service is designed to help purchasers of industrial products find suppliers, but you can use it to find customers. Use it to create a list of businesses that make specific products of which your product is an already-known component.

Another approach is to use an online index of patents to see whether your product is potentially an input for a newly pat-ented process or product. Your search could isolate patents that specifically refer to your product. Then obtain the name of the invention (or process), a summary of how your product is used in the invention or process, and information on the identity of the inventor and the assignee, often the business employing the inventor. The result should be a list of firms that may be interested in your firm as a source for this product. Also, you may find new applications that allow you to think about developing new marketing leads through more traditional approaches.

Special Challenges

Summary

The variety of online services today enables you to easily track developments in industries related to your primary one. To use databases effectively, however, you should first become familiar with their operation and pinpoint what your objective and target answers are. Use a reminder like the online database checklist to focus your search. Having a clear focus for your search will save you time and money.

> ### CI ALERT: What does this tell you?
>
> "It's grown in six years from a two-person start-up to a dynamic organization of 35 employees with nine sales offices nationwide. . . .
>
> "The company's clients include AT&T, Motorola, NASA, DuPont, Squibb, Harvard University, Carnegie-Mellon University, and the Massachusetts Institute of Technology. . . .
>
> "Software Associates . . . plans to open an international office in Europe and implement a telemarketing program within a year."
>
> Source: Article, Business Digest of the Lehigh Valley, January 1990.

Notes

1. Stewart Brand, *The Media Lab,* New York: Viking Penguin, Inc., 1987, p. 205.

2. Michael Murrie, "Electronic Databases in the Newsroom," *Link-Up,* March/April 1988, p. 27.

Chapter 10

International Information

Special Challenges

This chapter explores sources of business information through foreign channels for selected, primarily industrial countries. We focus on Japan and Canada in particular. These two nations represent opposite ends of the spectrum in many ways. One is an English-language society; the other is not. One is near to the United States; the other is more distant. One is our economic peer (at the least); the other is less so. One is seen as relatively closed to outsiders; the other appears not to be so. They illustrate similarities and differences in collecting international CI.

The basic principles of collecting international information for CI are the same as those for all other types of CI, with a few small but important differences. The primary difference concerns *where* the data is located rather than *what* that data deals with.

The major issue you face is how to select the most efficient place to start among the potential sources of raw CI. In some cases, the problem may be to identify the sources themselves.

Beginning Your Data Search

As we previously discussed for domestic CI, there are two main approaches. One is to take a look at the potential sources of raw CI and pick ones that seem most likely to generate the data you need. The other is to think about the raw data you need, determine the most likely places it may be located, and then figure out how to extract it from those places. In practice, these two approaches tend to mesh.

Locating Sources of Raw Data

We will start with how to determine where raw data may be located. As you now know, a proven method for handling raw data collection is to visualize the data you are seeking as a commodity.

Basically, you can repeat the process described in Chapter 6 to determine who in the foreign competitor's business produces, collects, uses, and accumulates the data, and what other firms may transfer the data or have done your research for you. There are, however, some exceptions to the process that you follow for U.S. companies.

Say you are seeking out where the data is transferred and why, for imports to the United States from a particular country. You should think of that nation's export promotion authority as a potential source, as well as United States import data sources, such as the U.S. Customs Service.

CI CLOSEUP: "Poachers"

For many years, the U.S. government operated the Trade Opportunity Program (TOPS) as a staple of its export promotion activities. The program was designed to provide U.S. firms with trade leads. Overseas officials would identify trade leads from various sources and submit them all to a central database in Washington. From there, the U.S. government would attempt to find U.S. suppliers from among TOPS subscribers. An audit of the program showed that, although the over-all use of TOPS declined, "there is some evidence that major non-U.S. competitors were in the subscriber base and that they were responding to many leads intended for U.S. firms." Among the cases the auditors pointed to were Japanese firms responding to leads developed in Germany and a Swedish firm responding to one in Italy.[2]

Special Challenges
■ ■ ■

For users of the data, you are seeking out people such as securities analysts overseas, who themselves seek data from companies whose stock is traded on American and other stock exchanges around the world. The analysts produce their own company and industry analyses. For you, of greatest importance may not be the analyst's conclusions or projections, but the raw data (numbers or comments) provided to the analyst by the target company.

U.S. government agencies accumulate data on international firms that you may find important. A major source is the Commerce Department's U.S. International Trade Administration (ITA). At that level, you will generally, but not always, find aggregated data. Disaggregation, a process described in Chapter 12, may enable you to isolate significant data assumed to be masked by aggregation efforts.

Examining who else has an interest in the data you want may lead to such diverse resources as non-English language trade publications and academics. The publications may collect or even generate data similar to that you are seeking so they can show that their publications really represent their advertisers' audience. You may experience a language barrier, but finding a translator may help you uncover a treasure chest of data. Also, increasingly, some of the publishers of non-English language trade publications offer English-language summaries of their principal articles and features.

As in the United States, academics can be an interesting resource because of their relatively open access to data.

Keep in mind a couple of key distinctions. The first is between the location of the data and the subject of the data. The second is between company-level and industry-level data.

Data may be available in three types of locations:

■　　In the United States on foreign companies and markets—
　　　"inside looking out."

■ Outside of the United States on U.S. companies and U.S.-based operations of foreign companies—"outside looking in."

■ Outside of the U.S. on foreign companies and markets—"outside looking out."

The data you seek may be at the company level or the industry level. This distinction may be critical in focusing your research. On one hand, data on foreign companies from foreign sources exists, but it may be difficult to obtain. This reflects other countries' attitudes toward disclosure and public records that differ from attitudes in the United States. In many nations, government agencies may possess substantial data on national companies. Whether they are *willing* to part with that data may be critical, because they may be under no legal obligation to do so.

On the other hand, industry-level data from foreign sources on foreign targets may be substantially more detailed than that available in the U.S. Again, this reflects national differences, in this case, different attitudes toward the exchange of data among companies.

On the Inside Looking Out
When you collect data in the U.S. on foreign companies and markets, treat this research in the same way as domestic markets and companies.

For example, federal government records and resources can be valuable. The Securities and Exchange Commission makes available filings of foreign firms whose securities are traded on U.S. markets. The United States International Trade Commission (ITC) records contain extensive material on foreign companies and markets. This data is collected in connection with hearings on claims of unfair competition. Currently, its docket files contain data developed in investigations of non-United States industries ranging from footwear to stainless steel.

Special Challenges

The U.S. Department of Commerce can often be useful, depending on what you are looking for. For most countries, the country desk officer at the ITA, which is a part of the Department of Commerce, should have documents variously titled "Sources of Information on Doing Business in [Country]," "The [Country] Desk—A Guide to Information Sources," or "Sources of Country Market Information—[Country]." This type of free guide is an adequate but somewhat informal, basic introduction, usually more useful for the list of contacts it gives than for the hard data it contains.

ITA also markets a series of reports and studies, all of which are oriented toward export promotion. These include the following:

■ International Market Research Reports: These are in-depth analyses, including behavioral characteristics of the market, trade barriers, market share figures, end-user (or consumer) analysis, and trade contacts.

■ Country Market Surveys: These are 10- to 15-page summaries of the International Market Research Reports.

■ Product/Country Market Profiles: These are single-product multicountry or single-country multiproduct reports, including trade contacts, trade leads, and statistical analyses.

■ Foreign Traders Index: This is a database describing foreign firms, their long-term interests, and the types of activities they engage in. The database can be searched according to status (that is, agents, sellers, distributors, and users), by companies, by geographic location, and even by number of employees.

Because all of these materials are export oriented, they may be incomplete if you are using them as a source of data for any other purpose. They may also be dated.

Another, somewhat different, service is the Comparison Shopping service. Under this program, U.S. Commerce Department personnel overseas conduct on-the-spot interviews to determine several key marketing facts about a particular product, such as sales potential in the market, comparable products, distribution channels, "going price," competitive factors, and qualified purchasers. This service is not available for every country or product.

In the future you may see additional data resources at the U.S. Department of Commerce (DOC). The Omnibus Trade and Competitiveness Act of 1988 requires the DOC to create and maintain a "National Trade Data Bank" consisting of two different systems. The first is the International Economic Data System, which is planned to store economy-level data on entire national economies, exports and imports, and major domestic economic data. The second will be the Export Promotion Data System.

Those developing the International Economic Data System are struggling with the problem of developing and then keeping current data on an industry—and even on a company—level. Whether and how the DOC will do that is still unresolved. In January 1989, the U.S. General Accounting Office (GAO) indicated that it anticipates the DOC also faces some problems in developing and maintaining the Export Promotion Data System.[3] As late as August 1989, the GAO found that this project was "plagued with a host of operational, resource, and management problems."[4]

Merely because we stress the variety of resources of the U.S. Department of Commerce, do not ignore other federal agencies. For example, the U.S. Department of State publishes a continuing series of "Background Notes" on specific countries. These 5- to 10-page documents provide a basic orientation to the nation, its political system, and its economy. A useful companion might be the "Foreign Labor Trends" series prepared by the U.S. Department of Labor.

The Export-Import Bank of the United States maintains credit files on foreign firms with which it has had experience. If you call or write the Export-Import Bank, it will send you that information at no charge. It also has access to international sources of similar credit information.

At the state- and local-government level, you may find some assistance through industrial development offices. These offices arrange the funding for new construction of major facilities. If your target has recently begun construction on new U.S.-based facilities, the public records of the sponsoring industrial development authority may be very useful and revealing.

> *It is as important to understand what you are not looking for as what you are looking for.*

There are several ways you go about finding these offices. For example, you could call the governor's office in the state in which you are interested for the name and number of the state office. Or you can get a complete list of them, with addresses, telephones numbers, and directors, from the National Association of State Development Agencies in Washington, D.C. The state offices can give you the name and number of local agencies. You can alternatively call the county or city government.

Do not forget the target businesses themselves. If a foreign corporation's stock (or the stock of a subsidiary) is traded on the U.S. securities markets, it must file reports with the U.S. Securities and Exchange Commission. Some of these reports may disclose data about non-U.S. operations. An example is the 1988 Annual Report of National Westminster Bancorp Inc., a part of the United Kingdom-based National Westminster Bank Group. Although the annual report focuses on the U.S. operations, it also contains a limited amount of important data on the group's banking operations in the United Kingdom and throughout the world. In contrast, the 1988 Annual Report of Fujitsu Limited, one of Japan's largest computer makers, covers its worldwide operations and strategies, and even provides details on personnel and facilities throughout the world.

United States trade associations may also be useful in several ways:

■ Associations may have data on foreign-based competition, including specific competitors of U.S. member firms. That data usually is collected only if the association's members are facing actual or potential competition from imports.

■ Associations may have developed data on foreign companies and foreign markets as a part of their own export promotion efforts.

■ Associations may be able to identify foreign resources for you in their industry, a form of networking.

Increasingly, specialized media resources in the United States follow foreign-based markets and companies. For example, one electronics industry publisher, based in Japan, publishes an English-language digest of electronics news in Japan, which it distributes in the United States. Several European sources provide "off-the-shelf" English-language industry reports on European markets. Also, one of the largest banks in the world—Japan's Sumitomo Trust & Banking Co., Ltd.—publishes a series of English-language reports on economic trends in Japan and throughout the world, including reports such as "Recent Performance of Japanese Industries," which provided industry profiles ranging from ceramics to home electric appliances.[5]

Did you know you can follow Japanese business news, in English, from your own computer?

Special Challenges

Some of the vast numbers of online databases now available in the United States may be of use. Several examples spring to mind. One provides financial data on Canadian corporations through Corporate Canada Online and is available through the Dow Jones News/Retrieval service. A second indexes articles appearing in Canadian newspapers and magazines and is called Canadian Business and Current Affairs, which is available through Dialog Information Services. A third and fourth are English-language databases, covering company data and business news in Japan. They are entitled Japan Economic Newswire™ Plus, offered through Dialog Information Services, and Nikkei Telecom Japan News & Retrieval Service, accessible through Mitsui & Company. Such databases can be your electronic windows on businesses based in these countries.

Organizations with a special interest in a country may also be helpful in developing company-level data about U.S.-based operations. For example, the Japan Economic Institute, which is partially supported by the Japanese government, publishes numerous documents, such as "Japan's Expanding U.S. Manufacturing Presence," a report detailing, facility by facility, Japanese investment in the United States. This can be a very useful document if you are profiling, say, a division of Sumitomo Corporation.

Helpful information on the Canadian economy and Canadian companies may be found at such diverse locations as The Johns Hopkins University's Center of Canadian Studies or in the Library of the Canadian Consulate General in New York City, which is open to the public.

How do you find such organizations? There are numerous directories and other reference aids you can use for this, ranging from the *Encyclopedia of Associations and Organizations* to *Instant Information,* some of which are noted in Appendix B.

Of course, you should consider using consultants and other experts in a particular country's business climate. For example, one academic has a very extensive collection of Japanese-language business publications. These publications contain quite detailed information on companies and products. If you can read Japanese, they could be extremely valuable. If you cannot read Japanese, the professor can—for a fee.

A brief case study illustrates what we have covered here. Say your CI objective is to develop data on three aspects of residential construction in Europe and Japan:

■ The current state of roofing technology in those areas.

■ A list of major local manufacturers of roofing materials.

■ An idea of the current perception of European and Japanese roofing manufacturers about roofing technology in the United States.

You might look at sources of data in the United States on these foreign targets. Following are several sources you might turn to:

■ Foreign government offices in the United States.

■ Articles in trade and business publications.

■ Trade associations and related organizations.

■ U.S. government personnel in the United States.

Foreign Government Offices in the United States. If you contact the commercial attaches at the relevant embassies, you find your request referred to trade development offices, both in the United States and overseas.

In general, these offices are of little direct assistance, because their mission is to promote exports to the United States, not imports from the United States. However, if you are seeking this data to build a plant overseas to serve the European or Japanese markets, you may find these offices more cooperative.

Special Challenges
■ ■ ■

Articles in Trade and Business Publications. A check of likely publications, using online electronic databases, turns up nothing useful.

Trade Associations and Related Organizations. The use of directories, such as the *Encyclopedia of Organizations and Associations,* turns up two likely candidates:

■ National Institute of Building Sciences (NIBS)
■ National Association of Home Builders (NAHB)

NIBS turns out to have no data, nor can it suggest any leads, other than to call NAHB, which is already on the list. NAHB refers you to a separate branch, the NAHB Research Foundation. That office indicates that it collected data on imports to the United States. However, the staff suggests contacting a narrower-based trade association, the National Roofing Contractors Association, which is only concerned with roofing in the United States. The reasoning is that this organization might identify other resources through its own network of contacts.

Contact with the National Roofing Contractors Association indicates that the association does not track such issues. However, staff personnel are also asked about association publications. It turns out that this association publishes the proceedings of an irregular series of conferences entitled "Symposia on Roofing Technology" and the like.

Among the reports in those proceedings are

■ "Roofing in Europe" (1985)
■ "Roofing Technology in the Far East" (1985)

U.S. Government Personnel in the United States. Here, research leads to the U.S. Department of Housing and Urban Development (HUD), International Trade Commission (ITC), and U.S. Department of Commerce's International Trade Administration (ITA).

HUD has no materials or suggestions, other than to contact NAHB. The ITC has held no hearings on this industry.

At the ITA, however, you find some assistance. One office, the Market Research Service, prepared several background reports in 1985 and 1986 dealing generally with construction materials in Germany and Japan.

You ask the country desk officers to assist with data and company identification in each country. In general, the desk officers are only able to provide import data from those nations, as well as the names of foreign trade offices in the United States. In most cases, your request is forwarded overseas.

At this point we leave this case study, but we will pick it up again as the chapter progresses.

On the Outside Looking In
A second major source of data is located outside of the United States and deals with both U.S. companies and U.S.-based operations of foreign firms.

CI CLIP

"[A]lmost any person or any department in a Japanese company will pass out printed statistical information, and if a foreign investigator personally visits the company with any type of respectable credentials he can often get the information he wants."

Commentator on Japanese-Western business relations.[6]

Special Challenges
■ ■ ■

As alluded to before, what is "public" information to United States businesses may not be so in other countries. However, the reverse may be true, and this can work to your benefit.

For example, some governments provide special studies on imports and exports that are not available here. Canada, for example, manually checks import and export documents to produce specialized data on imports and exports (Canadian) on particular narrow groupings of products. Of course, it does not distribute data that illuminates only one company, but careful selection of products and markets, coupled with aggressive disaggregation techniques (see Chapter 12), may convert this macro-level data into company-level data.

This data is substantially more focused than the occasionally useful Custom Statistical Service offered by the U.S. Department of Commerce. This is because the U.S. service is based on existing data in broad trade categories, whereas the Canadian study is based on a manual review at a narrower level.

Again, foreign-based trade associations may collect, distribute, and exchange data with a level of detail that our antitrust laws make impossible in the United States. Further, in that detailed data may be facts about U.S. operations. That data may even be separately presented. A word about culture is important, because there is no requirement for trade associations to disclose this data. You may find that you have to convince the trade association to provide it. And to do that, you may have to show that the release of the data is in its members' interest.

Sometimes, looking outside the United States can help you see future events more clearly. For example, some European governments release partial patent data 18 months after a patent has been filed, even if the patent has not yet been approved.[7] In contrast, in the United States, all such data is embargoed until the patent is finally approved, a process that can take 2 to 5 years. Many companies file patents simultaneously in several countries, so you may be able to use the European window to track an as-yet-undisclosed parallel U.S. filing.

The foreign media can also be of help. Under the Canadian-U.S. Free Trade Agreement effective January 1, 1989, you can expect that Canadian business publications are tracking U.S. markets and companies with increased diligence. And, through online databases, much of that data is literally a telephone call away.

To resume the case study, say you are also interested in determining foreign perceptions of the current state of U.S. roofing technology.

This can be accomplished in several ways:

■   The conference proceedings mentioned earlier also included a paper on "Roofing Practices in North America." You can assume that the conference attendees took back this data.

■   A database search of databases based in Europe, such as URBAMET (a French-based database dealing with town planning), as well as U.S.-based databases, such as ABI/ Inform®, which are widely available in Europe and Japan, should show what research from their point of view is available.

■   Contacts are made with a "technical-commercial data bank" in Belgium, which apparently deals with manufacturers of construction materials. This data bank is identified as a result of the research done with foreign sources, which is covered later.

As it turns out, Europeans and Japanese, using the resources at their disposal, have a fairly good picture of the current state of U.S. roofing technology.

On the Outside Looking Out
The last category is locating data outside of the United States about foreign companies and markets.

National government offices, such as trade development offices, usually have access to much more company-level data than do

Special Challenges
■ ■ ■

their U.S. counterparts. However, that data is typically only on exporters, a narrow portion of the spectrum.

As just noted for trade associations, national attitudes may be critical. For instance, government agencies may be willing to provide data that advances some special interest (for them), such as export promotion or assisting companies to locate factories in their country. That is, presumably, the reason behind the increasing number of English-language publications and studies being offered in the United States by The Office for Official Publications of the European Communities. On the other hand, the agencies may be unwilling to provide data that appears to be collected in support of less-desirable ends, such as increasing U.S. exports to their nation.

In addition, getting company-level data on foreign companies from government offices may be an extremely sensitive undertaking in some nations. This is particularly true when the government has an actual ownership interest in the company, such as in Czechoslovakia, as well as when the government regards certain companies and industries as being affiliated with a "special interest," such as defense industries in many nations or electronics in Japan and Korea.

However, to counterbalance this, local newspapers and business publications, particularly non-English-language publications, often carry much more specific company-level data than is carried by their U.S. counterparts.

The types of data you can expect from non-U.S.-based corporations vary widely in quality and quantity. In general, most corporations are willing only to provide official statements, and are often unwilling to meet with representatives of the business press on a regular basis to provide detailed interviews.

One reason for this is that many of these companies are run by executives who travel substantially more than do their United States counterparts. That makes it hard for outsiders to communicate with them. Another reason is the corporate culture of many foreign companies. For example, commenting on the problems of getting business information from German companies, a columnist in London's *Financial Times* noted

> [T]his inaccessibility may have something to do with a general lack of spontaneity in German corporate life—an addiction to legalism and hierarchy. It may, too, be linked with the fact that many quoted [publicly traded] companies are still under family control and have traditionally not felt obligated to offer much information. Others have only a minority of equity in public hands, and there are not always voting shares. Managers answer, in effect, to the big banks, not to outside shareholders.[8]

However, such withdrawn attitudes are beginning to change. The forces bringing about such change range from the need to seek capital from world markets to pressures brought about by the opening of "Europe 1992" (the elimination of most tariff and trade barriers in the European Community), as well as from the need to communicate with distributors and suppliers, to a realization that a failure to communicate with the public may produce problems in terms of long-run public confidence.

Returning to the roofing case study, assume that you are also going to seek data on the overseas targets and markets *as well as* those in the United States. The sources include the following:

- ■ National trade development offices, that is, those promoting exports from the target country.

- ■ National industrial development offices that promote the creation of local employment by encouraging the construction of industrial facilities in the target country.

- ■ Local trade and labor associations.

- ■ U.S. Foreign and Commercial Service Offices in the United States, plus embassies in each target country.

Special Challenges
■ ■ ■

The names and addresses of the trade development offices and industrial development offices come from a number of sources, including ITA desk officers and the Foreign Trade Missions in the U.S. Foreign Chambers of Commerce in the United States. The local trade and labor associations were identified by all of these groups.

What you get from these sources varies widely in terms of timeliness and relevance. Typically, the offices that provide prompt and relevant data are the industrial development offices, because they understand that a response might lead to the creation of local jobs. The least responsive are the local trade and labor associations. This may be because they can see no way in which responding to such a request aids their members' interests.

The U.S. Foreign and Commercial Service Offices are located in each embassy, as well as in a number of major consultant firms. If you plan to write or call, you can find the addresses and telephone numbers in a number of resources, such as the *Worldwide Chamber of Commerce Directory*.

> *Don't forget about using your fax to make an overseas request. Your request can go out when you are ready (or can be sent at cheaper phone rates late at night), you can make it as clear as possible, your addressee will be able to read it that day or the next, and, if necessary, translate it.*

Supposing you decide to fax a request to each office. Now, where can you get these fax numbers? The answer is: in at least two places. At the ITA, you could contact each desk officer for the numbers, a slow process. As it turns out, this process will produce a large percentage of wrong numbers. Why? Evidently most ITA desk offices do not have routine access to fax machines to communicate with embassies but instead use the diplomatic pouch, so they do not always keep their telephone directories up to date. You could also contact the Business and Export Affairs Office at the State Department. Why? Because all of these people are in embassies. If you call the State Department, you will be able to get a current and accurate list of these numbers.

Now, what do you get for your trouble from the U.S. Foreign and Commercial Service Offices? Generally a lot. A typical response involves the contact person calling a local trade association or government bureau and faxing back a reply. And most replies give good solid data, as well as places to make additional contacts.

Case Study: Getting Data
from Government Agencies

This case study focuses on one particular topic: getting data from foreign government agencies—either ones located abroad or in branch offices in the United States.

As mentioned earlier, a key to getting data from any government agency, and particularly from a foreign government agency, is to seek data that the agency sees as being used to advance one of the interests of that agency, such as export promotion. This is true even if that is not your ultimate use of the data.

For example, you may be able to get company-level data on potential exporters to the United States, which would provide some aid in profiling the local market for the products they produce. The reason such data exists is to enhance exports from the host nation to the United States. Thus, data on nonexporters, even if it is available to the same office, would be harder for you to obtain. The reason is that this data might promote imports to the homeland and increased competition in the domestic market, neither of which is seen by foreign governments as a desirable national goal.

203

Special Challenges
■ ■ ■

Other keys are patience and advance planning. Data from governments—U.S. or foreign—rarely comes quickly, so you must plan to seek the data at the earliest stage of your project so that it may arrive in time to be of use. Such delays may also prompt you to seek the same data from different offices within the same agency. In fact, requests for the same data from different offices of the same agency may elicit different responses.

In one case, inquiries were made about foreign markets for construction materials both from the Washington offices of the ITA and from ITA representatives located in U.S. embassies in the target countries.

The difference in response time and quality of materials was staggering. In one instance, the local U.S. trade representative evidently called around and located a national trade association from which he obtained national-level market data, as well as the names and addresses of the local firms that controlled the market. The response was faxed the next business day.

A similar request for data made at the same time to the equivalent country desk officer at ITA in Washington was neither responded to nor forwarded overseas.

Another common situation that requires patience in seeking data from government agencies, either U.S. or foreign, is the "hand-off." This occurs when your request is forwarded to another office within the same agency, to another agency or agencies, or both. Staff of the office to which you directed your request asks those to whom the request has been forwarded to reply directly to you, thereby removing itself from the "loop." You, of course, are informed of this hand-off, so the initiating office can consider that it has responded to your request.

As you can imagine, each hand-off may generate its own additional intragovernment—or even international—hand-offs. The most frustrating situation for you is to find that your request is ultimately handed back to the agency you originally started with.

204

Summary

Three types of sources are available for your foreign CI data collection. You can search within the United States for facts about foreign companies and markets—the "inside looking out" method. You can look outside of the United States for data about U.S. companies and U.S.-based operations of foreign companies—the "outside looking in" approach. Or you can search outside of the United States for facts about foreign companies and markets—known as "outside looking out."

The two case studies in this chapter, one on roofing technology and one on obtaining data from foreign governments, illustrate how to tap the resources available to uncover CI facts about foreign competitors here and abroad as well as determining your U.S. competitors' actions here and elsewhere.

CI ALERT: What does this tell you?

"Effective October 2, PACCAR sold the Wagner Mining Equipment Co. to Atlas Copco of Sweden. . . . Many have asked why we sold Wagner, especially when the company has been doing much better. We sold because Wagner occupied a very narrow segment of the total mining equipment business—specifically the load-haul-dump market—whereas some of our competitors have LHDs plus compressors, drills, and drill bits. We did not think it would be possible to profitably add those additional products to Wagner; hence the sale to Atlas Copco, which lacked an LHD product line."

Source: Letter from the Chairman of PACCAR Inc. to Employees, Paccar World [company magazine], 1989, p. 4.

Notes

1. Commission of the European Communities, *Completing the Internal Market—White Paper from the Commission to the European Council,* June 1985, p. 31.

2. U.S. General Accounting Office, "Export Promotion: Problems in Commerce's Programs," GAO/NSIAD-89-44, January 1989, pp. 46-47.

3. U.S. General Accounting Office, "Export Promotion: Problems in Commerce's Programs," GAO/NSIAD-89-44, January 1989, Ch. 5.

4. U.S. General Accounting Office, "Export Promotion: Problems with Commerce's Commercial Information Management System," GAO/NSIAD-89-162, August 1989, p. 5.

5. Sumitomo Trust & Banking Co., Ltd., "Economic Trends—Special Report—Recent Performance of Japanese Industries," August 1988, No. 10.

6. Boye De Mente, *How to Do Business with the Japanese,* Lincolnwood, Ill.: NTC Business Books, 1987, p. 219.

7. "Superconductors: Japan Wages War by Patent in Europe," *Business Week,* November 28, 1988, p. 127.

8. Andrew Fisher, "The Need to Open Up Corporate Germany: The Business Column," *Financial Times,* February 13, 1989, p. 32.

Chapter 11

Subsidiaries, Divisions, and Closely Held Businesses

CI CLIP

"Intelligence production is essentially an intellectual process."

Former U.S. Army Intelligence Officer[1]

It is often inevitably assumed that you cannot develop accurate data as quickly on subsidiaries, divisions of large firms, closely held companies, and smaller businesses as you can on large, publicly traded firms. Yes, you can! The key is to apply the very same techniques to these CI targets as you do to any others. The most important step is to free yourself from the restraint that you *cannot* do it. You can.

Special Challenges
■ ■ ■

In fact, data on divisions, subsidiaries, and privately held businesses may be available and easy to find once you start looking for it. Take, for example, a book published in 1989, *Doing Business in New York City*.[2] In addition to a great deal of data about New York, this book features brief profiles on over 1000 divisions, subsidiaries, and private companies in the New York metropolitan area. If the firm you are targeting is one of them, some of your work has already been done.

Tracking subsidiaries, divisions, and private firms is not very different from tracking public firms, except that you do not *usually* check filings with the Securities and Exchange Commission. The key word here is *usually*. Some of these corporations must file documents with the SEC (where they are quickly available to you), even when that corporation's stock is not traded on a stock exchange. For example, Montgomery Ward & Company, Inc., the national retailer, is a wholly owned subsidiary of Mobil Corporation. However, in spite of this status, Montgomery Ward files a separate Form 10-K with the SEC, detailing its business activities and current financial situation. The reason this subsidiary of Mobil files its own reports is that Montgomery Ward has outstanding corporate debentures that are still traded on stock exchanges, which entail filings with the SEC. So, even if a competitor has been acquired by a publicly traded corporation, a privately held company, or has gone private, do not assume that there are no current SEC filings available to you. Check with the SEC first.

This chapter gives you some specific hints and examples of how and where you can develop CI on subsidiaries, divisions, and closely held businesses.

Subsidiaries and Divisions

CI from the Top
Just because the subsidiary or division you are seeking information on is a very small part of a larger whole, it is not always the case that you cannot find any important data. As a rule, the

higher up the source of your data, the less detail you can expect. However, the higher the source level of the data, the more likely it is that you will find a "gem," such as something that has been accidentally released.

Subsidiary: *A corporation that is owned by another corporation, known as the* parent.

Division: *One part of a business, separated for management purposes. It can be part of a corporation or even made up of several corporations.*

For example, take the case of The Greyhound Corporation, a $3-billion diversified conglomerate: "John W. Teets just couldn't contain himself. On a recent trip to Chicago, the Chairman of Greyhound Corporation disclosed to reporters plans to introduce a low-calorie line of the company's successful Lunch Bucket microwaveable meals. Never mind that he angered his marketing staff, which considered the project top secret. It was good news, Teets reasoned, and his Phoenix-based conglomerate needed some of that."[3]

Checking Out the Parent
One way to approach the problem of developing CI on subsidiaries and divisions is to determine whether the ultimate parent corporation itself issues publicly traded stock. If so, some of the parent corporation's own documents may provide the kind of data you are seeking.

For example, the Bank of Boston, in a quarterly report to its stockholders, summarized the details of its annual meeting of the stockholders.[4] Among other topics, that summary discussed the bank's overall strategic plan. The bank considers itself a decentralized corporation, with each of its business groups, or divisions, operating in different markets facing different kinds of competition. In his remarks, the bank's chairman specifically commented on the performance of *each* of the bank's business groups. Among his observations were the following details, which might help a competitor analyze the operations and goals of some of the bank's divisions:

■ The bank regards its National Banking Group as the "mainstay of profitability and growth" of the entire bank. That division was reported to have had its pretax return on investment increase more than 50 percent since 1985.

■ The bank's international operations are in a "turnaround" phase. That specifically includes "withdrawals from nonstrategic businesses and locations that reduced the number of countries in which the [bank] has offices from 40 to 27."

■ In the Real Estate Group, the four mortgage banking companies within the Group were "recently combined."

CI CLOSEUP: "You Don't Always Get What You Want"

In a study in 1988, the U.S. Securities and Exchange Commission reviewed the Management Discussion and Analysis portions of over 200 Form 10-Ks filed in 1987 and 1988. Only 12 companies passed the first review. Six were considered so misleading that they were referred to the SEC's enforcement staff, and more than 70 companies were ordered to amend their filings.[5]

Watching for Outbound Messages

Another approach is to determine whether the division or subsidiary in which you are interested is in a business, such as consumer goods, in which it communicates regularly with numerous independent firms, such as distributors or retailers. In such cases, the target division or subsidiary may give interviews to the trade or business press on its current operations. The purpose of these interviews is to give its distribution and retailing network confidence in both the target's products and its performance. To generate that kind of confidence, your target may need to release very specific data. Your goal is to find the channels into which that sort of information is released. Then you can review those communications for the detailed data you want.

A representative example is some of the specific comments made by a division head of a major manufacturing corporation in a trade publication interview[6]:

■ 30 percent of the division's sales come from products that have been in its line less than three years.

■ The division put into effect price increases during 1989 averaging 3 to 4 percent.

■ The division will create its own "high-end" department store line of products, either by adding more fully featured products or by adding features to its existing retail products.

■ The division does not plan to enter a specific (described) product market.

As another example, consider the variety of important data released at a regional level by a major food manufacturer about its management operations and operating philosophy[7]:

■ The parent company reorganized its entire U.S. marketing operations, creating 21 "mostly autonomous regional operations, each entirely responsible for local market planning and spending." To help these new regional managers, manuals of marketing data, keyed to regions of the United States, were given to each new regional manager.

■ Following that reorganization, all domestic food production plants were reorganized so that they were tied to the regional sales operations. The plants now are more involved in developing new product ideas and have drawn marketing and sales staffs into the production-planning cycle. These regional food production operations are not yet producing everything their respective sales regions need, but they "will all be self-sufficient within the next five years."

Closely Held Businesses

Closely held business: *A business whose stock is not traded on any stock exchange.*

A closely held business may be a corporation with a small number of stockholders, a partnership, or even a sole proprietorship. In any case, the business does not have to file materials with the SEC.

Reviewing Annual Reports

Although the company you may be tracking does not publicly trade stock, it may publish an annual report. Some companies whose shares are not publicly traded produce an annual report because they must do so. Others do so because it makes them look bigger or because it gives the impression the company competes head to head with publicly traded companies. If a privately held company perceives that acting like a publicly traded company is to its advantage, it may well act like a publicly traded company. This can include the publication of annual reports.

For example, mutual insurance companies are not publicly traded, because they have no stockholders. They are owned by all the persons who have insurance policies with the insurance company. However, these firms have to provide annual reports for their policyholders. Just as with the reports filed with the SEC by their publicly traded competitors, these mutual insurance company reports have widely varying levels of detail.

These reports can range from an abbreviated pamphlet, such as that produced by State Farm Insurance, which contains only highly aggregated financial data, to a lengthy, glossy document, such as that distributed by The Prudential Insurance Group, which traditionally details its operations and discusses some of its operating strategy.

CI CLIP

"What is big is easy to perceive; what is small is difficult to perceive. . . . [I]t is difficult for large numbers of men to change position, so their movements can be easily predicted. An individual can easily change his mind, so his movements are difficult to predict."

Seventeenth Century Japanese Military Strategist.[8]

In some cases, privately held companies prepare and distribute something similar to an annual report. A document available from ARA Services, the international provider of food and health services, provides a typical example. ARA's "annual report" is entitled "The Year in Review—A Report to Employees." In form, it looks quite a lot like the documents that ARA filed with the SEC before it became a privately held company in 1984. However, this document (and others like it) has several important differences from those preprivatization filings:

Special Challenges
■ ■ ■

■ There is no legal requirement that ARA even prepare this report or that, if it does, it must make it available to outsiders. Its very existence and availability to outsiders is optional.

■ The report is written for ARA's own employees. That means it is written for readers who presumably understand the context in which it is written. If you are not in the know already, the contents may be confusing to you.

■ The contents of this report are not subject to the legal requirements of the federal securities laws. That means there are no legal rules about the subjects that must be dealt with, the way in which they are to be treated, or the accuracy of any financial information provided in the report.

Reviewing Government Filings

You may be able to get substantial data on closely held firms from state and local government sources. For example, the provisions of a bill proposed in Pennsylvania in 1989 aim to ease the regulatory requirements imposed on people starting new businesses, which are typically closely held. The bill proposed to establish a "master application" so that persons starting a business would file only one application for all state-required licenses and permits.

Significantly, the bill also proposed that Pennsylvania Revenue Department Offices be required to "provide easy access to application information, enabling consumers, customers, and service providers to make a quick background check on the companies with which they deal."[9] Of course, once such a file is established, you could easily use it to develop CI on a new Pennsylvania business.

Remember that state government agencies require reports about company operations, particularly in highly regulated industries. In many states, portions or even all of these reports are available for inspection or copying from the state regulatory officials

214

responsible for supervising the industry. So, if your target is in a regulated business, determine what kinds of reports it must file, and with whom.

Local governments—cities, townships, and counties—may also be a source of additional data to help you understand what a particular closely held business is doing. The local tax and assessor's office's files typically can provide you with a complete description of the property on which your target firm has built its offices or plant. These files may include the property's approximate market value, as well as the amount of taxes being paid on it.

A local planning or license and inspection office may have other important data in its publicly accessible files. Such data is contained in routinely filed documents such as building permit applications, subdivision applications, and environmental impact reports. These documents may detail the type and level of planned operations at a particular plant or office.

Checking the Chamber of Commerce and the Better Business Bureau

Check with the local chamber of commerce; it may be able to tell you whether your target firm has more than one office in the community and how long it has been doing business there. The local better business bureau may also be able to tell you a little about the firm. For example, you can find out whether the target firm is a member. More importantly, you can learn about any record of complaints against that firm, regardless of whether it is a bureau member. The complaint record may help you to determine how well the company is being run, where its goods and services are being sold, or even what types of goods and services it sells.

Office of Corporations

Every corporation must file some information with a state agency if it is either headquartered in that state or has an office in the state. This filing is usually with a part of the Secretary of

Special Challenges
■ ■ ■

State's Office called the "office of corporations" (or sometimes called the "corporations division"). When a corporation incorporates or sets up an office in the state, it must file incorporation papers or something similar. These papers usually provide, at a minimum, information on the nature of the business, names and addresses of officers and agents, and the amount of capital stock in the corporation. In addition to this registration, every corporation must file some kind of annual report. These annual reports may contain financial data. Some states requires sales figures, whereas others just ask for asset figures. Whether these filings are available to the public, and to what extent, varies from state to state.

State Securities Office
The U.S. Securities and Exchange Commission, discussed at length previously, regulates some, but not all, corporations that sell stock. For some stock offerings, financial information is filed only with a state securities regulator. These state filings are somewhat similar to those filed with the SEC. Again, however, the documents required vary from state to state. A telephone call to the office in charge can often provide immediate information on whether a particular corporation has ever made a filing with the state. If it has, you can obtain a copy. Usually the office of corporations in the Secretary of State's Office can refer you to the state's securities regulator.

Reading Uniform Commercial Code Filings
Another good source of financial data can be taken from the competitor's Uniform Commercial Code (UCC) filings. These filings, usually made with a state office, detail loans made by financial institutions to the target whose repayment is secured by equipment and/or accounts receivable. The size of the loans secured may help you estimate the size of the target company; the type of equipment recently acquired may help to determine its production capacity and future expansion plans; the amount of credit granted against accounts receivable may help you estimate the target's current sales levels.

Estimating Data

If you cannot find all the data you need, you can try generating some of it. For example, assume that you have already determined, or at least estimated, the gross assets and gross sales of a target company. You have no idea of that firm's gross profit margin, however. All you can determine is that the firm is profitable now. One option is to turn to a source such as *IRS Corporate Financial Ratios.* In that publication, you can find data taken from corporate tax returns, broken down by industry and size of corporation.

That book may reveal that the gross margin of profitable corporations in your target company's line of business is 28 percent and that their net margin is 4.3 percent. This is already helpful. However, this book's data is often more refined than that. In many cases, data on gross margins and net margins is also provided by size of business. Thus, you might find that profitable firms that have less than $1 million in gross assets have a gross margin of 32 percent, higher than the industry average, but they have a net margin of only 3.7 percent, lower than the industry average. Using this refined ratio may help you begin to estimate how well your competitor is probably doing.

Consulting the Local Press

In addition to the resources already suggested, it is almost always advisable to search local business newspapers, magazines, trade publications, and newsletters, such as those found in databases (Datatimes, the Trade & Industry Index, and PTS Newsletter Database). Even privately held businesses seek out or are the subject of stories in these publications. And those stories can be a way to extract real nuggets of data taken from the source itself—your target firm.

Becoming Aware of the Data's Origins

When you deal with data on closely held businesses, however, you have to be particularly sensitive to the need to understand the true source of any data you find. This is particularly critical in eliminating disinformation and preventing false confirmations when dealing with this data. For example, the introduction to the *Standard & Poor's Register of Corporations, Executives, and Directors* notes that "The information in [the Register] has, with few exceptions, been obtained directly from the individuals and companies themselves. The nature and magnitude of the work, however, make it impossible for the publisher to guarantee complete accuracy."

The other sources of information identified as sources for these reports are "daily news services, press announcements, trade publications, Standard & Poor's own editorial staff, and. . . individual contact by interested members within the business community."

These are the same sources generally used as inputs for reports by business information services. In the case of closely held businesses, this means that the *vast majority of the data* available through such a service may come exclusively from the target company itself. If a closely held business does not complete the inquiry sheet sent by one of the business information services, such as Standard & Poor's—and it does not have to do so— numbers and other data will be provided, based on S & P's "other sources of information." What you read may be more than merely inaccurate. It may be disinformation.

Summary

To find CI data about subsidiaries and divisions of companies, your search should include the parent company's publications, if that company's stock is publicly traded. Also, materials intended for a company's distribution and retailing network provide insights to its competitive position.

Although many closely held businesses are not held to the same federal government filing requirements as are publicly traded firms, many issue some types of annual reports and file reports with their state and local governments. Local governments, chambers of commerce, and better business bureaus are often repositories of data about a company's local dealings and history of operations. The local press is another likely source.

A special caution applies to information you obtain about closely held businesses: Always consider the source of information to be suspect, because it frequently comes from the target competitor itself, not an independent source.

CI ALERT: What does this tell you?

"Travelers announced Dec. 22 that it will continue to pursue the sale of its subsidiary, Travelers Mortgage Services Inc. (TMSI). The company is working with Salomon Brothers, its investment advisor, to identify interested purchasers.

"Travelers previously announced that it had accepted an offer for the purchase of TMSI from Hyperion Partners LP and the management of TMSI. That offer is no longer under consideration."

Source: Article, The Travelers Tribune [company newspaper], January 1990.

Notes

1. Washington Platt, *Strategic Intelligence Production,* New York: Frederick A. Praeger, 1957, p. 273.

2. Thomas Crain and Jeffrey P. Levine, *Doing Business in New York City,* New York: Dow Jones-Irwin, 1989.

3. "The Other Greyhound Isn't Winning Any Races," *Business Week,* June 19, 1989, p. 53.

4. Bank of Boston Corporation, *Report to Stockholders for the Quarter Ended March 31, 1989*. That report noted that a transcript of the annual meeting is available for inspection at the bank's headquarters office.

5. "Annual Reports: The SEC Cracks the Whip," *Business Week*, April 10, 1989, p. 74.

6. "Heiner: B&D Plans 'Same Old Success'," *HFD*, May 1, 1989, pp. 87, 90. This is a story featuring an interview with the president of Black & Decker's Household Products Group.

7. "Pushing Decisions Down the Line at Campbell Soup," *Business Month*, July 1989, pp. 62-63. This article is based on an interview with the president of Campbell USA, a division of Campbell Soup Company.

8. Miyamoto Musashi, *A Book of Five Rings* (translated by Victor Harris), Woodstock, N.Y.: The Overlook Press, 1974, p. 44.

9. Charles Jaffe, "New Bill Aims to Aid State's Entrepreneurs," *The Sunday Call*, March 12, 1989, p. C-1.

Part IV

Turning Data into Actionable Information

Chapter 12
Evaluating and Analyzing Data

Chapter 13
Using What You Know

Chapter 14
**Beyond the Obvious: More Sophisticated
Applications of CI**

Chapter 15
Defending Against CI

Chapter 12

Evaluating and Analyzing Data

CI CLIP

"Collecting information is only part of the job; there also has to be interpretation and analysis."

Director of Corporate Analytical Research, Motorola, Inc.[1]

Both evaluation and analysis are steps critical to the CI process. It can be somewhat difficult to distinguish exactly where they begin and the process of collecting raw data ends.

Without diving too deeply into the abyss of statistical theory and terminology, in this chapter we illustrate ways you can test how reliable the data you obtain from your CI program is, how to eliminate false confirmations from data sources, and how to make correct inferences as you guard against disinformation.

Evaluating Raw Data

Once you have gathered your raw data, you cannot merely assume that all that data is accurate. You must establish the probable accuracy of that data for it to have any meaning at all to you. Lacking that platform, you may be basing your CI on a concoction of very good data, marginally correct data, bad data, and even disinformation. Even if you find that you can draw some sort of conclusion from that mishmash, you risk drawing a wrong conclusion. However, once you have a sense of the relative accuracy of the individual pieces of data, you can then begin to analyze all of your data properly.

Evaluation: The process of studying the raw data as you are collecting it.

Analysis: The study of raw data in context to turn the data into intelligence.

For example, suppose that you have located an article about your target company in a publication whose articles have been quite reliable in the past. However, later, you find that this data appears to be contradicted by a report whose source you generally consider to be unreliable. Given these two facts, you should conclude that the article is likely to be correct. The fact that it was contradicted by an unreliable source may make it all the more likely to be correct. You can then minimize the impact of the other, less reliable, data in your analysis, or even ignore it completely. In fact, a conflicting account from an unreliable source may make you more secure in your reliance on relatively reliable data.

As this example shows, in evaluating raw data, you are engaged in several different tasks. You have to try to establish the reliability of the source of the data that you have. To do that, you should try and determine exactly where the data was produced, because the identity of the originating source may help you to estimate the reliability of the data.

CI CLIP

"When addressing questions of verifiable fact, it was scrupulously accurate; reporters could rely on anything we said about sales, profits, miles per gallon, and other technical or particular subjects. But we often sidestepped facts we thought embarrassing, and we hadn't the slightest compunction about misrepresenting what we knew and felt about the issue at hand."

Former member of major automaker's public affairs staff.[2]

You also have to estimate the accuracy of the data itself. Sometimes you do this by comparisons. For example, is one piece of data confirmed by data from an independent source? If so, it *may* be accurate. Before you jump to that conclusion, you should complete other steps, such as spotting and then eliminating false confirmations of data.

As you can see, there are three basic steps in evaluating the accuracy of raw data:

1. Identify the actual source of the data so you can evaluate the reliability of the source.

2. Estimate the data's accuracy so you can classify the data.

3. Eliminate false confirmations.

Turning Data into Actionable Information
■ ■ ■

Establishing the Reliability of the Source

To conduct a good evaluation of any data, you must have at least a sense of its ultimate source. Figure out why the data was produced, collected, and released. You have to understand the origin and history of each piece of data, because those facts are critical to its analysis.

Reliability: In CI, the believability of the source of your data. You estimate how much you can believe any data coming from a particular source, based on its past performance.

Accuracy: In CI, the correctness of the particular piece of data you have. You are estimating how correct the data is, based on factors such as whether it is confirmed by data from a reliable source as well as the reliability of the original source of the data.

Essentially, you can assume that all data is produced and released for some *certain purpose.* For example, if the Electronics Industry Association (EIA) releases market share and growth rate data on its members, it may have collected those facts for a hearing before the International Trade Commission (ITC). The EIA may have gone to that hearing to convince the ITC about the potentially severe impact of future electronics imports on the U.S. economy. The data presented to the ITC and that sought by EIA will support this position. It will tend to be presented to the ITC in a light that advances the EIA's case. This does not mean it is "wrong," just that it was collected to make a certain point.

> *To understand data, understand the reason for its existence.*

However, each of the EIA members that provided data for the ITC hearing may also produce its own market share and growth rate estimates in its annual report. These estimates may seem to differ from the EIA's estimates. Why? Is one wrong? No. They are different because they were produced for different purposes and two different audiences. To use either or both sources, you first have to understand the origins of the data. Then you can decide which you should use, if either. So, when you begin to analyze raw data, keep in mind the need to tie your evaluation of the raw data to the reason it was created, not to the reason you are seeking it.

You must not ignore the origins of data, either. Data is only as good as its source. With the earlier example, the electronics industry data you get from, say, the files of the ITC or a report by the ITC does *not* have the ITC as its real source. That is where you found it. Instead, the data's real source should be considered to be the member companies that provided the raw data, as well as the EIA itself, if the organization performed any analyses of the data from its members.

Keep in mind this informal rule: Unless you can establish otherwise, *assume* that every place from which you get data has its own point of view that permeates any data from that source. You might think a source such as a securities analyst might be an automatic exception to this rule. It is not. Research indicates that security analysts, as a group, tend to be overly accepting of management's projections of the future performance of corporations about which they write.[3] Some believe that this is because they generally write about firms whose stock their employers trade or in which their employers make a market. That caution does not mean that you should overlook security analysts as a resource. Just remember "where they are coming from."

Estimating the Data's Accuracy

One way to look at CI is to visualize a jigsaw puzzle. You start with many individual pieces of data that initially seem to be meaningless and unconnected. When you put them together correctly, however, they produce a picture—valuable CI. One key difference between CI and a jigsaw puzzle is that, when you deal with CI, you may have to remove some of the pieces and not use them.

CI CLIP

"The paper you read is shaped by unstated, implicit values and biases which you must recognize. I admit that the mirrors we [journalists] use to reflect reality are inevitably flawed by our own presuppositions and prejudices. You must correct the 'spin' those twists impart to what you read. The clues are in all the subjective elements—phrasing, word selection, story placement, sourcing—that shape a particular reporter's or paper's version of the news."

Newspaper Reporter David S. Broder.[4]

Once you have assessed the reliability of the data source you are looking at, you next estimate its accuracy. This involves classifying the data you get as to relative degrees of accuracy. As you collect more data and involve others in collecting and analyzing it, you might find that you need some systematic way of marking individual pieces of raw data to identify both their likely accuracy and the probable credibility of their sources.

One way is to use or adapt a two-character classification system, shown in Table 12.1.

Table 12.1

Data Classification System

Reliability of the Source	Approximate Truthfulness of Past Data (%)
A. Completely Reliable	100
B. Usually Reliable	80
C. Fairly Reliable	60
D. Not Usually Reliable	40
E. Unreliable	20
F. Reliability Cannot Be Estimated	50

Accuracy of Data	Probability of Accuracy (%)
1. Confirmed by Other Reliable Sources	100
2. Probably Accurate	80
3. Possibly Accurate	60
4. Of Doubtful Accuracy	40
5. Improbable	20
6. Accuracy Cannot Be Estimated	50

When you evaluate the reliability of a source of data, consider both the original source of the data (source) and the source from which you actually obtained it (provider). For example, information you get from the current distributors of a target firm may or may not be reliable. Its reliability depends on the attitude of the particular distributors toward their supplier, their view of the use to which the information they are giving you may eventually be put, and their access to current data of the sort you are trying to get from them.

Similarly, data from a competitor's suppliers, even those with whom your firm also does business, may be influenced by conflicting factors. These include the desire to please you, reluctance to discuss other customers, or a lack of perception on the part of the individual providing you with the data.

The past track record, if available, of both individual and institutional sources of data is generally a good basis on which to estimate current reliability. A supplemental test is one dealing with the *likelihood* that your source could actually have the specific data you have obtained from it. That is, ask yourself whether, under the conditions facing the specific source, that source could have actually obtained the specific data within the limitations of time, access, and financing that the source faces.

In applying the two-character classification system noted in the table, a few guidelines may prove helpful:

- If the source of the data is friendly (that is, one not seen as hostile to your interests) and is also an informed one, you can usually assign an "A" rating when that source of data is known to have a long and extensive background with the type of data reported. Use the rating "B" for friendly, informed sources that lack the background experience but are of known integrity. Assign a rating of "F" when there is no adequate basis for estimating the reliability of the source. This might include, for example, information that has accidentally come into your possession but that does not have a clear source, so you cannot evaluate the source's track record at all.

- If you get data from a source that is regularly collecting this type of data—whether it be a business information firm, such as Standard & Poor's, a market research department in your firm, or a CI firm—rate the data based on two factors. First, rate the source based on its current state of training and experience. Second, rate the source that generated the data in the first instance. When you have given the source of a piece of data and the collecting unit different evaluations, give the lower rating of reliability to the data that came through both of them. That is the most conservative approach.

■ If you can say with certainty that reported data originated from a source other than the one that already provided the data being confirmed, then the data can be classified as "confirmed by other sources" and rated "1."

■ If, as you apply the same test, there is no reason to suspect that the confirming data comes from the same source as the data being confirmed, then you can consider it as "probably true" and give it a rating of "2."

■ If your investigation discloses that raw data for which you have no confirming data yet available is consistent with the behavior of the target as you have observed so far, the data received is "possibly true" and rated "3."

■ Classify as "doubtful," with a rating of "4," reported but unconfirmed data, the contents of which contradict estimated or known behavior of the target, as long as that data cannot be disproved by available data.

■ Reported data, unconfirmed by other available data and contradicting experience, is classified as "improbable" and should be given a rating of "5." The same classification would be given to reported data that contradicts existing data already rated "1" or "2."

■ If your research discloses no basis for allocating any of the ratings of "1" through "5," the reported data should be classified as "6," because you cannot judge its truth.

Always keep in mind that, under this system, the ratings of accuracy and reliability are independent of each other. For example, a highly reliable source may report data which, when compared with other data that you know to be true, appears to be improbable. Its evaluation would be "A5." On the other hand, an evaluation of "E1" could be given to data from a source of unknown reliability when, through confirmation from other, reliable sources, the data is determined to be of proven accuracy.

Eliminating False Confirmations

False confirmation: A situation in which one source appears to confirm data obtained from another source. In fact, there is no confirmation because the first source may have obtained its data from the second source, or they both may have received it from a third source, unknown to you.

Confirming data serves to assess its accuracy. In the long run, it also serves to assess the reliability of its source.

An example will illustrate how false confirmations work. Assume that you are trying to develop some CI on a publicly traded company. You might think that one way to confirm data you obtain from Standard & Poor's would be to check that data against data from other sources. One might be a database such as TRW Business Profiles online. The TRW Business Profiles combines credit information, corporate financials, and other information. However, looking at it might confirm what you found from Standard & Poor's, but it would be a false confirmation. Why? These records contain, in TRW's own words, "Standard & Poor's balance sheet figures and operating statement . . . plus S&P COMPUSTAT® and REGISTER® information. . . ." In other words, a good portion of the TRW file comes from S&P and thus cannot confirm the S&P data's validity.

The same is also true when you deal with trade and professional publications. These narrowly focused magazines and newspapers offer both benefits and disadvantages as sources of data. On the plus side, the fact that these publications have a specialized focus allows them to present stories with a degree of detail that is almost impossible to find in the more general media. On the other hand, many trade publications depend heavily on press releases issued by companies in their industry, often printing them verbatim. That means that the same report in two trade publications may only mean that both have printed the text of the same press release. Again, this results in a false confirmation, due to a common source for the data.

Determining Whether All Your Data Is Relevant

Finally, you must eliminate data that is not relevant to your CI needs. It is almost always the situation in CI collection that large amounts of valuable raw data are brought in by an effective collection effort. However, typically, these same collection efforts create large amounts of "good" data that is not directly relevant to the assignment.

You have to put irrelevant data aside once you see that it does not directly pertain to your assignment. Drawing an analogy from communications, you must avoid drowning out the crucial data with the "noise" generated by irrelevant data.

Conducting Supplemental Data Gathering

A logical follow-up to the first round of data evaluation is to develop a plan to continuously identify any supplemental data you need to collect. Typically, the kind of data you will need is narrow, enabling you to answer new, highly focused questions that have arisen as you have done your research and analysis. But do not forget that just because the data you need is supplemental, a "gap-filler," you cannot ignore the CI processes outlined throughout this book. You may find that narrow, highly focused questions may be harder to answer than were the broader questions you started with.

Turning Data into Actionable Information
■ ■ ■

If you need some supplemental data, by all means seek it out. But do not use this as an excuse to redo your earlier collection efforts. When a step is done, go on.

Analyzing the Data

Although CI cannot be conducted without acquiring raw data, the analysis is what converts that often relatively useless raw material into really usable information. The care with which the analysis is conducted is just as important as the quality of the data collected. For example, when you analyze the raw data, be careful not to project your own biases and preconceptions onto the data. If you don't avoid that, you can render even the best data worthless to your analysis.

What Are General Analysis Procedures?

How do you analyze the raw data, once you have identified which is reliable and which is not? It is like any other analysis—legal, financial, or medical. You must start to work knowing that you may lack complete data. In fact, you may never have all of the data you need.

CI CLIP

"The issue isn't acquiring enough information. The issue is, how do you choose from all the information that you've got?"

Vice President, Strategic and Marketing Planning, AT&T.[5]

Competitive intelligence analysis is also similar to these other types of analysis, in that you must remember that some of the data you have is contradictory, some only appears to be contradictory, and some of it is flat out wrong.

Organizing the Data

Analyzing the results of research is a different process for each project because the analysis is a function of the task, the data collected, the audience for which it is being done, and your experience. A number of organizational techniques can help you here:

- Structure your preliminary research results to help you conduct your analysis.

- Be imaginative and alert to the importance of detail.

- Identify and eliminate disinformation.

- Locate patterns and determine their significance.

- Seek out anomalies and understand why they occurred.

- Try isolating the vital data using disaggregation.

- Be sensitive to data that should be there but is not.

- Be sensitive to data that should not be there but is.

- Don't make assumptions—find out.

- Review your results to ensure completeness and consistency.

- Separate your data from your conclusions.

Typically, in a CI project dealing with one or more of your competitors, your raw data can be classified in three basic categories:

- What your competitors say about themselves.
- What one competitor says about another.
- What third parties say about your competitors.

CI CLOSEUP: "Analysis Styles"

How do you formally handle the analysis? That can vary. For example, at Pfizer, Inc., the pharmaceutical company, the manager of competitive analysis was faced with a problem of determining the threat posed by generic drug products. To accomplish this, a company task force was set up. It included personnel from corporate strategic planning, the domestic pharmaceuticals group, the research and development staff, the corporation's Washington office, and the credit department.

This group held formal meetings, with each participant providing a piece of the analysis. The topic was discussed, and supplemental data sources, such as security analysts, were tapped for data. At the end, each participant prepared a separate report, all of which were assembled as a package for Pfizer's president. It was followed up with a series of later, narrow reports dealing with related issues.

In contrast, at the Adolph Coors Company, the sales and marketing operations handle this task differently. There, the director of sales and marketing operations estimates that he and his staff spend 40 percent of their time in data collection and 60 percent in analysis and reporting. Coors has experimented with a number of analysis techniques, including pattern recognition, scenario development, assembly and reassembly of pieces of information, game playing, and content analysis.

Coors' personnel concluded that, for them, the most useful method is a simple one. As Coors' director of sales and marketing operations describes it, the key is the "periodic think-tank session": "We use technical, marketing, sales, and planning people to analyze information for our planning process. We gather about 10 people in a room, twice a month, in long sessions—anything from three hours to a couple of days. The sessions have no formal structure. We examine and massage the latest competitor and industry information to determine where things are going and what we should be doing."[6]

When you reorganize the data by area of coverage, such as dividing it among categories including costs, markets, consumer relations, and financial strengths, you may find that data in one category appears to be dominated by one of these three categories of sources. If that is the situation, decide what that means and whether it is significant.

For example, if virtually all of the information about a competitor's manufacturing costs comes from third parties who are not also competitors, that may tell you something about the quality of the data. Among the potential conclusions could be that the cost data is not likely to be accurate, because you can find no way in which outsiders could have derived it. Alternatively, it could mean that the outsiders were provided data by your competitors, so that you have data that is quite accurate. To determine which alternative is more likely, you will have to immerse yourself in the data and put yourself in the place of both the outsider and your competitor.

> *Before you draw a conclusion, organize your facts in different ways: by source, by subject, by time, and by perspective.*

Structuring search results also enables you to put together seemingly isolated pieces of data and achieve an unexpected result. For example, note how a business reporter described finding out about changes in the product line of a major brewery: "On Page 6 of *The Wall Street Journal* . . . was a three-column photograph of former Pittsburgh Steeler Franco Harris holding a bottle of Barbican beer (identified as an import from Bass Ale. . . . Not until examining the small print are the facts revealed that the nonalcoholic beverage is distributed by Great Northern Imports Ltd. in the Stroh Brewery Co. brewery in Fogelsville (Pennsylvania)."[7]

CI CLOSEUP: "No News Is Bad News"

A chemical company reportedly suffered a "serious setback" when a competitor introduced a more effective product. The damage was severe for several reasons, among them that the product accounted for a high percentage of the company's profits and that the company was unaware of the development of the competitor's product. In reviewing why the company had been taken by surprise, its managers found that one problem lay in its intelligence activities. Early intelligence had been available to it both through published sources and through its own employees, such as buyers and salespeople. The problem was that no one was responsible for collecting, analyzing, and distributing this information.[8]

That small bit of data then led the reporter to find out that Stroh's had established a new subsidiary, Great Northern, in the past six months. The reporter also tied another brand of beer to Stroh's when he found that the address of the company making that brand was identical to Stroh's. If the reporter had not put all of this information in proximity, he might not have seen these connections. But he did, and the result was a story about forthcoming changes affecting a major local employer. None of the information the reporter found was hidden, nor was the story explosive. However, until the information about beer brands was sorted properly, there was no story.

Assembling the Data

How do *you* assemble *your* data to produce *your* analysis? One way is to use an outline. The outline format is particularly easy to handle if you are using a word processor. First, create an outline of the topic you are analyzing. Then, as you review the raw data, insert each piece of data as many times as needed under every appropriate heading. Do this for all of your data. Then read it, section by section. What conclusions do you see? What problems? What gaps?

Another hint is to separate your data from your conclusions. In fact, when you have finished a draft report, go through it with a highlighter and mark your data in one color and your conclusions from that data in another. Then go back through it and make sure you have enough data to support each of your conclusions. If you don't, add the data you did not include in the right place or drop the conclusions as unsupported. Verify that you have drawn conclusions from all data you assembled. Otherwise, why did you include it in the first place?

> *Draw a conclusion based on facts; then attack it, using the same facts.*

In addition, be careful that you understand exactly what has been said and what has not. Increasingly, many businesses and industries use their own private language. Sometimes, this provides clarity and precision for those who use data. In other cases, it only serves to keep outsiders from understanding what is actually going on. The jargon may even be intended to create desired impressions in targeted groups.

Sifting Out Disinformation

Because CI involves converting your data into a cohesive picture of a competitor, you must beware of business disinformation. You must also develop tools to identify and handle it.

> *Disinformation:* Something that looks like information but is not information. It is designed to mislead others. The word itself comes from the world of intelligence and international politics, where the term encompasses both fraud and forgery.

As the text of a secret U.S. government document on disinformation (itself released to the press from an unknown source) is reported to have said, disinformation "combines real and illusory events . . . with the basic goal of making [the target] *think* what the initiator wanted." According to this document, among the objectives of a disinformation plan is to keep the target "preoccupied" and "off balance."[9]

Disinformation in the business world is not as expansive as it is in politics and espionage, because it falls short of fraud. You can look at disinformation in two ways: active versus passive and purposeful versus accidental.

Active business disinformation intentionally misleads people with erroneous or exaggerated information. *Passive business disinformation* involves concealing relevant information. In each case, business disinformation is aimed at establishing false value judgments, creating erroneous impressions, diverting attention from defects or problems, or hiding facts. This is just a way of looking at disinformation based on its content (or lack of content).

Another way is to see it in terms of the way it came about: purposeful versus accidental.

Purposeful business disinformation can best be understood by looking at how and where it develops. Business disinformation usually originates from the business itself. For example, a firm may have one of its officers give an interview to a local newspaper to improve the firm's community image. During the interview, the reporter's expected questions about the firm, its plans, and its future are answered, with great care, by the officer.

The reporter leaves with notes, quotes, handouts, and impressions. When the article is written, all of these go into the final product. In writing the article, the conclusions drawn by the reporter may not be precisely correct. In fact, the person giving the interview may have worked quite hard to have the reporter draw certain conclusions without ever stating them as facts. This enables the reporter, not the officer of the business, to make the disinformation public.

If the conclusions do not hurt the firm, the firm usually has no incentive to seek a correction. In fact, even if a correction were requested and eventually printed, the damage has been done. Retractions and corrections rarely catch up with those who read the original story.

The article then can become an important input to the "trades," to investment analysts, and to others following the firm or the industry. In turn, these sources may generate a second level of disinformation based on the first level of disinformation.

Accidental business disinformation can also arise. For example, due to the rise in interstate bank mergers, many small regional banks have been reviewing their long-range plans to see whether they should seek to be acquired, prepare to oppose an acquisition, or seek to make defensive acquisitions themselves. As a part of this review, they often hire outside consultants to advise them on their options.

241

Turning Data into Actionable Information
■ ■ ■

In one case, a bank holding company retained such a firm. The bank did not intend to publicize this fact. The firm was hired to provide general advice; this was not a step in either an acquisition or a sale. However, the firm that the bank hired did not "get the word" about avoiding publicity. In fact, the firm issued a press release about its retention by the bank, publicizing its hiring in order to get future business. The press release was printed by the business media.

Some who saw the resulting article came to the erroneous conclusion that the bank was really seeking to be acquired. They assumed that the bank had arranged for the publicity. Why else, they concluded, would the bank release this information, particularly in publications serving areas that none of the bank's subsidiaries served?

The result was that the bank was misidentified as a potential acquisition target. As a result of the undesired attention, the bank had to take steps to protect itself against a possible takeover while deciding whether it should even actively seek a takeover.

C: CLIP

". . . Machiavelli thought that a general's interest should not be restricted to purely military actions; he ought also to devise efficient methods of deceiving the enemy and employing ruses—like the spreading of false rumors—to discourage him."

German diplomatic historian.[10]

Sometimes, business disinformation is generated specifically to *mislead competitors*. For example, in many industries, the development of new products and processes is costly and time-consuming. If you believe that a competitor is ahead of you in a particular area, you might abandon your firm's work in that area, reasoning that you could never catch up.

For example, to determine the technological status of competitors, companies have routinely used online databases to identify competitors' new patents as they are issued and new products as they are released around the world. In some industries, this practice has reportedly been met by a countermeasure: intentional business disinformation. Some companies are reported to have patented "mistakes" to throw their competitors off the track. Others make product announcements allegedly rife with false information, seeking to lay claims to markets before their technical or sales forces can actually produce the product.

In some cases, business disinformation is generated to *make the sourcing company look good*. It also has as one of its effects the misdirection of competitors. For example, a manufacturing firm was planning to expand its production capacity by building more plants. To do this, it sought joint venture partners. However, it seemed that it was going to take time to put all of these facilities in place. The company sought to gain time for its expansion plans to take hold by keeping out potential competitors until its new capacity was in operation. It also wished to project a very positive image of its strength and progress to reassure its current investors and joint venturers as well as to bring in new ones. The result was business disinformation.

It was produced by arranging for stories on new production capacity that overstated the status of new projects. The company did not engage in actual fraud—such as misrepresenting the status of these projects on its books in a material way—so this move was not illegal. It was just business disinformation.

Being aware that disinformation really exists and trying to decide whether a competitor is using it is like analyzing a test for a disease:

Turning Data into Actionable Information
■ ■ ■

■ If you don't check whether disinformation is present, and it is there, it can be destructive. You may not recognize its destructive effect until it is too late to counteract it.

■ If you look for the disinformation, you may not spot it, even if it is present. In that case, known as a *false negative,* your CI analysis is affected by the disinformation, but in a direction and to a degree you cannot appreciate.

■ You may find what you think is disinformation, when it is not really there. In that case, known as a *false positive,* you simply become more suspicious about the credibility you assign to what is really accurate data and more reluctant to rely on it without further confirmation.

■ You may be correct in spotting the disinformation. In that case, handling it properly permits you to avoid its damaging effect on your business's planning and marketing operations.

CI CLIP

"Historically there have always been people who used the business press. But over the last five years, the sophistication of sources who want to use the press has multiplied manyfold."

Former reporter for The Wall Street Journal.[11]

If you have identified data that appears to be disinformation, treat it as follows:

1. Note whether the reason for your characterization is the data source or the nature of the data itself. If the reason is a questionable data source, this cause should help lead you to other sources to verify the data and to avoid ones that might

provide no assistance at best or a false confirmation at worst. If your concern is the nature of the data itself, you should be seeking confirmation or contradiction for data from all sources, including the original source.

2. Seek alternative sources of data to confirm or discredit the potential disinformation. Be particularly sensitive to the danger of false confirmation here.

3. If you are not sure whether the data is disinformation, try to estimate the likelihood of its accuracy and then assign a probability of accuracy to the data. This may enable you to use it even if there is a question about its validity.

4. Analyze why the potential disinformation was created or permitted to continue. If you cannot determine why the firm probably would have created it or permitted it to exist, it may not be disinformation. On the other hand, if you can deduce why it was created or permitted to continue, you may not only have identified disinformation, but you may know what the firm was trying to accomplish. This can be important in determining this firm's strategy and methods of operation. It may also help reveal the actual facts. If you know what isn't true, you may be able to determine what is true.

5. If there remains any question about data you have, it is generally better to treat it as disinformation.

6. Don't overreact. Remember, every business wants to put on a good face. It is up to you to be sensitive to the distinction between a good image and disinformation.

Assessing the Consistency of Your Data

Merely because you have consistent data does not mean that you can immediately draw a conclusion based on that data. You will soon find out that when your research seems to provide consistent estimates, it can mean one of several things:

Turning Data into Actionable Information
■ ■ ■

- ■ The data and your conclusions really are valid.

- ■ No one ever questions this "revealed truth" in an industry.

- ■ All the data has a common source, so there is no real confirmation, merely a false confirmation.

Look at the data in question and analyze it, keeping all of these possibilities in mind. Make sure you know why data is consistent before you rely on it.

In evaluating consistency or dealing with possible inconsistencies, one of the easiest mistakes to make is to confuse similar terms that are really used to mean widely differing things. You can avoid this by paying careful attention to definitions. For example, in the area of food marketing, certain phrases have fixed meanings and others do not. If you are an outsider to this industry, compare in your own mind *lean* with *lite* or *no preservatives added* with *organic*. The first terms in each set have specific legal meanings; the second do not.

Under the rules of the U.S. Department of Agriculture, *lean* meat or poultry cannot have more than 10 percent fat by weight. Generally, products labeled as *lite* just have fewer calories or fat than some other product. On the other hand, it may only mean that the product is light in taste or in color. *No preservatives added* means that there are no synthetic preservatives in the product, but the product can still contain artificial coloring. In comparison, the Food and Drug Administration considers the term *organic* as undefinable; the label *organic* on food does not always mean that the food is free from chemical fertilizers and pesticides.

Noting Patterns
Always start by looking for direct indications of what you are seeking. For example, in a high technology business, is your competitor hiring more researchers, building more new facilities, being awarded more patents, or devoting more funds to R & D than in the past? In practice, you should not really expect to find

246

such directness. What you will generally find is data that involves indirect hints.

In that case, it is important to identify patterns and determine their significance. Pattern recognition is critical. For example, reading the annual report of a corporation for one year may disclose that a particular operation is a separate division. But reading these reports covering a period of years might reveal that the prominence with which the results of that division are reported has changed radically. This may, in turn, reflect a change in the relative importance of that division to the parent corporation. You can think of it as a corporate form of "Kremlinology." Kremlinology is the science (or art) of watching who stands where on the May Day reviewing stand in Red Square, comparing the lineup with the previous year's, and then drawing conclusions about the past performance and political future of key Soviet bureaucrats and politicians.

Finding Omissions and Displacement

What is *not* present after you have finished your research can often be as significant as what is present. Omission is the seeming lack of cause for a business decision. For example, you may find that a competitor is planning to sell a particular manufacturing operation. From your own experience, you may have found that this operation is a highly profitable one. If you can find no reason for the proposed sale, you should consider that a significant omission.

Try to establish what the most plausible reasons might be for this action. In this example, there may be two: a possible need by the parent company for cash for its other operations or a technological breakthrough by a competitor that might make this operation less profitable or even obsolete. To determine which reason is more likely, you have to evaluate and analyze other information about this competitor. That could mean studying the financial results of your target's other operations, checking for new patents granted or personnel changes signaling changes in research or manufacturing operations.

Turning Data into Actionable Information

■ ■ ■

> *The absence of something expected may be an important fact.*

Compare these facts with other data and watch for omissions. In one case, a major corporation was concerned about the strength of a competitor that operated two separate but related businesses. The first was in the consumer sector; the second, the raw materials division. The consumer business seemed strong, but raw materials seemed weak. However, a close look indicated that each division had the same promotion track and equal representation on the board. Comparing this company with others similarly structured disclosed that this company did not price intercompany transactions on the same basis. The company used the cost of the raw material, not the market cost, as its competitors did. The result was that the consumer division was made to appear more profitable and the raw material division less profitable than they actually were.

Displacement is a related concept that involves facts or operations that should be there but are not. It involves a substitution for expected behavior. This substitution is like the Sherlock Holmes exchange about the significance of a dog barking during the night.

> "Is there any point to which you would wish to draw my attention?"
>
> "To the curious incident of the dog in the night-time."
>
> "The dog did nothing in the night-time."
>
> "That was the curious incident," remarked Sherlock Holmes.[12]

When a company has a consistent pattern of behavior and suddenly changes that pattern, the resultant change deserves close examination.

Drawing Inferences

When you study raw data and try to come to a conclusion about what it all means, one tool is drawing inferences. Basically, that process involves coming to a conclusion in light of both logic and your own past experience. However, that same process also may cause you to fit incoming data into your own preexisting beliefs or to perceive what you expect to be there. In other words, your own experience acts as a screen on the data as well as an aid in analyzing that data.

CI CLIP

"Prejudice on any question, or its milder form, conventional wisdom, whether out of bureaucratic self-interest, ignorance, habit, or intellectual bent, is death to analysis. On the other hand, fear of disaster (or its obverse, a passionate thirst for victory) can overcome decisions about the focus of analysis, compel critical examination of prejudice, and diminish the relative importance of bureaucratic self-interest."

A staff member of the U.S. Senate Select Committee on Intelligence.[13]

Just being aware of the difficulty of dealing with inferences can help you avoid its problems. However, at least one source has suggested a brief test to see whether you are having a problem dealing with inferences. Ask yourself, as each new fact comes in, which of the following is your reaction:

■ "That fact *is* incorrect" or "That fact *is* correct."
■ "That fact *must be* incorrect."[14]

Turning Data into Actionable Information
■ ■ ■

If your response is the second, you may be fitting the data into your preexisting beliefs rather than testing it to see what it really means.

When you are analyzing data and trying to draw a conclusion you are using inductive reasoning, not deductive reasoning. The difference between these can be seen as the following:

■   With deduction, you infer the particular from the general.
■   With induction, you infer the general from the particular.

The difference between these two types of reasoning is more than just words. In inductive reasoning, you contend that the premises you use give *some* support for your conclusion. In deductive reasoning, you contend that, if the premises are correct, the conclusion *must* be true. Because in CI you are not dealing with revealed truth, you are using *inductive* reasoning.

Checking for Anomalies

Anomaly: *Data that does not fit; usually an indication that one's working assumptions are wrong or that an unknown factor is affecting results.*

Seek out anomalies and figure out why they occurred. Something out of the ordinary should not be automatically rejected as an aberration or even a mistake. It may just be an anomaly.

If you spot an anomaly, first ensure that it is not actually a mistake in the way the data was presented or collected, such as transposed numbers or a misquotation. If it is not a mistake in that sense, look for other data that indicates that this is something which is true or could be true in the future. What you are doing is actually attacking your assumptions by using the anom-

250

aly to test them. The existence of an anomaly may indicate that your basic assumptions about what is true or what is possible are not correct.

An example of an anomaly and the potentially revealing conclusions drawn from it can be seen in a case involving some "futures" researchers. One such group is reported to have predicted significant and imminent engineering developments based on an anomalous remark by President Reagan in his 1986 State of the Union message. It concerned development of a jet that would fly at 15 times the speed of sound or faster. According to these researchers, conventional jet fuel cannot be used for aircraft flights over 5 times the speed of sound. That remark, coupled with information from technical journals, led them to the conclusion that a hydrogen fuel will soon be available for jet flight.

The anomaly in President Reagan's remark is that he was talking about developing a plane for which there was *no* fuel. The State of the Union Address is a carefully prepared, written document reviewed by many government advisers. The remark, if it existed in the written copy of the State of the Union Address, the researchers concluded, could not have been a casual slip.

Keeping alert for anomalies has another benefit. Specifically, by doing so, you help prevent yourself from falling into a common trap for those involved in handling CI: the predisposition to subconsciously reject a deviation from a known trend or situation until a new trend or situation has been conclusively established. As a U.S. military text on intelligence has observed, "This is a predisposition which is likely to be reinforced by the experience that such an expert turns out more often to be right than wrong, just as the weatherman in many climates can be more often right than wrong if he always predicts today's weather for tomorrow. Unfortunately, the analyst who is unconsciously given to this sort of pragmatism is most likely to be wrong when it is most important to be right."[15]

Isolating Company-Level Data Using Disaggregation
As indicated in earlier chapters, you may only be able to obtain aggregated CI data. If you can derive estimates of some of the components, however, you can eliminate them and draw closer to having facts about just your target. Even if partially disaggregated data is not conclusive, it may serve to confirm an apparently unsupportable estimate obtained from another source.

For example, if you cannot find out about the aspects of a business in which you are interested, step back and look at the entire operation. Then eliminate all data dealing with areas in which you have no interest. What is left may be indistinct, but it shows you the outlines of what you seek. That is a form of disaggregation.

As another example, say you cannot determine what your competitor is spending on new research facilities. If you can find out its total financial picture, then eliminate expenditures for nonresearch facilities, you have a good start. What is left sets the outer bounds of the competitor's spending on research. In one case, CI research located a Ph.D. thesis that had been written based on confidential data. The data was aggregated to conceal company-specific information. Other data had also been published, by a U.S. government department, but it was aggregated in a different manner. By studying each set of data and using other sources of specific data, estimates of company-level data could be generated.

The process of disaggregation can be seen in the following problem.

Alpha Corp., Bene Inc., Charles Co., and Det Ltd. are all in the same industry. You know that one of the firms has a profit margin for a particular product of over 25 percent, one is at about 15 percent, one at 5 percent, and one is losing money on the product. You do not know from the data which is which. You also located some relative data. From the data you have, you want to find out which firms are operating at what profit levels, and if possible, what each one's market share is. You know the following relative data:

1. Alpha Corp. and Charles Co. are both making money.

2. Bene Inc. is the second largest firm in terms of market share.

3. The two largest firms together have 75 percent of the market.

4. The least profitable company has the largest market share.

5. Charles Co. is more profitable than Bene Inc.

6. Alpha Corp. is the largest firm, with 40 percent of the market.

7. Det Ltd. is the smallest firm in terms of market share.

8. The breakeven point in this industry is estimated to be at 12.5 percent of the current market.

9. Charles Co. has 15 percent of the market.

To keep track of the facts and conclusions in this puzzle, one of the best ways is to use a matrix to show each possibility and then fill it in. That is a form of disaggregation.

The chart you would use should look like Exhibit 12.1.

When you have concluded that the firm named at the left is the one described at the top, you would mark the appropriate box Y. If you conclude that the firm cannot have the named percentage, put an N in the box.

In this puzzle, you can immediately infer from statement 1 that neither Alpha Corp. nor Charles Co. is losing money, so you put an N opposite their names in the third column. From statements

	+25%	+15%	+5%	Losses
Alpha Corp.				
Bene Inc.				
Charles Co.				
Det Ltd.				

Exhibit 12.1:   Empty Matrix for the Profitability Problem

4 and 6, you can infer that Alpha Corp. has a profit margin of 5 percent, the smallest in the market. So you would put a *Y* in column 3 by Alpha Corp.

Given these, also fill out Alpha Corp. across with *N*s. By process of elimination, you can now see that Bene Inc., Charles Co., and Det Ltd. are not at 5 percent, so mark *N* by their names in column 3.

The matrix now looks like Exhibit 12.2.

Next, according to statements 3 and 6, Alpha Corp. is the number 1 firm in size, and thus the number 2 firm in the industry would have 35 percent of the market. By statement 9, Charles Co. has 15 percent of the market. By statement 7, Det Ltd. has the smallest share of the market. This means that Bene Inc. is number 2 with 35 percent of the market. In turn that means Det Ltd. has 10 percent of the market.

Now, given statement 8, Det Ltd., with 10 percent, is not breaking even, so you mark a *Y* in column 4 next to Det Ltd. and fill in *N*s next to the others in that column and across the bottom of the matrix.

	+25%	+15%	+5%	Losses
Alpha Corp.	N	N	Y	N
Bene Inc.			N	
Charles Co.			N	N
Det Ltd.			N	

Exhibit 12.2:   Matrix with Partial Answers Entered

Continuing, by statement 5, Charles Co. is more profitable than Bene Inc., so you can finish the matrix. It now looks like Exhibit 12.3.

To complete your analysis, you also know that Alpha Corp. has 40 percent of the market, Bene Inc. has 35 percent, Charles Co. has 15 percent, and Det Ltd. has 10 percent.

	+25%	+15%	+5%	Losses
Alpha Corp.	N	N	Y	N
Bene Inc.	N	Y	N	N
Charles Co.	Y	N	N	N
Det Ltd.	N	N	N	Y

Exhibit 12.3:   Completed Matrix

Turning Data into Actionable Information
■ ■ ■

Unlike our puzzle, in actual CI situations you may have only estimates or approximations to deal with. What you do in that case is take the best estimates or approximations, then proceed to fill in the missing pieces of data. Even if you do not know what the answer in each case should be, you may know a range, so that you can test whether each item is approximately correct.

Drawing Conclusions

Your ultimate goal is to draw a conclusion. That conclusion should be logical, but it may not be in all cases. If, for example, you are trying to determine what a competitor will do under certain circumstances, your goal is to anticipate how that competitor thinks. That is in turn based on its track record, its corporate culture, and how it perceives its competitive environment. To you that perception may not be careful and realistic, but that is not the concern here. The issue is whether that is what the target perceives. As a vice president of general development of W. R. Grace & Co. said, "[Y]ou can't assume that the competitor's moves are rational. If you do, you may make a countermove that is a waste of time."[16]

Summary

Through evaluation, you study CI data as you collect the facts, eliminating unreliable or inaccurate data, falsely confirmed data, and irrelevant facts. Then you conduct supplementary data collection to fill in the gaps.

It is only by analysis that those facts remaining are converted to usable information. You organize and assemble the useful data, sifting out disinformation or inconsistent facts. From what remains you look for patterns that reveal your competitor's strategies, checking for omissions and displacements that mask the real intentions of your target. Then you are ready to draw inferences about the competitor's moves and determine the significance of anomalies in your information. You may need to disaggregate your target's facts and figures from industry-wide or corporate-wide totals.

Finally, you are ready to draw conclusions about the competitor from the solid information you have established.

CI ALERT: What does this tell you?

"Employees: 2,900

Sales & Marketing	19%
Engineering	25%
Production	31%
Administration	25%"

Source: NEC America, Inc., "Fact Sheet" (1989).

Notes

1. The Conference Board, Inc., *Competitive Intelligence*, Research Report No. 913, 1988, p. 27.

2. Paul H. Weaver, "Evade, Obscure, Fudge," *Business Month*, April 1988, pp. 63-64, 67.

3. See, for example, Gretchen Morgenson, "How Reliable Is Your Broker's Research?," *Money*, December 1984, pp. 149-54, and "Some Need 'Info' Before Investing in Stocks," *Business Digest of Lehigh Valley*, June 1989, pp. 15, 17.

4. David S. Broder, *Behind the Front Page*, New York: 1988, Simon & Schuster, Inc., p. 366.

5. The Conference Board, Inc., *Competitive Intelligence*, Research Report No. 913, 1988, pp. 35–36.

6. The Conference Board, Inc., *Competitive Intelligence*, Research Report No. 913, 1988, pp. 22, 31.

7. Dan Shope, "Diverse Sources Reveal Changes at Stroh's Brewery," *The Morning Call,* June 11, 1986, p. B13.

8. Benny Gilad and Tamar Gilad, "A Systems Approach to Business Intelligence," *Business Horizons,* September-October 1985, pp. 65-70.

9. Bob Woodward, "U.S. Reportedly Deceived Gadhafi," *The Washington Post,* reprinted in *The Morning Call,* October 2, 1986, p. A26.

10. Felix Gilbert, "Machiavelli: The Renaissance of the Art of War," in E. M. Earle (ed.), *Makers of Modern Strategy,* New York: Atheneum, 1970, p. 14.

11. John Crudele, "Takeover Artists Adept at Using the Press," *The Sunday Call,* January 1, 1989, p. D3.

12. "Silver Blaze," in A. Conan Doyle, *A Treasury of Sherlock Holmes,* Garden City, N.Y.: Nelson Doubleday, Inc., 1955, p. 395.

13. Angelo Codevilla, "Comparative Historical Experience of Doctrine and Organization," in Roy Godson (ed.), *Intelligence Requirements for the 1980s: Analysis and Estimates,* Washington, D.C.: National Strategy Information Center, Inc., 1980, pp. 11-36.

14. Robert Jervis, *Perception and Misperception in International Politics,* Princeton, N.J.: Princeton University Press, 1976, p. 145.

15. Jack Zlotnick, *National Intelligence,* Washington, D.C.: Industrial College of the Armed Forces, 1964, p. 39.

16. The Conference Board, Inc., *Competitive Intelligence,* Research Report No. 913, 1988, p. 5.

Chapter 13

Using What You Know

This chapter shows ways to revise your planning, strategic position, and competitive stance based on the outcome of your CI investigation. You will see some practical applications of CI in everyday business that can make your business objectives and operations more effective. Our goal here is to provide some useful examples of ways you can employ CI; however, many more applications exist.

Where to Use CI

As you saw in Chapter 2, The Conference Board, Inc.'s, survey showed that its members felt that pricing, strategy, new products and services, and acquisitions were the *best* examples of business decisions they made, relying on monitoring their competitors.[2]

CI CLOSEUP: "Marketing"

At Leo Burnett Company, Chicago's largest advertising agency, researchers use online databases to answer a wide variety of questions in support of new client development. Among the wide variety of questions answered are how much certain celebrity spokespersons are paid for endorsements; who wears branded clothing; what colors are expected to be "hot" in the next two years; and even information on the popularity of certain breeds of dogs. The researchers also check local newspapers to keep track of potential clients.[3]

Defining Your Competitive Advantage

Before you set out to define your competitive advantage, you must make three key commitments. The first is to view your own company impartially and objectively. The second is to accept what your defensive CI tells you that your competitors think about you. The third is to accept what you find out about your competitors, even if it does not agree with your own preconceptions.

Without that kind of honesty, you will not make effective use of the CI you have developed. Also, you will not get good CI on which to base your decisions.

CI CLIP

"A regular feature of the weekly group meeting in Japanese companies is the 'competitor comparison,' in which competitors' strengths and weaknesses are matched against the strengths and weaknesses of the group's company."

President of a firm specializing in developing
information on Japanese industry.[4]

Once you have accepted the importance of these commitments, you can begin to define your competitive advantage by taking the following steps:

1. Establish the business context.

2. Know your strengths and weaknesses.

3. Determine your competitors' strengths and weaknesses.

Establishing the Business Context
Use CI to develop hard data about the business and regulatory context you are in now or will enter. This can include developing shadow market plans (discussed in Chapter 14) of your key competitors and determining the present and future regulatory and financial environments facing both you and your competitors.

261

Turning Data into Actionable Information

■ ■ ■

Once you establish the business context for your competitors, you should be able to develop a competitive scenario to assist in preparing your own plans. A competitive scenario is an analysis of what one or more competitors can be expected to do in response to changes in market and other conditions affecting the activities of each company.

CI CLIP

"He who has a thorough knowledge of his own conditions as well as of the conditions of the enemy is sure to win in all battles. He who has a thorough knowledge of his own conditions but not the conditions of the enemy has an even chance of winning and losing a battle. He who has neither a thorough knowledge of his own conditions nor of the enemy's is sure to lose in every battle."

Sun Tzu, Chinese Military Strategist.[5]

The analysis is based on a profile of the competitor, including estimations of its intentions and capabilities, derived from a study of its past actions. The analysis considers the perceptions, style, and behavior of the competitor's current and future management. Each competitor's expected actions are measured against the same set of expected market conditions and changes.

A case from the luggage industry may help to illustrate. Each year, a trade publication, *Travelware*, releases a survey of luggage manufacturers. In that survey, the manufacturers identify their best-selling product for the previous year and also what they expect will be their best-selling product in the current year.

However, before you rely on what the survey says to guide you, remember that you cannot just accept this survey at face value. For example, consider whether the firms are likely to be completely frank in identifying their best-selling product for the prior year. For the *Travelware* survey, manufacturers probably are truthful, because the sales levels probably can be informally verified by interviews with retailers.

Do not automatically assume, however, that competitors' projections of the bestseller for the current year is just as accurate. One firm may have many reasons to identify a product as a major seller when it does not really expect it to be a significant success. For example, the firm may be trying to mislead its competitors about its own decision to move into (or out of) a higher-priced market.

Not all firms are always accurate in the predictions they make. To decide whether the prediction is probably correct, compare last year's predictions with the results announced this year. You might find that these firms vary widely in their relative ability to predict what happens in their own markets. Make sure that you are not misled by their errors, even if your competitors are.

> *Do not overestimate your competition; they may draw the wrong conclusions from the same data.*

Knowing Your Strengths and Weaknesses

Do you know just what your strengths and weaknesses are? Using CI can help you spot them in time to do something about them. For example, consider the case of Xerox Corporation, the corporation that invented the modern plain paper copier. In the 1970s Xerox found that it was rapidly losing market share to Japanese manufacturers. At first, Xerox denied that such a threat even existed, but finally, in the early 1980s, Xerox began to respond.

Turning Data into Actionable Information
■ ■ ■

We will cover benchmarking in more detail in Chapter 14.

In formulating its response, Xerox decided that it "needed to understand everything we could about our competitors, so we [at Xerox] started benchmarking." The benchmarking project was designed to determine the answers to many critical competitive questions, including the following:

■ What was the per-unit manufacturing cost of each of its competitors' products?

■ How many people did its competitors have working on each project?

■ What were the distribution costs of its competitors for each product?

Benchmarking: *A process for comparing one company's operations against those of other firms, both in and out of the market. Typically, the comparison is made with those firms believed to exhibit the most efficient operations.*

After Xerox determined areas in which a competitor performed better than it did, the corporation established them as areas needing improvement.

Among Xerox's specific findings from the benchmarking were that its copier prices were up to 40 percent higher, its per-unit manufacturing costs were "significantly out of line" compared with its most efficient Japanese competitors, and Xerox's internal infrastructure was "not cost effective." Armed with this data—the results of a hard and honest look at its own operations and those of its competitors—Xerox began a major campaign to reduce these costs.[6]

**Assessing the Competitions'
Strengths and Weaknesses**
The Conference Board, Inc.'s, 1987-1988 survey found that 90 percent or more of the corporations surveyed rated the following types of CI about competitors as either "Very Useful" or "Fairly Useful":

Expansion Plans
Key Customers
Market Share Changes
New Product Programs
Pricing
Sales Statistics
Strategic Plans[7]

Having identified your present competitors, you should focus on what they have going for them. How do you do that? Review the CI you have acquired about each competitor as a means to answering the following question: "What is this company's single greatest competitive asset?"

Sometimes you hit that one piece of data that provides a key insight into your competitor's strategy. More often, however, this process involves a careful review of larger amounts of data. You are combing for little signs that add up to something big.

Here are a few examples of how small facts add up.

■   One major corporation annually listed its major areas of activity at the back of its annual report. That by itself does not provide a lot of data about its strengths and weaknesses. However, a comparison of reports and other competitors' documents over time showed one line of activity was progressively put further and further down the list. This, in fact, reflected an unannounced corporate decision to gradually deemphasize that activity. To the corporation's rivals, that may mean this activity will be less of a future competitive threat.

265

Turning Data into Actionable Information
■ ■ ■

■ A request for capability materials from one company was met with the reply that there were no materials of that kind now available, but that they would be available in about four to six weeks. The reason was that these materials were being substantially revised as a part of a new marketing approach. Although this reason was not given at the time, the temporary unavailability of materials was a hint of a forthcoming significant change in marketing direction. To the company's competitors, this may be a warning to avoid committing themselves until they know the new direction. Alternatively, it may mean that competitors have a temporary opportunity to go after new business while the company is at a disadvantage.

■ A call was made to one division of a company using the phone number found in a current business directory. However, a second call was required, to another, newer number. That number, assigned to a new office location, was an overt consequence of a yet unannounced divisional restructuring.

CI CLIP

"[T]hink of the enemy as your own troops. When you think in this way, you can move him at will and be able to chase him around. You become the general and the enemy becomes your troops."

Seventeenth Century Japanese Military Strategist.[8]

Another aspect of assessing strengths and weaknesses is to determine whether or when your competitor is about to make a mistake. For example, during the 1980s we saw some examples of mistakes in marketing and management strategies that, if they had been spotted by competitors, might have made substantial differences in competitive performance. Take, for example, the cases of Montgomery Ward and Sears Roebuck, two major retailing chains, during that decade.

Montgomery Ward was acquired by Mobil Corporation in 1974 for $1.8 billion. During the next 12 years, in spite of infusions of additional capital, Montgomery Ward lost money. That changed in 1985, when an experienced retailer was brought in to run it. One observer has concluded that the reasons Mobil's acquisition of Montgomery Ward resulted in poor performance for so long were that Mobil did not know anything about retailing and that it did not get the talent to run Montgomery Ward at the same time it acquired the company.

During the early 1980s, Sears Roebuck & Company changed its marketing strategy, moving toward an upscale market and away from an emerging trend toward discounting of national brands. The result was that over a short period of time, Sears' nationwide market share fell from 18 percent to 13 percent. The reason for this, according to an observer, is that Sears was trying to fight a historical trend that was obvious to most observers in the industry.

During the period that Montgomery Ward and Sears were having difficulties, other companies—specifically Wal-Mart and K mart—expanded rapidly. A knowledge of what the troubled giants were facing and would likely be facing may well have contributed to the growth of Wal-Mart and K mart.[9]

Structuring an Attack Plan

Your plan of attack should now grow almost naturally out of the CI you have already developed. In general, your plan of attack will be developed in your planning process, in your marketing efforts, or—more often—in both places.

> ### CI CLIP
> *"Nearly all of the battles which are regarded as masterpieces of the military art . . . have been battles of maneuver in which very often the enemy has found himself defeated by some novel expedient or device, some queer, swift, unexpected thrust or stratagem."*
>
> *Winston Churchill.*[10]

Using CI in Planning

Injecting CI into your business's planning requires that the CI you get have a direct relevance both to the planning process and its objectives. In deciding on the CI you need, you are really also fine tuning your business planning process. Similarly, when you define the objectives of your business plan, you are, in part, defining the data needed for that plan from reliable CI in the future.

To show where CI can fit into your existing business planning process, you have to distinguish among planning at the corporate, business, and functional levels.

At the Corporate Level

In your corporate-level planning, CI can be used to develop the following data, all of which is vital for establishing a competitive strategy for each industry in which your corporation participates:

- Projections of the future size of the market and rates of growth for each industry.

- The cost structure for each industry, trends in its key cost components, and technological threats and opportunities.

■ The nature of competition in each of these industries, including

   ■ intensity of the competition.
   ■ the dominant firms.
   ■ the dominant firms' shares of the market.
   ■ potential new competitors.
   ■ barriers to entry to the market.
   ■ your competitors' perceptions of the competitive nature of each market.

At the Business Level

In business-level planning, you can incorporate CI to develop the following data, all of which is vital to establishing a competitive strategy and to making frequent tactical decisions for each line of business:

■ The market's size and your company's relative market share.

■ The comparative quality of your business's product or services.

■ Perceptions of the relative quality of your firm's products and services, as well as of your competitors, among both existing and potential customers.

■ The strength of both current and potential competitors. This requires you to find out who your potential competitors are and why they are potential—rather than actual—competitors.

■ Recent personnel changes in key positions or recent purchases of new equipment or facilities by competitors.

■ The strategic elements and strength of each competitor's marketing plans and the tactics being used to implement that plan.

Turning Data into Actionable Information

At the Functional Level

In functional-level planning, CI can be used to develop the following data, which is vitally needed when you make frequent tactical decisions:

- Technological developments by competitors.

- The probable direction that your competitors' research and development efforts will take and the likely short-term impact of these developments.

- The overall financial strength of your competitors as well as their relative financial strength.

- Likely changes in the regulatory environment affecting both your firm and your direct competitors.

- The marketing tactics being used for each product line, as well as actual and potential results.

Applying yet another common distinction among plans, that is, the difference between strategic and tactical plans, you can see where CI should fit into your current plans and planning efforts.

In developing your strategic plans, among your key considerations should be the following:

- A means of anticipating and assessing uncontrollable social and economic factors that impact your business. To do this, you must determine what these factors are, such as energy prices or trade barriers, and identify their importance to your plans. Then use CI to identify the historical variations these factors have faced and to evaluate potential future fluctuations.

  For example, A. D. Dasler KG, the German manufacturer of Adidas athletic footwear, decided to manufacture its footwear in the United States. There were at least two reasons for this decision. First, Dasler felt that a foreign label would find it difficult to compete with American-made products for consumer acceptance. Second, Dasler felt that establishing a plant in the United States would permit the company to overcome existing trade barriers to the import of athletic footwear. Following Dasler's decision, however, U.S. trade barriers lowered, so that the German firm then faced severe competition from non-U.S. athletic footwear. Apparently no one at Dasler noted the likelihood that the current administration in Washington would not support trade barriers and would in fact lower them if possible. Also, Dasler was evidently not made sensitive to the fact that, in many markets, Americans prefer foreign-made goods to American-made products. In this case, preliminary CI might have led the manufacturer to a less-costly solution.

■ Determine profit margins for various segments of your businesses, the past and expected future growth rates for each, and their relative stages in product/service life cycles.

■ Determine probable responses by your competitors to your potential competitive strategies. This is particularly important in industries where one or two firms dominate. Using CI can help to evaluate potential competitive responses so that you can take advantage of them. For example, a CI analysis may show that the largest firm in a particular market is unlikely, based on its track record, to retaliate to competitive moves that do not threaten its total sales, as distinguished from its market share. That means an effective strategy might involve attempts to capture new business while leaving existing business untouched. The goal is to avoid provoking a sudden and costly response.

Also, use CI to get data on a competitor's responses to your activities and to keep abreast of changes in conditions that might cause you to change your own plans. By doing this regularly, you should be able to improve your ability to respond to changes in the business environment by modifying your plan, as well as by making the corrections in your plan and tactics needed to keep your plan on track.

Turning Data into Actionable Information
■ ■ ■

Using CI in Marketing

Competitive intelligence has myriad uses in your marketing activities. The ones described here include test marketing, determining trends, facilities location, advertising and product line strategies, and talent selection for endorsements.

> ## CI CLIP
>
> *"The emergence of new non-Western trading countries . . . creates what I would call adversarial trade . . . in which the aim is to gain market control by destroying the enemy or to gain such predominance in a market that it would be almost impossible for newcomers to challenge the market leader."*
>
> Peter F. Drucker.[11]

By this time, you should have an appreciation of the ways CI can help you in your marketing program. We have touched on some of those ways in previous chapters. Here, we will give you some specifics, stressing what CI you need.

Looking for Opportunities

For your test marketing efforts, double check what the databases you already access can do for you. Too often, we forget just how useful the databases we use routinely can be. Take, for example, PTS MARS (Marketing and Advertising Reference Service™), which you can access to help you track a competitor's test marketing activities.

MARS abstracts over 75 publications in the following categories:

■ Core advertising sources, such as *Adweek.*

- Consumer-oriented trade publications, such as *Video News.*

- Newsletters.

- Business methods journals, such as the *Journal of Advertising Research.*

- Advertising columns and sections from major metropolitan newspapers.

CI CLOSEUP: "Drugs"

A small drug company, Alza Corporation, credits aggressive CI with helping it to grow. Its Technical Information and Publications Department houses over 450 journals, plus thousands of books and monographs, a collection regarded as "one of the best biotech collections in private industry." Alza places "great importance on immediate access to diverse information resources," even to the point of employing a research scientist to manage its Literature Search Services. The goal is to find and use this information to identify drugs suitable for delivery in non-traditional ways, that is, other than tablets or capsules, and then establish joint ventures for development and marketing.[12]

Among the specific codes you can use to search this database is one that specifically indexes test marketing products. If you run a periodic search using this code together with your competitor's name or its product names, you can spot any references in these publications to test marketing activity, both efforts currently under way as well as some in the planning stages.

At this point, you might consider your own countermarketing campaign. You are also in a position to track the results of the test by monitoring the company's other activities—such as hiring a new advertising agency or opening a new plant—that might be related to that competitor's plans for the future of the product that was test marketed.

CI marketing data can help you spot emerging national trends. A small Minnesota advertising agency used databases to develop information for marketing daycare. In one search, the firm's employees found 190 articles that gave them a "national picture of daycare trends."[13]

The Dayton-Hudson Corporation is one of the country's largest general merchandise retail companies. In making decisions about where to locate its new stores, it uses the following:

■ *Census data*. This is used to identify specific trends and levels of population growth, the numbers of young families, income levels, owned or rented housing, numbers of young children, and educational levels, among other things.

■ *Interviews*. Dayton-Hudson's personnel talk with local city and county planners, the local chamber of commerce office's director of research, and with the advertising and research department of local newspapers. The goal is to gain both hard data on the target area as well as a "feel" for the community.[14]

CI data can track some sophisticated advertising moves, as well. The vice president in charge of an information center for a major advertising company, DDB Needham Worldwide, uses commercial databases for the following purposes:

■ *"Environmental scans"* are conducted for clients who are launching new businesses or products. First, competitor financial records are located and reviewed, as are business publications dealing with those competitors. Then, business publications are reviewed to develop some overall demographic information on the markets in question.

■ *Recent competitor activity* is tracked using databases that feature very current reports, such as DJNEWS on the Dow Jones News/Retrieval Service. Generally, headlines on all of the stories dealing with any of the competitors are reviewed, so that they can spot important announcements.

■ *Competitor profiles* are developed, using a combination of financial, news, and business information services databases.

■ *"Product scans"* are run if a client is preparing to introduce a new product. These are designed to supplement background research that has already been done by the agency's market research division. These scans involve watching for recent stories or other announcements dealing with specific products.

■ *Test marketing.* When the firm is planning to test market a product, news from local publications covering the areas under consideration is reviewed. Presumably DDB Needham does this to see whether the areas selected are still appropriate for test marketing the product.[15]

Finally, you can use CI to find out what a celebrity spokesperson for a competitor is paid for endorsements. Developing this single fact may greatly assist you in conducting any cost/benefit analysis of your competitor's advertising campaign. In addition, databases that access trade magazines dealing with sports or show business can help you follow the relative recognizability and popularity of the personality in question.

Preempting the Competition

> ## CI CLIP
> *"By observing the spirit of the enemy's men and getting in the best position, you can work out the enemy's disposition and move your men accordingly. You can win through this principle of strategy, fighting from a position of advantage."*
> Seventeenth Century Japanese Military Strategist.[16]

Marketing plans tend to require micro-level, not macro-level, data. Also, they generally need current, rather than historical, data. For example, good marketing planning generally requires some (or all) of the following CI to be really effective:

■ *The identity of a firm's competitors.* It may seem astounding, but many firms, particularly in the services field, do not actually know who their current competitors are. This should be among your first CI assignments.

■ *Relative market share and total market size, as well as overall market trends.* CI should be the source for this. Too many firms use and update some prior year's gross estimates or use some anecdotal data for next year's market plan. The better the data here, the better your firm will be able to evaluate its true position in the current market.

■ *An analysis of each major competitor's market position and strengths.* CI can be invaluable when it provides this kind of data. For example, knowing that the major participant in your market has financially weak unrelated businesses may create an opportunity for you to assault a previously sacrosanct market. This CI would suggest that your competitor probably cannot respond to an assault by seeking additional

276

funds from the parent corporation. If that's the case, it improves the likelihood that your assault will succeed.

■ *An evaluation of the likelihood of indirect competition from other products or services.* Too often, businesses do not see potential competition coming because they are not looking for it. Engaging in ongoing CI monitoring of markets, firms, and technologies may be an effective way for you to avoid being surprised by new competitors in your markets.

■ *Technological trends and your competitors' responses to them.* Here, effective and current CI may serve as an early warning system for your marketing department. Tracking a competitor's research and development efforts, for example, may be one of the best ways that you become aware of a major new product *before* its introduction is announced.

CI CLOSEUP: "Window of Vulnerability"

In a conversation with a retailer, the chief executive officer of Dana Imports Inc., an importer of lamps and office furniture, learned that a competitor had just raised prices on a line of upscale office lamps in the South. He immediately faxed this information to his sales force, together with a list of all accounts in the territory. The sales force was on the telephone the next day and they "definitely . . . won new business."[17]

Learn from others' mistakes. Use CI to check on your competitors' track records. If they have already tried and rejected a marketing approach you are now considering, find out why they did so. That may save you from making the same mistake. Then you can proceed in another direction without incurring the same costs your competitors did when they tried this approach. On the other hand, if their failure was related to a problem you have already dealt with, you will not be diverted from what may be a potentially valuable approach by misunderstanding their failure.

Use CI to determine what market objectives your competitors have established. If your competitors have different objectives from yours, you cannot just assume that they will behave as you would against new competitive situations. Also, knowing what their objectives are may help you to modify your own marketing objectives so that you can take advantage of areas that are no longer critical to your competitor. In fact, if your strategic objectives differ enough from those of a major competitor, it may mean that a particular firm is no longer a direct competitor.

Summary

CI information should be treated impartially to be maximally effective. CI data can be used to establish your business context. This big-picture perspective can help you develop alternative competitive scenarios.

To structure an attack plan, CI results are integrated in all other forms of your company's planning at the corporate, business, and functional levels. CI also helps you anticipate the impact of factors out of your control, which is invaluable for your strategic planning.

Areas in which CI results assist marketing efforts include test marketing, determining trends, facilities location, advertising, and endorsements. CI even helps you preempt the moves of your competitors by evaluating their potential competitive moves and possible technological trends.

Integrating CI results in both your planning and operations can help avoid repeating your competitors' mistakes and might minimize the impact of their successes.

> ### CI ALERT: What does this tell you?
>
> *"Du Pont said it plans to sell its virology blood screening business and give greater emphasis to its core diagnosis business. . . .*
>
> *"The sale is the first step in a strategy calling for increased spending in Du Pont's core diagnostics business while divesting some nonstrategic diagnostic product lines developed or acquired in recent years. The company said it will increase research and development expenditures five-fold in 1990 for its clinical chemistry business that manufactures and markets instruments and prepackaged chemical reagents for hospitals and reference laboratories."*
>
> Source: Article, Focus, January 10, 1990.

Notes

1. The Conference Board, Inc. *Competitive Intelligence*, Research Report No. 913, 1988, p. 28.

2. The Conference Board, Inc., *Competitive Intelligence*, Research Report No. 913, 1988, p. 20.

3. Noreen O'Leary, "Electronic Information Gives Agencies the Edge," *Adweek*, September 7, 1987, pp. 27-28.

4. Alan K. Engel, "Number One in Competitor Intelligence," *Across the Board*, December 1987, pp. 43-47.

5. Sun Tzu, *The Art of War,* New York: Oxford Press, 1963, p. 82, quoted in Howard H. Stevenson, "Resource Assessment: Identifying Corporate Strengths and Weaknesses," William D. Guth (ed.), *Handbook of Business Strategy,* Boston: Warren Gorham & Lamont, 1985.

6. "How Xerox Zapped the Japanese," *Business Month,* June 1989, pp. 81-82.

7. The Conference Board, Inc., *Competitive Intelligence,* Research Report No. 913, 1988, p. 16.

8. Miyamoto Musashi, *A Book of Five Rings* (translated by Victor Harris), Woodstock, N.Y.: The Overlook Press, 1974, p. 82.

9. Stephen W. Quickel, "Hard Lessons of the Eighties," *Business Month,* June 1989, pp. 64-65, 68.

10. Winston Churchill, *The World Crisis,* London: 1923, Vol. II, pp. 5-7, quoted in Harvey A. DeWeerd, "Churchill, Lloyd George, Clemenceau: The Emergence of the Civilian," E. M. Earle (ed.), *Makers of Modern Strategy,* New York: Atheneum, 1970, p. 293.

11. Peter F. Drucker, "The New World According to Drucker," *Business Month,* May 1989, pp. 58-59.

12. "Meet Alza Corporation," *Inside Business,* Winter 1988, p. 12.

13. "Advertising & Marketing Pitches," *Dowline,* Second Quarter 1989, p. 28.

14. "Spotlight on: Joan Finch," *The Information Advisor,* May 1989, p. 6.

15. "Advertising & Marketing Pitches," *Dowline,* Second Quarter 1989, p. 29.

16. Miyamoto Musashi, *A Book of Five Rings* (translated by Victor Harris), Woodstock, N.Y.: The Overlook Press, 1974, p. 74.

17. Mark Robichaux, "'Competitor Intelligence': A Grapevine to Rivals' Secrets," *The Wall Street Journal,* April 12, 1989, p. B2.

Chapter 14

Beyond the Obvious:
More Sophisticated Applications for CI

CI CLIP

"No matter how committed they are to developing their business, managers must allocate 10 percent to 20 percent of their time to reading trade journals, The Wall Street Journal, and to attending industry trade shows."

Business crisis management consultant.[1]

This chapter explores the benefits of using three more advanced applications of CI: shadowing, competitive benchmarking, and reverse engineering.

Shadowing

Among the new applications being developed for CI is the shadowing of specific markets. Shadowing is composed of three separate but related activities: shadowing markets, the development of shadow market plans, and defensive CI. Each can be an effective supplement to business planning, particularly the marketing oriented planning vital to so many businesses.

Shadowing markets is a term whose origin is not clear. It implies a regular observation of markets. To a limited degree, this is true. However, the concept is broader, probably originating with the British political concept of the "shadow cabinet." In the United Kingdom, a shadow cabinet is created with members from the largest political party in the Parliament that is not a part of the government in power. The party not in power is known as the Opposition. Each shadow cabinet member is assigned a government department to follow. It is the shadow cabinet member's duty to

■   Prepare to take on the management of the target department when the Opposition takes power.

■   Track all key policy and personnel changes in the target department.

■   Help the Opposition to develop its own policies to respond to government policy initiatives.

■   Be a resource for the Opposition, able to anticipate key policy and personnel changes in the target department *before* they occur. In that sense, the shadow cabinet becomes a model of the government's department.

Similarly, shadowing a company involves tracking key information about that company. Shadowing markets takes one of two different forms, which can be carried on at the same time and by the same people. The first is preparing a *shadow market plan.* The second is engaging in *shadow market planning.*

282

The Shadow Market Plan

Developing a shadow market plan is usually a one-time assign-ment. The goal of the process is to produce a document that is as close to the competitor's market plan as possible. You can do this whether or not your competitor actually has a marketing plan of its own, because the point is to analyze what the competitor will do, even if your competitor does not have a specific, written document.

> *Can you get a copy of the contents of your com-petitor's marketing plan? If you cannot, you should develop a shadow market plan.*

It is not necessary to access your competitor's planning docu-ments themselves to get an insight into how, when, and why that competitor is planning to act. How individual products, cam-paigns, and departments are arranged, developed, and operated by the target's management can be strong and useful evidence of the general marketing strategy the target company employs.

Do not assume that you cannot actually find out what the competitor's plans are. First, try to learn whether any details of that plan have been made public. You may be surprised how often that occurs. If you cannot find data directly detailing the plan itself, however, you must immerse yourself in that competi-tor, its philosophy, operations, and history. From that data, you try to construct a picture of what your competitor is probably doing and why. You then estimate what that competitor will be doing over the next several years under certain sets of facts. This analysis of your competitor is a shadow market plan.

Your goal here is not actually to reproduce the physical text of your competitor's document, assuming that there is one, but rather to understand the competitor's plans and capabilities *as the competitor understands them.* To make sense, you may want to restate them using concepts with which your own firm is more comfortable, rather than the competitor's own concepts and terms. It is probably best to have the shadow market plan parallel the form and presentation of market plans used by your firm.

Shadow Market Planning

Engaging in *shadow market planning* involves the regular monitoring of the elements that contribute to the competitor's marketing and market planning. The goal is to enable one or two persons to act as if they were the competitor and to be able to respond to "what if" competitive questions on a current basis.

Shadow market planning requires you to estimate what your competitor is planning in its marketing efforts and to estimate its capabilities to carry out that plan. This is, of course, based on CI that you develop about that competitor. Typically, if you are producing a shadow market plan you have to put yourself in the place of the competitor you are shadowing and try to duplicate what that competitor's market plan would be.

> *Try putting yourself in your competitor's place. What would you do if you were there? That is the essence of shadow market planning.*

A shadow market plan differs from shadow market planning in that the former is a project-oriented operation and the latter is a process. The dividing line is not hard and fast. For instance, a unit can produce shadow market plans while also engaging in shadow market planning.

In its purest form, shadow market planning requires one or two people to "become" the competitor being shadowed. This role can be likened to the role of aggressor squadrons in most air forces. These squadrons are made up of top pilots who operate equipment as similar as possible to that which a potential adversary would use. The pilots are then trained to think and respond in the same way that the adversary's own pilots would, using their preferred tactics and subject to their command limitations. The goal is to provide an opponent for pilots that duplicates, as closely as possible, the way the adversary's pilots and equipment would respond in combat and other situations. Interestingly enough, the most common nonmilitary application of this technique is found in football. Some teams have players learn to duplicate the "look" of an opponent's offense or defense, so that the first team and coaches can practice "against" that opponent before a game.

CI CLIP

"To become the enemy' means to think yourself into the enemy's position. . . . In large-scale strategy, people are always under the impression that the enemy is strong and so tend to become cautious."

Seventeenth Century Japanese Military Strategist.[2]

In business, shadow market planning requires the same dedication as you find in aggressor squadrons or in football. The person or people who will monitor the competitor must, in a very real sense, become the competitor. They must become familiar not only with financial statements but with virtually everything involving that competitor on a regular, perhaps even daily, basis.

Shadowing Your Own Company Through Defensive CI

Businesses involved with CI have gradually become more aware of the benefits of CI in areas such as evaluating potential acquisition targets. This is an "offensive" use of CI. However, competitive intelligence can also be applied "defensively."

> **Defensive CI:** *The process of monitoring and analyzing your own business's activities as your competitors and other outsiders see them.*

The difference between the offensive and the defensive use of CI is somewhat subtle. For example, using CI offensively might involve shadowing the marketing activities of three direct competitors on a regular basis. As your firm is already in the market in question, that also means you are checking on your own relative position as a part of this assignment, even though the project is not focused on your firm.

The difference in perspective is critical. You are not trying to evaluate what your firm can do or is doing. Rather, you are trying to develop data on how others see your business, *even if you think that their perception of your business is wrong.*

Because it creates a different perspective from offensive CI activities, defensive CI usually involves collecting larger amounts of less focused data than are collected with offensive CI. However, the data collection phase still requires the same steps and standards as for offensive CI.

> *How do your competitors see you? That is the essence of defensive CI.*

Defensive CI is not the same as, and should not be confused with, defending against CI (discussed in Chapter 15) or employee security countermeasures. Employee security countermeasures range from efforts to lessen employee theft to hiring an investigator to locate the source of confidential data that is being sold to competitors. Because defensive CI involves understanding what CI your competitors are getting on you, handling defensive CI may be one of the missions of an internal CI staff unit.

The Defensive CI Process

To conduct defensive CI, apply basic CI techniques to your own firm's activities. The goal is to find out what *your competitors* probably know about *you*. In turn, this means that you can better understand what they may do, given what they think they know about you. From this perspective, defensive CI may be something that you want an outsider to do for you. This may ensure that the data gathering and analysis is not influenced by the personal knowledge of one of your own employees. You may be surprised by exactly what information, or even disinformation, is already in the public domain.

In fact, undertaking a regular defensive CI review may also be a way of evaluating how good your own CI operations and techniques really are. Comparing what you can find about your own firm with what you actually know about your firm may help to evaluate the strengths and weaknesses of your own CI program.

Some examples of where defensive CI might have made an important difference may be helpful. In one case, a Fortune 500 corporation found out that it had been targeted as a prime potential takeover candidate by a major New York investment firm. One reason for that designation was that the corporation was unwilling to sell several of its operating divisions to become more efficient. The corporation became aware of this investment report sometime after it was released. By the time the corporation found out about the analysis, large blocks of its stock had already been acquired by speculators. The corporation was then forced into a rapid and relatively unplanned restructuring to keep from being acquired. That restructuring included the sale of some of its operating divisions. This was done to prevent the completion of what threatened to become a self-fulfilling prophecy: its takeover.[3]

Defensive CI, such as monitoring the recommendations of key investment advisers, might have disclosed the takeover warning before the acquisitions of large blocks of stock by speculators. Thus the company could have avoided the unplanned sale of some of its divisions.

In another case, a major U.S. natural resources corporation bought U.S. rights to an important new process developed in Europe. Before the U.S. corporation had even registered a trade-name for the new process, stories on that new process appeared almost simultaneously in a major national news magazine and on both network and cable television reports. The U.S. corporation felt it had to make some kind of public statement about the new process, even though this was well before the products that this process was to produce would even come to market.[4]

The corporation was reluctant to make any announcement. This was probably due to the fact that it had to announce the process without being able to coordinate that announcement with a marketing campaign. In this case, merely monitoring announcements made by the European firm following the licensing agreement would have revealed the licensing firm's unexpected announcement about its new U.S. licensee. Knowing that, the U.S. corporation could have at least prepared for the time when it would have to respond to media reports.

To protect yourself against this type of problem, credit your competitors with being at least as good as you are in gathering CI. Use your own CI skills and resources to monitor information about your own business just as you monitor that of your competitors. That means going to the same sources with the same regularity as you apply to your own offensive CI work.

For example, do you read your firm's materials the same way that your competitors do? Take a moment to read, carefully and objectively, some recent PR materials, interviews, product advertising, and other stories released by your company. If you also have an internal newsletter that might be read by others, read that as well. You may be surprised at the amount and kinds of useful data that you are already disclosing to your competitors.

If you find that you are inadvertently disclosing potentially critical information to competitors, consider ways to halt that. At this point, you have shifted from defensive CI to defending against CI, a subject we cover in detail in Chapter 15.

Case Study on Defensive CI

According to the marketing vice president of a major U.S. corporation (Corporation), a top executive with a key competitor (Competitor) toured a non-U.S.-based plant owned by the Corporation. The vice president discovered this later, because he received and reviewed a list of the people who had taken that plant tour. He spotted the name of a former customer, now with Competitor, on that list. The Corporation's plant tour personnel did not stop the visitor, because his position was with a holding company that owned Competitor, and not with Competitor. Plant tour personnel did not make the connection between the holding company and Competitor.

The vice president described one result of this unexpected penetration: "Our people argued back and forth about whether that was legitimate behavior. We decided it was. It was legitimate for him to try and legitimate for us to stop him at the gate, if we had recognized him as a competitor. As a result, we've been a little more specific with tour invitations."[5]

Hints for Shadowing Markets

The CI process has five major phases, all of which were covered in detail earlier in this book. To recap, the process consists of

Turning Data into Actionable Information
■ ■ ■

1. Establishing CI needs
2. Collecting the raw data
3. Evaluating the raw data
4. Analyzing the results
5. Distributing the results

If you are shadowing markets, whether you are shadowing a market or shadowing your own firm, you have to go through each of these phases. Once you have decided to shadow a market, you have established your CI needs, the first phase. Shadowing markets has unique aspects, however, that require a few specific remarks on each of the remaining four stages.

Collecting the Raw Data
Whether you are trying to develop a shadow market plan or to employ shadow marketing planning, first try to locate and use data already collected by your people in your own firm for their market and strategic planning efforts. However, you should *not* automatically incorporate any of their underlying assumptions or the conclusions they have already drawn in your efforts to shadow markets. Unfortunately, this may be difficult to do, but it is very important.

Good Sources of Data for Shadowing:

Trade shows.

Competitor advertisements and newsletters.

Trade press.

Consumer publications.

Your own employees.

Local newspapers.

Licensing and regulatory proceedings.

There is one main reason for ignoring your assumptions and conclusions: The competitor you are shadowing will be applying its own assumptions to the raw data it collects, and those assumptions may differ from assumptions made by people in your own firm. This does not mean that either your colleagues or your competitor is necessarily wrong; the assumptions are just different.

What kinds of data should you be collecting if you are shadowing markets? Typically you want to use some or all of the following techniques, in addition to the other steps discussed throughout this book:

■ Attend trade shows so you can meet your competitor's personnel as well as outsiders important to them, such as ad agencies and distributors. By doing this, you can evaluate strengths and weaknesses of your competitor's personnel as well as gather important new data.

■ Collect and read as much materials *generated by your competition* as possible, from new product brochures to company newsletters and from advertising to annual reports. In that view, consider how a few insurance companies develop very basic information on their competitors and competitive products: "They get competitive policy illustrations and brochures from agents and brokers (who get them from clients and product mailings). They get financial data (like dividend history, surplus position, and gross rates of return) from company financial reports, filings, and other public documents; and they get product tips from conventions, trade publications, and casual conversations."[6]

■ Find stories about the target competitors in the trade press, as well as in publications in related areas, such as those directed to your target customers. If you are preparing a shadow market plan, you might want to use online databases for this. On the other hand, if you are involved in shadow market planning, it may be more cost effective to use a clipping service for this form of tracking.

Turning Data into Actionable Information
■ ■ ■

■ Debrief your employees who have any current contact with your competitor. This can include salespeople who have lost sales to that competitor; employees who work with employees of the competitor on industry and other committees; dealers who carry a competitor's products in addition to your own; and your own marketing consultants, who may be aware of the capabilities of the competitor's new advertising agency.

■ Interview any of your employees who have had prior contact with your competitor. These might be people who actually worked for the competitor in the past or those who have observed the competitor from another angle, such as from the perspective of a retailer or a wholesaler.

■ Study your competitor's track record and prior history in this and other markets. As a part of your study, determine where your competitor's key personnel came from and what experience they brought to their current position.

■ Track personnel changes at your competitor's firm that involve the operations of particular interest to you. This requires finding out about these people, perhaps from local papers or company news releases. Don't forget to track personnel changes in other operations, such as upper management, which might eventually impact the operations you are shadowing.

■ Track regulatory proceedings in which your competitor is involved, such as licensing matters or consumer protection enforcement actions. In the process of handling them, your competitor may reveal important information.

Warning: *Avoid contaminating your analysis with preconceptions about your competitor.*

Avoid preconceptions at any stage when you are shadowing markets. The problems of preconceptions in analysis should be obvious, but they can cause problems in gathering raw data too. Preconceptions about what data is available, where it is, or what your competitor is probably planning may cause you to automatically filter data as it is being sought and collected or even to miss important sources of data altogether. In turn, this omission of data sources limits the data you eventually get to analyze. That means the entire CI process can be distorted, because the data (naturally) reflects and supports what may be a (dangerously) erroneous preconception.

Evaluating the Raw Data

You may find that some data you have collected is contradictory. Normally, this implies that some of the data is correct and some of it is not. In shadowing markets, however, you are often dealing with the intentions of a number of people. Contradictory data means that your competitor is sending contradictory signals that reflect, perhaps, internal indecision.

> *When you are shadowing markets, if you come across contradictory data, all of it may be right.*

In addition, don't immediately reject a seemingly outrageous piece of data or conclusion. Again, remember, you are trying to determine intention. For example, you may conclude that the competitor is planning to undertake a marketing strategy that seems so risky that you cannot take it seriously. Yet, that strategy may be under consideration by your competitor *because* it believes that other firms, including yours, will discount a high-risk operation as impossible. Your competitor may expect you to believe that the strategy is too risky to undertake. The target may be counting on that, so that it has a window of opportunity within which to move, thereby minimizing the risk of failure.

Turning Data into Actionable Information
■ ■ ■

Chapter 16 details how you can use outside professionals to evaluate data if your resources or time constraints dictate.

Analyzing the Data
A few more warnings are in order for shadowing markets. Remember at all times that your goal is to think as the competitor thinks. Not only should you be able to provide current information on what is going on at the competitor but you should also be able to provide a fairly accurate estimate of what might happen.

This means avoiding three critical snares:

■ Again, make sure that you are not contaminated by your own firm's preconceptions. Just because you or your firm would not respond in a particular way must never influence your estimate of a competitor's potential response. As has been observed in the context of analyzing competitive marketing strategies,

> Although there is clearly no certainty that the competitor would in fact respond as you would if you were in his or her place, it is generally a reasonable expectation that rational managers will respond in similar ways to a given situation. If one's competitors have in the past acted in what at least seemed to be an irrational manner, such a pattern must, of course, be taken into account. In many cases, *what seems to be irrational competitive behavior may, however, simply suggest that one does not really understand his or her competitor's situation.*[7]

■ Don't be surprised if you cannot always come up with a consistent analysis of your competitor's probable future behavior. Your inability to do that may not be a failure; it might mean that the competitor *itself* has not made a decision. Such evidence of indecision may be critical CI.

■ Over time, if your competitor finds out or merely suspects that it is being closely shadowed, it may get more difficult for you to develop new data. Your target competitor may even try to mislead you. Keep that in mind.

Distributing the Results

A former U.S. intelligence officer has observed that "[M]arketing intelligence to policymakers takes a combination of doggedness, ingenuity, humility, and—on occasion—monumental gall. . . . [T]he trick is to bring policymakers the bad news without seeming to attack the entire policy."[8]

This applies particularly when you are shadowing markets. For example, in preparing a shadow market plan, you may want to include an evaluation of how the targeted competitor probably perceives your own business. Providing such insights can be quite difficult, because it requires you to make a concentrated analysis of the competitor's people and exactly what they think they see and how they think. Although the results may tend to be more sketchy than other parts of a shadow market plan, they can be extremely useful.

If your firm wants this perspective, you may want to consider having an outside firm specializing in CI prepare this portion, in case the results are startling or unpleasant. For example, if you are a manager at the Beta Consumer Goods Company, are you going to feel comfortable telling your supervisor, "Our major competitor, Kappa Appliance Corporation, does not regard Beta as a serious competitor in the major appliance market"? How would you feel about reporting, "Kappa believes that Beta is poorly managed, with a harmful focus by senior management on short-term results at the expense of long-term stability"? Such potentially disturbing news may be better delivered by an outsider. It is also more likely to have a receptive audience if it comes from outside.

The ways to use outsiders beneficially in CI are discussed in Chapter 16.

Case Study for Shadowing Markets

A brief example of how some of these concepts are applied may clarify their importance. Assume that the CI assignment is to develop and determine the shadow market plans of a major bank. To do that, you might consider some of the following initially:

■ Review branch banking applications (or even merger documents) that have been approved at the federal or state level. Your competitor may have discussed its own expansion plans or hinted at its underlying strategy.

■ Open an account with a competitor bank. You will be on that bank's mailing lists for cross-selling efforts. In addition, you may receive other data, such as announcements of forthcoming "improvements," in its customer newsletter.

■ Visit a branch office to see what services and promotional materials are featured in the lobby. Take copies with you.

■ Monitor local advertising—radio and TV spots and newspaper ads—to watch for evidence of new campaigns or changes in emphasis compared with previous advertising.

Using these resources might disclose, for example, that the bank is planning to initiate an aggressive campaign to expand its credit card operations. This might be inferred from a story announcing the hiring of a direct marketing firm that specializes in credit cards. In addition, as a depositor, the newsletters for customers you receive may note the opening of a new telemarketing facility and/or announce the hiring of a new executive who has directed a credit card marketing unit.

After evaluating and confirming the accuracy of the data and its sources, you can combine the results with other information about the bank's past actions and its current attitudes toward the market in question. This might be data developed on the bank's overall corporate strategy and past record, such as whether it regards consumer operations, such as credit cards, to be more important than its commercial lines.

The result might be a shadow market plan that concludes the bank is planning a major campaign to market credit cards to young adults as part of a new effort to expand retail banking operations. The plan notes that the campaign will rely heavily on direct marketing.

Once you develop the shadow market plan, you can use some of the same techniques to track the bank's progress. For example, you might want to arrange to monitor mailings and other solicitations by your competitors. Announcements by vendors, such as insurers, can reveal in the vendor's own industry publication the sales level of their enhancement products to that bank. Also, you can monitor ads in consumer publications aimed at the market you now believe is being targeted by the bank to confirm that the predicted campaign is underway.

Competitive Benchmarking

> *Competitive benchmarking:* The process of comparing your company's operations against those of other firms.

Typically, benchmarking comparisons are made with those firms regarded as having the most efficient operations. The firms against which a comparison is made may be in or out of your market. For example, Xerox reportedly studied L. L. Bean's order processing and fulfillment operations to improve its own order handling for copier supplies and parts.

The key to benchmarking is to select the most appropriate operations against which to compare your own operations. It is also vital to obtain the data needed to make that comparison work. Without CI to supply the relative cost or efficiency data, benchmarking can degenerate into a series of subjective and inexact comparisons, producing no real benefits. Good CI can drive an effective benchmarking project or process.

Turning Data into Actionable Information
■ ■ ■

> *The key to effective benchmarking lies in properly selecting the other firms with which you will compare your own operations.*

Benchmarking can be used at almost any level, from the product level to overall corporate operations. For example, your business may use benchmarking in the same way it would use reverse engineering. That is, you can focus on a particular product and determine all of the elements that went into establishing its costs of production.

In benchmarking, unlike reverse engineering, the focus is on a comparison. Thus, to analyze how to most effectively compete head to head with a particular product, you figure out both your own and your competitor's manufacturing and distribution costs, taking into account matters such as the cost and yield of raw materials, and the number of staff hours and hourly rates involved. The goal is to determine where you have a relative advantage and then to exploit it.

Continuing with this example, suppose a benchmarking comparison discloses that while your hourly rate for labor is lower, you need more hours of labor to make each item. Thus, your total labor costs are higher per unit. Your solution might be to increase productivity rather than seek to transfer production to a labor pool with lower hourly rates, because your competitor has a better productivity level.

Similarly, a benchmarking study might also indicate that, although your competitor is not as efficient as you are in the amount of raw material it uses in its products, it has a relative advantage, because it pays less per unit for that raw material than you do. Here, the solution indicated might be to seek a better price on the raw material from your suppliers or to find lower-cost suppliers. Another solution might be to switch to another, less costly material where your own engineering and manufacturing efficiencies will grant you a competitive advantage.

Benchmarking can also be used to analyze your firm's efficiencies by comparing its performance against performance levels of a number of different firms. For example, you may want to compare your direct mail operations with those of a direct mailer in an entirely different business to see if your overhead costs are reasonable. Similarly, you might try to compare your bookkeeping operations with those of a retailer or with a bank's billing departments. By collecting detailed data on specific operations, CI can enable your firm to undergo a rigorous self-examination.

Another form of benchmarking can be used in comparing your firm's standards of operation with those of its competitors. The goal is not to determine the most efficient cost levels of each component of an activity. Instead, you undertake a process that compares your performance with that of another firm.

> *Don't forget to benchmark your operations as well as your material and manufacturing costs.*

For example, in one case, a firm (Company) was concerned about the productivity of its sales force compared with that of a major competitor. Company chose to approach its problem by benchmarking its own operations against both a major competitor in its own industry (Competitor) and sales operations of an efficient manufacturer of similar, non-competing, equipment (Outsider).[9]

Company found that its sales representative costs, as a percent of its revenues, were competitive with those of Competitor. However, the analysis disclosed that Outsider paid substantially higher commissions than other firms in its own industry. Out-

sider seemed to obtain better productivity from its sales representatives than did either Company or Competitor. Dissecting the
sales management system through benchmarking disclosed that
Outsider was focusing its attention on new accounts and used
formal new-account quotas.

This benchmarking brought on a review and eventual restructuring of Company's sales management and marketing program.
Company's sales force was divided so that certain sales representatives focused on new accounts, and others serviced existing
accounts. Commission rates were increased. The result was an
increase in productivity and market share for Company.

The message here is that you must have effective CI to provide
the detailed information needed for benchmarking. What occurs
otherwise is a study focused on internal information only.

"Reverse Engineering" Products and Services

Reverse engineering: Purchasing and then dismantling a product to identify how it was designed and constructed. This process enables an
investigator to estimate costs and evaluate the
quality of the product. In the case of nonpatentable processes and devices, it can also provide information on how to produce a competitive or substitute product.

Reverse engineering may give you some engineering "cues." For
example, it may show you how to pack and ship your products
at a lower cost or with less damage for the same cost. It may show
you that there are less costly ways to accomplish similar ends, in
terms of the costs of raw materials or the manufacturing techniques used.

CI CLOSEUP: "Tire Wars"

Several years ago, it was reported that Bridgestone Tire Corporation of Japan had hired a firm to help it compete in the U.S. tire market. Whenever Goodrich or Goodyear released a new model of tire, Bridgestone requested the U.S. firm to ship one tire to it. After a period of time, the firm offered to provide the same service to Goodrich and Goodyear. The U.S. firms declined that service, explaining that they "knew exactly what was going on." One result was that Bridgestone soon captured an increasing percentage of the U.S. tire market from Goodrich and Goodyear.[10]

The same analyses can provide important marketing hints. For example, reverse engineering may show you that a competitor's products are very costly for it to make. In turn, this, coupled with other data, may tell you that the competitor's profit margin is lower than you had anticipated. You can then use this data to help develop a new marketing campaign, aimed at pricing your own product below your competitor's manufacturing cost but above your own manufacturing cost. The result of this might be a significant impact on the targeted product's market share.

Reverse engineering can deliver even more CI. For example, numerous firms have found that, by regularly buying a competitor's products from the same sources, they can tell at what capacity competitor factories are operating. One clue often is that each product from a particular plant has a unique, consecutive serial number. If the output from a key plant is found to be routinely distributed through one distribution center, the serial numbers may show relative production. Thus, buying the same item there each week is a way of sampling the factory's output. Comparing the serial numbers over time can give a firm an estimate of how many units the factory produces each month.

Turning Data into Actionable Information
■ ■ ■

Reverse engineering can also convince your own people that a particular innovation or modification really *is* possible. As a General Motors official once put it, "It's pretty difficult for an engineer to argue that something can't be done if you can bring him down here [to a reverse engineering center] and show him that it is already in production. . . ."[11]

Reverse engineering techniques can be applied effectively to services as well as products. In that context, marketing professionals or other experts replace the engineers. Working with a CI professional, the experts get data on the service being analyzed and then proceed to "tear it down" to its basic steps.

For example, for a firm competing in the insurance industry, reverse engineering annuity contracts could follow this process:

1. You obtain copies of a competitor's annuity contracts from a state insurance department, where they are filed as a matter of public record.

2. To learn the premium rates, you just call your own agents, review industry data books, or call someone who is selling the product to get a quotation.

3. Information on supporting marketing efforts is obtainable from publications such as *Advertising Age* or *American Banker,* both of which are indexed in online databases.

4. You obtain information on the commissions paid on sales— probably in part from your own agents, if they are selling both your products and those of your competitor.

5. Next your company's actuaries determine how much each element of the coverage would cost you and should cost your competitor. The marketing personnel would determine the loading factors required to cover commissions and current levels of marketing support.

6. These estimated costs are then compared with the actual pricing to determine the probable minimum levels of sales needed to keep the product on the market and profitable.

7. Now your company is able to compare its own products with those of your competitor, adjusting for product differences, so you can determine relative competitive strengths and weaknesses. Also, your marketing personnel can sample consumer satisfaction with the product, adding an additional important element to the reverse engineering.

The result is a profile of a competitive service, here an insurance product, which indicates its costs and profitability. In turn, this profile helps you make more effective marketing decisions, select among the options of introducing an identical or substitute product, or even decline to compete in this market segment at all.

Summary

Shadowing activities include shadowing markets, shadow market planning, and shadowing your own company for defensive CI. Competitive benchmarking is useful when you want to check your pricing structure or standards of operation against those of competitors. Besides its value as an engineering aid, reverse engineering can reveal marketing and manufacturing strategies of your competitors. Services can also be reverse engineered.

CI ALERT: What does this tell you?

"*Peavy Electronics Corporation, a leader in the manufacture of sound equipment, has an immediate opportunity for a design engineer. Responsibilities include the design of mixers, musical instrument amplifiers, and related products using CADCAM and CBDS.*"

Source: Advertisement, Atlantic Tech, Dec./Jan. 1989/90.

303

Notes

1. "Caution!: Business Pitfalls Ahead," *Partners,* Winter 1988, p. 16.

2. Miyamoto Musashi, *A Book of Five Rings* (translated by Victor Harris), Woodstock, N.Y.: The Overlook Press, 1974, p. 75.

3. Douglas M. Barnes and Roger W. Kapp, "Strength and Strategy in a Proxy Contest," *Directors & Boards,* Summer 1985, pp. 19-25.

4. Analie Adler Ascher, "'Embalmed' Plants Will Stand Tall," *The Baltimore Sun,* reprinted in *The Morning Call,* May 31, 1987, p. G5.

5. The Conference Board, Inc., *Competitive Intelligence,* Research Report No. 913, 1988, p. 15.

6. Linda Koco, "Who Watches the Product Watchers?," *National Underwriter* (Life & Health/Financial Services), February 29, 1988, pp. 13-14.

7. "Competitive Analysis," Harvard Business School Case 9-576-158, HBS Case Services, 1976.

8. Herbert E. Meyer, "Marketing Intelligence to the Boss," *Across the Board,* April 1988, pp. 7-8.

9. Timothy R. Furey, "Benchmarking: The Key to Developing Competitive Advantage in Mature Markets," *Planning Review,* September/October 1987, pp. 30-32.

10. Jeffrey L. Kovach, "Competitive Intelligence," *Industry Week,* November 12, 1984, pp. 50-53.

11. James Risen, "GM 'Spy Center' Dissects Competition," *The Los Angeles Times,* reprinted in *The Morning Call,* December 6, 1987, pp. D1, D3.

Chapter 15

Defending Against CI

A separate and distinct issue from developing CI for your business is that of defending against CI directed against you and your company.

Defending against a competitor's CI is not strictly a part of defensive CI, which was covered in Chapter 14. This is because the operational details involved, principally controlling the unauthorized release of valuable data to competitors, differ from external acts of tracking what competitors and others are saying about you. Thus, you may visualize defensive CI as a part of your business's ongoing concern about employee and internal security. Because many of the same analytic skills are needed to determine where your company is vulnerable as are needed to obtain CI on your competitors, the two types of CI are related.

There are two prime areas of concern in defensive CI: company publications and publicity, on the one hand; and trade shows, conventions, and conferences on the other.

Company Publications and Publicity

Every business needs to communicate to survive. However, what your business releases may help your competitors. Clearly, you should review both what your business releases and to whom information is released. Try to find out in advance what will be distributed at a conference or other public or industry meeting attended by employees of your firm. If possible, have someone not involved with preparing or distributing the materials review them.

The same is true with the following materials, all of which can be valuable sources of CI for competitors, if they can get access to them (and they usually can):

■ Articles and interviews in the trade press.

■ News stories and features in local news and business publications.

■ Newsletters and other house publications.

■ Press releases and media kits, both from you and from those working for you, such as advertising agencies.

■ Speeches and technical papers.

For example, materials in a media kit describing forthcoming high technology products may hint at or even disclose data that your Research and Development Department would not want in the public domain. Be realistic, however. Remember, at one point, the Stealth Bomber was such a top secret that the Pentagon did not even acknowledge that it existed. Despite those protestations and using only public sources, the investment community was able to figure out who was building the Stealth Bomber and how much it cost; a science magazine produced sketches of it; and a model company made a kit to build a model Stealth Bomber. If the Pentagon could not keep it secret, you cannot hope to keep everything from leaking. But you can try to control the leaks.

How to do this varies from company to company. What you must ensure is that policies designed to defend against CI do not keep your employees from doing their jobs, or that rules are not so rigid as to invite noncompliance. Among the options you should consider are the following:

■ Limiting distribution of house publications to employees only—at the office only—and *not* in the lobby.

■ Making announcements of major developments in employee publications only when these same announcements will be made to outsiders. An option is to post these announcements, not use a publication for that purpose.

■ Marking documents given to sales personnel, whether employees or independent contractors, as "company confidential," "not for duplication or redistribution," *only* when that is what you mean.

■ Asking all publications that run articles based on interviews with company personnel to send you a copy of the article as actually run.

■ Requiring that employees participating in surveys know the identity of the firm taking the survey and inquire whether the company will receive a copy of the results in exchange for its cooperation.

307

Turning Data Into Actionable Information
■ ■ ■

Trade Shows, Conventions, and Conferences

Some firms make extensive use of trade shows, conferences, and other meetings as a primary source of raw data for their own CI. The firms encourage employees to attend the events as a way of getting data from both attendees and the exhibitions and presentations.

This is legitimate. Attending meetings, making and participating in presentations, and listening to discussions can and should be used to increase your knowledge about your industry and its players. And, of course, critical information may slip out.

> When you go to a trade show or association meeting, watch out for *The Phantom Interview, The False Flag Job Seeker, The Seduction,* and *The Nonsale Sale.*

There are some techniques used in connection with trade shows, meetings, and conventions, however, that should raise your guard. In fact, due to the use of some of these questionable techniques, some professionals have concluded after conferences, shows, and trade meetings that future employee attendance at such events should be strictly limited or eliminated. This is not because key personnel may inadvertently disclose critical information. Rather, the professionals are concerned that their employees may actually be pumped for CI by competitors.

Those CI probers who pump employees use a variety of tactics, including the following:

■ *The Phantom Interview.* Here a potential employer, one of your competitors, talks with your key people and pretends to be interested in filling an empty position. In fact, the va-

308

cancy does not exist. The goal is to get data on you through your employee's understandable efforts to explain what he or she does in the best possible light.

■ *The False Flag Job Seeker.* This is the converse of the Phantom Interview. Here, a trusted employee of a competitor approaches you seeking a job. The employee actually has no interest in changing positions. Rather, the goal is to use the employment process to learn more about your firm.

■ *The Seduction.* Here an employee is encouraged to talk about how important or technically proficient he or she is—by flattery. The goal is to encourage the employee to disclose key data about your business.

■ *The Nonsale Sale.* Here a competitor talks with those nonemployees associated with your business, such as distributors, franchisees, suppliers, or licensees. These firms may be led to believe they are being courted to carry a competitor's line of goods or services. Whether or not this is true, there is an additional, hidden agenda. They are being pumped for hard information on topics such as your current pricing structure or level of customer service.

CI CLOSEUP: "Security"

The manager of meetings and conventions at a Sony Corporation location organized an international management marketing meeting where confidentiality was seen as having "paramount importance." In addition to having the room swept for electronic listening devices, the manager had the simultaneous translation delivered through a wired system, instead of a wireless one. The reason: The wireless translator might have transmitted the proceedings outside of the conference room.[2]

Turning Data Into Actionable Information
■ ■ ■

Although such tactics have caused some firms to question the value of employee attendance at conferences and meetings, the benefits of attending these meetings generally outweigh the risks of disclosing critical information to competitors.

Among the key benefits of attending meetings such as trade shows, trade association meetings, industry seminars, and training sessions are the following:

■ Participation in professional and trade associations is one way many in the private sector can keep their credentials updated. Participation by employees in a trade or professional association tends to help your firm identify itself as being at the cutting edge in an area. This may make it easier to keep key employees, to recruit new employees, and to keep credibility with your own customers.

■ Most meetings can serve as a forum for your firm to enhance existing business relationships and to add new clients.

■ The reason that some firms improperly exploit meetings— because they are a prime source of CI—is the reason that it is important to go to them in any case. By associating with those active or seeking to become active in a trade or a field, you are in close touch with trends before they become evident in trade publications.

Don't avoid industry and technical meetings because of a fear that your competitors will turn them into an espionage campaign. Because the benefits of attending are substantial, adhere to a few simple rules and you can avoid any major damage.

Attending Meetings Safely
To benefit from meetings and also feel comfortable about limiting the amount of CI that can be developed about your firm, consider the following. These tips also apply when you or your employees are dealing with outsiders in other contexts, such as over the telephone:

■ Don't disclose anything to employees that you do not want competitors to know about unless you at least warn the employees about confidentiality in advance. For example, several years ago it was reported that an employee of a major express package company accidentally disclosed the company's plans to expand into Europe. The disclosure came during a discussion at a training meeting attended by representatives of major competitors.

■ Don't travel with any sensitive materials to work on while you fly or stay in your hotel room. These papers could be accidentally distributed, destroyed, or duplicated.

■ If you have contracts or work rules concerning trade secrets or noncompetition, or have a code of conduct dealing with protecting confidential business information, remind your employees of the agreements.

■ Brief key employees on what to say about critical issues. Do you want certain things disclosed?

■ Caution your employees about the dangers of talking too freely with people who have no identified affiliation or whose affiliation is with an unknown firm.

■ Have your employees listen critically and report on what they hear. What they tell you about a competitor's CI efforts may indicate what your competitor knows about you.

■ Warn your employees about the traps discussed earlier and give them guidance on how to deal with them:

  ▪ The Phantom Interview. If an employee suspects he or she is being pumped instead of interviewed, the employee may be able to smoke the false interviewer out, without losing the chance for a legitimate position, by asking questions such as, Who is doing the job now? Why is the position vacant? If the interview is a ploy for gathering CI, the answers are often evasive.

311

- The False Flag Job Seeker. Remind your employees that anyone interviewing them is not bound to protect your trade secrets. Employees should be careful if the interview seems to be directed to discussions about the work they will be doing in the future and away from the individual's qualifications. Watch out for indications that an unnecessary facility visit is being sought.

- The Seduction. Remind your employees that an *excessive* interest by prospective employers or the media in *exact* job duties should be suspect.

- The Nonsale Sale. A phony sale of goods or services is the most difficult to deal with. To stay in business, you and your distributors must respond to requests for pricing, quotations, and the like. However, if you are sensitive to the existence of this ploy, knowing that you and your distributors are being contacted for quotations from new sources may indicate that a competitor is closely monitoring your activities. That in turn may help you figure out what the competitor's next moves might be.

The key to defending against CI is common sense. For many employees, merely alerting them to the dangers of disclosing critical, confidential information is enough. For other personnel, you may have to outline the tactics they may face and suggest appropriate responses.

Of course, at some point defending against CI shifts into defending against industrial espionage. For example, is a sign warning employees to use a shredder or not to give out information over the telephone to strangers defensive CI or an effort to stop industrial espionage? It is probably a little of each.

However, do not let what your competitors know or may learn about you become overwhelming. Remember, half of what your competitors think they have learned about you is probably wrong—and vice versa.

312

Agreements Not to Disclose
Confidential Information or Trade Secrets

When an employee does not know that information is confidential, and the employee has not been told that it is confidential, that employee may not be obliged to keep it a secret. Because of this, employment, consulting, and independent contract agreements often provide that those signing the agreement agree not to reveal or to use any of the business's trade secrets.

This contract restriction is growing in popularity for several reasons. Among them are that more businesses are sensitive to the importance of protecting themselves against the leak of confidential information to competitors and that these agreements have been relatively easy to enforce.

However, what is confidential or a trade secret is a very important issue in using these clauses. For example, courts have ruled that a company cannot sue former employees to stop them from using trade secrets if these were not actually treated as trade secrets by the company seeking to enforce the clause.

Some companies try to get around this by asking for an agreement to bar the "use of any and all information gained" during employment or while a person is under contract. Such broad clauses are usually seen by the courts as unreasonable. For that reason, the courts will not enforce them, because to do so could forbid the disclosure of information that is actually common knowledge.

Turning Data Into Actionable Information
■ ■ ■

Summary

Prime sources of competitive intelligence about your business are your company publications and publicity materials. Brief or train staff about sensitive information and what types of data are confidential.

Avoid the four common ploys of CI investigators at trade shows, conventions, and conferences. Head off attempts to pump employees by teaching them about The Phantom Interview, The False Flag Job Seeker, The Seduction, and The Nonsale Sale.

Do not avoid meetings and conferences for fear your competitors will turn them into an espionage campaign. Following a few simple rules will help you avoid accidental disclosure of vital facts about your firm.

CI ALERT: What does this tell you?

"Drivers undergo a 22-day training period that includes three days of classroom instruction followed by close work with a supervisor. Each of the UPS's district offices throughout the country offers not only a training room but a training manager."

Source: Article, Corporate Planner, December 1989.

Notes

1. The Conference Board, Inc., *Competitive Intelligence*, Research Report No. 913, 1988, p. 15.

2. Amy Teibel, "Prudence or Paranoia? Meeting Planners Tackle Corporate Espionage," *Meeting News*, October 1988, pp. 1, 59-60.

Chapter 16

Going Outside for Information

CI CLIP

"One of the most important, but clandestine, functions of public relations agencies in Japan is industrial espionage."

Commentator on Japanese-Western business relations.[1]

This chapter explains how to screen and contract with outside consultants to assist you with your CI program. The chapter addresses where you find CI consultants, how you can learn to pick the consultant who is right for the job, how to express what you want done, how to maintain the confidentiality of the results, and what type of fees to expect.

317

When to Go Outside

In general, there are several reasons to seek outside assistance in gathering raw data and conducting CI:

■ Your company lacks expertise or lacks experienced personnel to handle a particular project, *and* the nature of the project does not warrant hiring full-time or even temporary personnel. An outside firm can offer a concentration of specialities and experience that makes its use a relative bargain.

■ You are short of available staff, either because of hiring restrictions or financial limitations. An outside firm can help to supplement your staff and other resources.

■ You are short of time and cannot meet the timetable established for the project without some outside assistance. An outside firm can be a useful resource that can focus substantial resources on your project in a very short time.

■ You need an "objective" or "outside" point of view. For internal reasons, it might be preferable to have someone who is not enmeshed in your firm's management or policies and who can bring fresh insight, guidance, and analysis, or even to have someone not on staff deliver an unwelcome message.

Sometimes in particularly sensitive situations you may prefer to have the CI provided by an outside firm on a "cut-out" basis, even if none of the above criteria are met. The cut-out means that the CI is given to someone other than you, usually to an intermediary who is not the ultimate user. While it can be useful, you should resort to this tactic infrequently, because CI is most effective when the analyst is aware of all the key facts. Sometimes it is vital for a consultant to know the identity of the client. The cost of concealment may be a lack of completeness.

The question of whether to use an outside firm is particularly important when you are shadowing competitors, as discussed in Chapter 14.

When you are involved in shadowing, it might appear to be more cost-effective for you to do the work inside, for several reasons:

■ Because shadowing is often an ongoing operation—you benefit most by doing it again and again—the long-term cost of doing it inside may be lower than the costs of contracting it out.

■ You may want to be able to call on those who are playing your competitors at any time, so these people can answer your "what if" questions right away.

■ It is easier to prevent your own personnel from working for competitors in the future by the use of employment contracts than it is to control outside consultants and the consultants' personnel.

On the other hand, it may be wiser to use an outside consultant to develop a shadow market plan, for these reasons:

■ You do not have to train your personnel in shadow marketing techniques. By going to outsiders, you are buying the time of trained personnel, not paying for training.

■ You can minimize the number of people who know about the shadow market plan project.

■ The final shadow market plan may include conclusions about the probable actions of a competitor at odds with your firm's conventional wisdom. It should be easier for an outsider to deliver and defend this conclusion than it might be for an insider.

Managing Your Own Program
■ ■ ■

Which Outsiders Can Do the Job?

As businesses have begun to use CI, they have also come to
appreciate the need for assistance in finding raw data, as well as
in analyzing that data. As a result, some firms began to seek out
CI specialists to locate competitive data, analyze and evaluate it,
draw conclusions from it, and prepare it for presentation. From
those projects has grown up a small, specialized industry.

CI CLOSEUP: "Too Much Data"
*Sometimes, you can have too much of a good
thing. In one case, a company called in a consultant to help with its CI program. When the
consultant arrived, he was shown 13 file cabi-
nets "chock-full" of undigested data on the
competition. The client asked what the company should do with it. The consultant's response
was "It's a bit late now, isn't it?"[2]*

As one who uses, or will soon be using, CI, you have numerous
resources for help in getting CI. Each outside source of raw data
and finished CI has its own pros and cons. One of the major
distinctions you should try to make is between sources whose
primary interest is the mere collection and processing of data and
those that have a larger interest.

Existing Professional Relationships
You might consider using some of the following people and
services that already work with your firm to help you find some
raw data: distributors, advertising agencies, and marketing firms.
However, they are all most efficient in helping you locate raw
data only as that data or its location directly pertains to their

profession. Getting CI is not their primary expertise, so their ability and willingness to help you get the data will be uneven at best.

In addition, the most effective and impartial CI should be obtained from sources that do not have any other interest in your business. In particular, your source for CI should have no financial interest in seeing that a particular transaction or even any change in planning goes forward. This is not to question the objectivity of professionals such as attorneys, accountants, investment bankers, and banks. Impartiality, however, is both an objective and a subjective matter. An outsider with no financial or career interest in a particular transaction or decision may provide a needed impartiality, both actual and perceived.

Sources for Raw Data

If you are just looking for raw data, using firms specializing in obtaining business data may be a good option. These are known variously as "information brokers" or "document retrieval services," depending on their reliance on online databases or on hard-copy material. This category also includes services that specialize in obtaining documents from U.S. government files under the Freedom of Information Act or from government agencies' public information and publications centers.

> *Possessing facts does not provide information, only the potential for information.*

Whatever the source of the data, the strengths of such specialists lie in obtaining, but not analyzing, the data. Once they have provided the raw materials you seek, you should have the data and documents evaluated and analyzed, either inside your business or by other outside experts.

Managing Your Own Program
■ ■ ■

The most reliable method of obtaining CI, as distinguished from raw data, from an outside source is to hire a firm that treats CI as a speciality. Using outsiders for CI can have additional benefits. Outsiders providing you with CI will be more likely to remain anonymous from your competitors. In turn, this makes it less likely that the inquiries and research being done on your behalf will trigger unnecessary and harmful speculation by your competitors about your strategy and intentions.

What Do Outsiders Do Best?

The services an outside CI professional provides depend on what you ask to have done. In deciding whether to seek outside assistance, you should be aware that, *in general*, a CI specialist is able to develop certain types of data on competitors better than you can. In such cases, the CI specialist should be seen as the primary source of your competitive data. In other cases, however, you can better use your own internal resources for a CI task, so you should consider using the CI specialist to supplement your own research work.

Outsiders should be able to significantly contribute to developing CI in the following broad areas of competitor analysis:

■ Data on the overall competitive environment, including the industry's structure, potential entrants and future competitors, and market shares and profits of existing competitors.

■ Data on your competitor's financial and legal positions, including sources of financing, profitability, and major lawsuits and regulatory actions affecting the competitor.

■ Data on your competitor's personnel, resources, and facilities, including its sources of raw materials, the level of its quality control, and planned facilities.

■ Data on your competitor's strategies, objectives, and self-perceptions, including how strategy is made and implemented, what markets it is targeting, and how the company sees itself.

■   Data on how other competitors and customers see the targeted competitor.

In the following broad areas, outsiders providing CI will probably be able to make significant contributions to developing CI on competitors, but in some cases, that contribution may only be supplemental to what you could develop from inside sources:

■   Data on the owners and managers of the competitor, including data on how decisions are made, who makes them, and corporate politics.

■   Data on emerging technology, research and development, current manufacturing methods and processes, and access to outside technology.

In the following cases you are usually better off developing CI from your own internal resources. They are ones for which an outside source of CI can serve as a regular supplement:

■   Data on products and services offered by competitors, including customer service and performance, and products or services likely to be introduced or eliminated.

■   Data on marketing, including market shares by product lines, marketing approaches, and probable future changes in marketing directions.

The following broad areas are ones for which an outside source of CI can supplement, sporadically, what you can develop from your own internal resources:

■   Data on sales and pricing policies, including topics such as pricing strategy; price levels and flexibility; and credits, discounts, incentives, and special pricing policies.

■   Data on the competitor's sales force and customers, including the type of sales force, its organization, training and compensation, the number of customers, and an analysis of the most important customers.

Managing Your Own Program
■ ■ ■

What Should You Expect in Working with Outsiders?

In selecting and using any outsider for your CI work, you must appreciate that how you proceed and how you define the task have a major impact on what the outside firm does. The major steps involved are the following:

1. Define your problem, what you need, and what you expect to get.

2. Locate several potential firms.

3. Evaluate the firms and their proposals. Select your firm.

4. Monitor your assignment.

5. Evaluate the results of the assignment.

Defining Your Problem
In defining what you expect a CI consultant to do, you first have to settle upon the following:

■　Is the consultant to carry out the assignment alone?
■　Is the consultant to carry out the assignment working with you?

In each case, you should identify what data you have already collected and what, if any, you will be releasing to the consultant.

Also identify exactly what you expect the consultant to provide. It may be any or all of the following:

■　Ongoing advice.
■　A written report.
■　Interim written or oral reports.
■　Copies of specific materials, such as product brochures.
■　All notes of interviews.
■　A formal presentation.

324

From there, to define your problem, you will use the same tools we presented in Chapter 5.

Finding a CI Consultant
In seeking a CI consultant, you are subject to constraints you may not always face in searching for a new employee. For example, you may not wish to advertise openly for a firm with CI expertise, because this almost certainly alerts your competitors about your future business intentions and capabilities.

> *How do you find a CI specialist if you can't just advertise for one?*

CI consultants may be identified and located through a combination of the following:

■ Research the trade press covering your industry, as well as the more general business press, for discussions of the activities of consultants and consulting firms working in CI.

■ Review directories of CI, research, and related service organizations for leads.

■ Survey key employees for their suggestions.

■ Check for articles or books published by principals and employees of consultants. This can lead you to their firms. However, you should first read them. Do their skills match your needs?

Each of these steps should turn up some names of individuals or organizations. Your search should not stop here: Expand that list before you close it. For example, individuals identified with one firm several years ago may now be with another firm, making that new firm a candidate for your consideration.

Managing Your Own Program
■ ■ ■

In looking for names of CI consulting firms, avoid the trap of going only for the "old, established consulting firm." Just because a management consulting firm is large and has been around a long time does not mean that it provides CI services or that it can provide the quality of services you want on a cost-effective basis.

For reasons of efficiency and equity, seek out more specialized firms. Being smaller, they may be more responsive; being newer, they may be more aggressive; being specialized, they may be more cost-effective.

There is another pitfall to avoid—assuming that every firm does everything well. If you are seeking research, look for a firm that does CI research. If you are seeking in-house training and consulting, look for that. If you want to go to a seminar on CI, find out who presents seminars and how good they are. If you want to buy search aids and directories, look for organizations that sell them. If your need is for an information broker using databases, find those specialists. If you just need someone who runs a clipping service or can get reprints, look for that type of firm. Another need might be for prepackaged reports. If so, that is what you should seek. Although all of these activities are elements of CI, it is extremely unlikely that you would find all of them being done equally well by the same organization.

In fact, you may want to look at the types of CI services you may need as falling into one of three broad categories:

■ *Raw materials:* Reprint and clipping services, information brokers, document retrieval services, and directory publishers.

■ *Processed products:* Prepackaged reports and public seminars.

■ *Custom services:* Collecting and analyzing data, and helping individuals and companies to perform their own CI.

326

A firm that is active in one area should be able to assist you in another one but probably cannot function equally well in all three of these areas.

Once you have a list of potential CI consultants, evaluate them. That means contacting the targeted CI firms for indications of their qualifications to conduct the kind of research you want and their ability to consider taking the assignment within the time and cost constraints that you face.

These firms should be told up front of any special limitations, such as important time constraints, work at a specific location, or provision of CI based only on interviews, not on secondary research.

Evaluating the Consultant

After you clarify the qualifications and interest of the firms on your list, review them to decide which firms should be contacted for additional discussion. These discussions may be as elaborate as interviewing key members of the firm or requesting each firm to submit a complete proposal and price for the assignment. The follow-up may be as simple as sending a contract to one firm and asking whether the firm will sign it and start to work.

In initial discussions with potential CI consultants, begin by presenting the problem or assignment directly to the consultant. That a consultant understands the problem and says that he or she can solve it is not enough. You should clarify several items before you decide whether to retain a particular consultant, including

■ General information on the consultant and his or her experience.

■ Specific information on key individuals employed by the consultant who would be working on the project. It cannot be overemphasized that, if you are hiring an individual for his or her particular experience, you should always ensure that this specific individual will be working on or at least supervising your assignment.

■ What references the consultant can provide, other than clients or completed projects (for reasons of confidentiality).

■ Whether the individuals to be assigned to your project are the same individuals who have worked on similar projects for other clients.

You should feel free to compare one consultant with another.

You and the consultant should discuss openly exactly what the consultant will need from you, covering not only fees and costs but also your commitment of other resources, such as your time or the time of other key employees and executives. You must be frank in deciding whether you are willing and able to commit your time or that of others, particularly if you are overcommitted already. If you cannot or will not commit the resources required by the consultant, you may have to consider a radical change in the nature of the CI work to be performed.

Beware of the "prepackaged" solution to your CI problems.

A trap to avoid—and one not always easy to spot—is the retention of consultants with prepackaged approaches. In such cases, you will typically find that the consultant is very assertive, pointing to how it handled similar problems for other clients with the same approach time and time again. Determine whether the approach suggested to each of these is basically the same, regardless of the unique characteristics of each assignment. If that is the case, the consultant is probably selling a product (its own predetermined approach) and not a process (a way to handle your research in the best and most cost-effective way).

Another key point is reporting and communication. You should be wary of a consultant who indicates that he or she will take an assignment and only report back at the end, but does not see any need to provide interim communications, progress reports, or other feedback. Be particularly wary if the consultant appears reluctant to keep in regular communication with you.

Monitoring the Assignment

If you are working with a consultant for the first time, or the assignment is one that will take a long time to complete, you may want to monitor the assignment as it is being done. However, if you anticipate doing this, make sure that the consultant is aware of this *before* the assignment is begun. Remember, from the consultant's point of view, your firm's monitoring activities (or its need for regular reports) may increase the time the entire project takes or increase the effort that the consultant expends. That translates into fees and costs. For this reason, it is not fair to impose a substantial monitoring/reporting requirement *after* an assignment has begun.

Evaluating the Results

To evaluate results, make sure that you compare what you expected to receive from the consultant with what you finally received. One way to do this is to compare the final report (if any) with the written proposal given you by the consultant at the beginning of the assignment. However, make sure you account for any later changes in the assignment due to requests that you made. Do they match? If not, why not? In what ways?

If the consultant is providing services, rather than a report, find out from those in your company with whom the consultant worked whether they were satisfied with the consultant. Was the consultant cooperative, prompt, and effective?

Confidentiality and Conflicts of Interest

Two additional steps apply to your prehiring screen of consultants. You should make arrangements up front to ensure the confidentiality of the CI investigation any outside consultant performs for you. Do not limit this protection to what the consultant's contract states. Also, verify that the consultant you hire—and his or her firm as a whole—has no direct or indirect conflict of interest in assuming your assignment.

Confidentiality
In working with a CI consultant, a critical issue is what access the consultant will have to your information and how the consultant will handle that information. A related issue is how the consultant will treat the results of your assignment.

To perform effectively, in many cases a CI consultant may have to have direct, continuing, and unimpeded access to corporate records and other information that is highly sensitive. The issue, then, is not merely protecting the confidentiality of your information while the assignment is being conducted, but in some cases protecting your information from being disclosed after the fact.

> *Does your potential CI consultant have a list of satisfied clients? Do you really want your name on that kind of a list?*

The key here is a clear understanding between you and the consultant that the data you provide will be kept confidential and that the assignment being conducted for you will also be kept confidential. In addition to language in the consultant's proposal or agreement covering this point, look for the following as evidence of the consultant's ability and willingness to keep this kind of commitment:

■ How many people in the consultant's organization will actually know the identity of the client?

■ If you provide the consultant with materials during the assignment, will they be returned to you, uncopied?

■ Do client names appear on copies of work kept by the consultant?

■ What does the consultant do with the work files accumulated during an assignment? Are they kept intact or are they destroyed?

■ Does the consultant name other clients and detail assignments conducted for them? Will it refrain from doing that with your company's name and its assignment?

The point about descriptions of past assignments raises what is an often-ignored issue: the identification of former clients by a CI specialist. Some firms involved in CI research and in related areas disclose past and even current clients, usually in the hopes of generating additional business. We believe that such a disclosure, except at the express request of the client for whom the work was done, is improper and unethical. The CI client necessarily seeks confidential research and analysis. The fact that a firm retains a CI specialist may itself be valuable confidential information that the client may not want disclosed.

Conflicts of Interest
This is an extremely important issue for CI specialists, but one where very little guidance can be given. That is because the facts of each case have a powerful influence over defining what constitutes a conflict.

As a general rule, an ethical CI specialist avoids any conflict of interest or the appearance of a conflict of interest. Although most people think of a conflict of interest in the context of being hired to develop information about a current client, it is important to realize that this issue can emerge in many other, less-direct areas. Avoidance of a conflict of interest also requires adhering to the following rules:

■ A CI specialist should not use the *results* of any work done for one client as data for another. For example, if an assignment has resulted in a client changing its marketing plan, that result should never be disclosed to a competitor unless and until it has been made public.

■ A CI specialist should not use any *information* received in confidence from one client as data for work done for another. For example, if a client has developed internal cost data on its own operations that it released to the specialist, that data should never be revealed to any other firm.

■ A CI specialist should not disclose the *analysis* or conclusions it has given to one client to any other client. For example, if you have advised Company, Inc., that a particular market is vulnerable to imports, you should not tell Industrial Concern, Inc., that you have drawn that conclusion and given it to another business.

■ A CI specialist should not be involved in *both sides* of a transaction. For example, the specialist should not work for one corporation that has targeted a current client for a takeover.

How Much Will It Cost?

An article in *The Wall Street Journal* observed that consulting fees for CI "can jump to $100,000."[3] That may be true, but it is just as fair to observe that the fees can be as low as nothing. As with so many broad statements, the truth lies somewhere in between.

> *One key to controlling costs is to be clear on what you want—and don't want.*

In evaluating the cost of outside CI services, you must take into account several factors:

■ CI services are intangible products.

■ CI services cannot be turned on and off like a faucet without additional costs.

■ CI services are driven by *what* you seek and *when* you need the information.

This means that the better you define your problem and what help you need, the better you will be able to control the cost. You must be frank with a CI consultant about the terms of the services needed, the timeframe of the project, your budget, and the nature of the final product. If you try to go in "cheap," you will often find that you have cost yourself more money, not saved it.

This also means you are buying something before you or the consultant knows exactly what the result will be (and whether you can get it). If you are not satisfied, the consultant cannot "repossess" the CI and recover its costs; once completed and provided to a client, CI is out of the consultant's control forever.

Some tips are in order:

■ Determine what you can afford to spend for the CI you need and figure out what the absence of that CI could cost your firm, as well as what its presence could mean in terms of profits and benefits. Then you can do a cost/benefit, cost/ risk of loss analysis to see if you are being realistic.

■ Target what you would like if you could get everything you wanted. Then establish what will be "enough" for you to get in order to be able to operate. If the ideal is unattainable or too expensive, shift to the fallback position.

■ Consider breaking an assignment into tiers. That is, when you have the results of the first tier of work, you can narrow down what you need in the second tier, and so on.

■ Arrange to keep in close touch with your CI consultant.

■ Establish how much data is already on hand that the CI consultant can access and use.

■ Consider using the CI consultant only as a guide, while you and your own personnel do most of the work.

■ Get a written proposal with a quotation covering a range of fees. In general, try to avoid a research proposal or quotation given in terms of dollars per hour plus costs. In that case, you have little control over the final cost. If that type of pricing is unavoidable, such as with on-site consulting services, work with the consultant to establish formal or informal controls, such as having the consultant call you before fees and costs exceed a predetermined level.

■ Consider sharing the costs of a CI consulting firm with other units in your company who can use its services, particularly if what you are obtaining may benefit several units.

Summary

Hiring an outside consultant for CI is preferable when internal resources are limited or when the CI is better presented by an "outsider." The nature of the task should help you determine whether to use professionals who have existing relationships with your firm or to hire CI specialists. Another decision involves whether to have the consultant develop or supplement most of the data.

Steps in pinpointing (and achieving) your expectations about consultants include defining your problem, needs, and expectations; locating several potential firms; evaluating the firms and their proposals; selecting the firm; monitoring your assignment; and evaluating the results.

A vital process in screening consultants is verifying that they will maintain the confidentiality of your CI program and that they have no direct or indirect conflict of interest in assuming your assignment.

CI ALERT: What does this tell you?

"[The owner of a competitor-intelligenced firm] won't reveal names of [the firm's] current clients, but he casually identifies past clients. They include CBS, Campbell Soup, Colgate-Palmolive, and GTE Sylvania."

Source: Popular Computing, March 1983.

Notes

1. Boye De Mente, *How to Do Business with the Japanese,* Lincolnwood, Ill.: NTC Business Books, 1987, p. 218.

2. "George Smiley Joins the Firm," *Newsweek,* May 2, 1988, pp. 46-47.

3. Mark Robichaux, "'Competitor Intelligence': A Grapevine to Rivals' Secrets," *The Wall Street Journal,* April 12, 1989, p. B2.

Chapter 17

Developing an Ongoing CI Program

CI CLIP

"If you talk to a Japanese executive, he says, 'Of course information gathering is a part of the job.' If you ask a typical Harvard MBA, he says, 'It's the company librarian's job'."

President of a Firm Specializing
in Research on Japanese Industrial Topics.[1]

This chapter integrates all the techniques described in Parts I through IV to illustrate how you can initiate an ongoing competitive intelligence program in your business. It also covers practical issues of how to set up, staff, and maintain an intelligence unit and explains how your other staff should interact with internal CI personnel.

Managing Your Own Program
■ ■ ■

Why Have a CI Unit?

During the last several years, there has been increasing interest in many corporations in creating separate CI units. In part, this is the result of the reported actions and presumed successes of firms such as IBM, General Motors, Texas Instruments, and Citicorp, which have operated CI-type units for years. The interest also reflects a growing appreciation of the benefits of CI.

The most common reason given for having an internal CI unit, instead of relying on outside sources for all CI, is that the more formal the process for producing CI is, the better the resulting product will be. This can be true. However, when such a unit has not proven successful following its creation, there appear to be a couple of reasons contributing to its failure:

■ Cost is a large factor. Creating a CI unit involves setup costs and may involve operating costs much higher than operating under a more informal system, where information is obtained outside (or from insiders) on an as-needed basis. Usually the problem is not the total fixed and operating costs of the unit, however, but management's failure to anticipate the full scope of such costs.

■ Creating a new, specialized CI unit may result in stress between departments. A new CI unit might be perceived as a threat to existing units, such as marketing, planning, finance, and law, which may see some of their functions usurped by the new unit. In addition, creating a formal CI unit occasionally gives rise to misconceptions by management, stockholders, and the public that the business uses "spies." Fortunately, the latter problem is becoming less and less frequent.

For your own CI unit to operate most effectively and efficiently, ideally you should staff it with people who have direct experience in every area of the industry you expect the unit to monitor. In turn, this means that the departments that may be most dependent on CI—whether manufacturing, planning, finance, engineering, or marketing—may find that they are called on to provide skilled personnel to staff the new unit. In some companies, some of these departments have been reluctant to release highly skilled individuals from their positions to serve with a permanent CI unit.

CI CLOSEUP: "Insurance"

A medium-sized insurance company, Indianapolis Life Insurance, first organized its competition unit in early 1986. When the unit was formed, there was so little information available on such units that the unit's director had to travel to the few insurance companies that did have such units to get ideas on how to start one. Within two years, it grew to four full-time people who keep files on almost 700 companies and financial comparisons on about 200.[2]

Management Issues

If you decide to create an internal CI unit, you must first be prepared to handle a host of interrelated management issues that are unique to the creation and operation of an internal CI system. Some of these arise out of the demands of the CI process we have already described in this book. Other issues surface because your internal CI unit must function both as a supplier of and as a recipient of data from many other departments.

The following observations apply to a CI unit, both when it is first being established and once it is in operation. These issues reflect the most common types of management problems the authors have seen associated with actual CI units. At each point you may have to make a decision.

Managing Your Own Program

Staged Development

Staged development means bringing your CI program online one step at a time. Typically, this might involve gradually moving through the following start-up steps:

1. Require all business and marketing plans to include a profile of key competitors.

2. Begin collecting materials produced by competitors, such as product brochures and advertisements.

3. Routinely check online databases for articles about your competitors.

4. Distribute copies of key new information to executives who can use it.

5. Convince personnel who have regular contact with your competitors to report back, informally, on any new developments.

6. Interview new employees who have joined your business from a competitor.

Is the staged development of an internal CI program appropriate? In many cases, staged development enables a unit to grow in responsibility and effectiveness. It also permits it time to develop a track record and internal organizational support. In many corporations, however, it is difficult for new units to "evolve." Either they come into existence fully grown and strong, or they soon wither away.

Visibility

How visible should your CI unit be, both within your firm and to outsiders? Specifically, should you call it a competitive intelligence section—a name that accurately reflects what it does? Or should you give it a more neutral (but less accurate) title, such as information support or marketing reference services?

What Work Goes Outside the Unit?

How should the work of your CI unit be divided between your own personnel and outside sources? It is extremely unlikely that any internal CI unit will be able to handle all of your firm's CI needs. As we noted in Chapter 16, using an outside firm for CI may be appropriate only to handle peak work loads. Or you may want some CI work to be contracted out in special circumstances such as merger and acquisition transactions, when the internal security of sensitive information may be especially important.

CI CLOSEUP: "A Collection of Clients"

Dow Chemical Company, a multibillion dollar international company, operates a centralized Business Information Center where only one manager and a staff of three collect information on products, industries, and companies for marketing and management information. According to the manager of the Business Information Center, the Center's three major customers are Dow's Market Research, Economic Planning, and Sales Departments. Much of the data they need is provided through the use of online databases.[3]

In any case, it is always easier to set a policy on when and what CI to contract out *before* a CI unit begins its operations. Like any business unit, a CI unit may see as a threat to its growth or even its existence efforts to contract out "its" work. Making these decisions at the beginning may minimize such a conflict.

Managing Your Own Program
■ ■ ■

Staffing Up

Where do you recruit people to do your CI? For example, you may need to hire people with broad experience in your business as well as in your industry to work in your CI unit. These people are typically the very ones seen as candidates for rapid promotion and long-term development within the corporation in other areas. To attract them and keep them in the CI unit, you must avoid creating a dead-end position.

A promotion line from the CI unit upward must be established and a decision made about where the unit is located and to whom it is administratively responsible—*before* the unit is created, if possible. If good employees see no way out of a new unit, they will not volunteer to join that unit. If they are transferred in, they will make their own way out—usually to competitors.

Who Should You Place in Charge of the Unit?

Where will your CI unit be located in the organizational hierarchy? A decision must be made about the level of the unit and to whom it is administratively responsible. A "special" unit or joint supervision rarely works. Your options are varied. Typically departments such as marketing, business development, and strategic planning can all make a strong case for having the CI function report to them. A chief information officer (CIO) may also be a logical candidate to supervise and direct a CI unit. This is because of the CI unit's heavy reliance on information gathering and management, and its need to provide reliable support to a wide number of corporate functions, all of which may dovetail with the charter of a CIO.

Who Initiates Data Gathering?

How should data gathering be allocated between the internal CI unit and other corporate units? Here, you may have a choice between a cooperative and an authoritarian model, which are described in the following box.

In the former, the CI unit seeks to obtain data in exchange for useful CI. It takes longer to initiate a meaningful program this

Models of CI Units

From an overview perspective, it can be said that there are two basic models of CI units: the authoritarian and the cooperative. The authoritarian model (sometimes seen as the revolutionary model) is one that owes its creation to the decision of one person (or at most a handful), at which point it must begin to justify its services. Someone says, "Let it happen," and it does. The cooperative model (also sometimes seen as the evolutionary model) is one that owes its creation to a need for its services, and then must justify its continued existence.

Their basic characteristics usually strongly influence their creation, growth, manner of operation, and ultimate survival. Typical characteristics are described below.

Authoritarian Model:

Hits the deck running.

Has a corporate sponsor from the beginning.

Survival is often dependent on the career of the sponsor.

Internal cooperation easily mandated and enforced.

Staffed up quickly; career path (or lack of one) quickly evident.

Success rate not an immediate factor in acceptance; therefore has time to mature.

Initial audience for its services is usually clear and centralized, such as strategic planning.

Use of its output is usually mandated at the same time it is created.

Name given the unit reflects its purpose, such as marketing intelligence.

Available funds for its operation must be openly appropriated or come from another source controlled by sponsor.

Authoritarian Model (continued)

Substantial protection from problems of accepted/expected failure.

May quickly cross the line from analysis to policymaking.

Quickly seen as clearly neutral, a "special pleader," or a control device.

Cooperative Model:

Slow starter.

Develops without a powerful sponsor.

Survival not generally tied to that of others, but it is highly dependent on being successful—quickly.

Internal cooperation must be earned; that takes time.

Staffing up takes time; career paths (or lack) not usually evident at the beginning.

Success rate is often critical to corporate acceptance; may not be given time to mature.

The audience for its services is often unclear and is usually in a unit not at the center of decision making, such as a part of the marketing department.

The unit usually must "sell" the need for its services to other units within the company.

The name given the unit often reflects its previous mission, such as information support.

Funding is initially available if this is an expansion of an existing unit's functions.

Often lacks protection from problems of accepted/expected failure.

Usually does not face opportunity to be involved in policymaking.

Takes some time for its neutrality (or lack thereof) to be discerned.

way. However, this path may result in more permanent institutionalization of CI within the corporation.

In contrast, an authoritarian model enables a new CI unit to be up and running more quickly. However, the unit's continued existence and effectiveness may depend more on the future of the individual who created it than on its own track record for effective and supportive CI.

One way to help get a CI unit off the ground is to provide incentives for potential data providers to cooperate. For example, your sales force should be made aware of just how important you think current, accurate data is about both customers and competitors. The sales force should be able to provide important data about loyal, longstanding customers, about customers that have recently switched to competitors, about new customers, and about potential customers. In addition, the sales force should be able to provide at least partial data about potential new-product introductions by competitors, gained by listening to customers.

Once you have made the sales force aware of this, give the salespeople a reason to cooperate. That reason may be recognition at headquarters and by their supervisors, it may come in the form of receiving CI they can use, or it may be financial rewards. Without appropriate incentive, salespeople may feel that data gathering is just taking up time they could use to make sales, and they will not cooperate.

Dealing with Excessive Data Collection

How will you deal with those who are really good at CI? Here, consider one problem that is not recognized as much as it should be. People who are good at CI tend to be retentive, in a psychological sense. That is, they seek out and retain *everything* they can, on the basis that "some day" it might be of use. The problem may start as one of too much data solicitation or of excessive data retention, but it ultimately becomes a problem of processing and storage.

345

These people seek data for the sake of collecting it—they are a kind of mental "pack rat." For example, one member of a CI unit may suggest that the personnel department inform him of the last place of employment of staff newly hired and of the place of next employment of all those leaving the corporation. This sort of data may be useful for monitoring a particular competitor's recruitment efforts to determine changes in research and development activities. If the data is not being collected for a particular end, however, you may not want to collect it at all.

> *Another issue you may have to face is dealing with the departure of an employee involved in CI. Can you (should you) "debrief" the employee? Was the employee subject to a nondisclosure agreement? If so, what did it cover? If not, why not? So far, there are no formal guidelines for this, because CI is still in its infancy. However, this issue will become prominent—soon.*

Collection Versus Analysis and Evaluation Responsibilities

One issue not often considered in setting up a CI unit, but a possibly important one, is who will evaluate the accuracy and reliability of the raw data you collect. Specifically, do those who collect it also analyze and evaluate it, or do you separate the collectors from the analysts? As with so many other elements of the CI process, there is no clearcut answer. What is important is that you recognize that it is an issue and deal with it.

Who Gets What?

Once a CI unit becomes effective, experience shows that the demand increases rapidly for its services by departments and managers other than the unit's originally intended recipients.

Thus, it becomes very important to establish, at the beginning, exactly who needs what information and how frequently.

Not only must you separate those who need to know from those who just want to know but you also may have to refuse to provide CI to certain units because of special considerations. These might include the need to keep your CI sources confidential.

Operating CI units soon discover that they must limit the number of assignments and establish priorities among them. The driving constraints are typically cost and time. The unit simply cannot afford to do everything it is asked to do. In terms of time, CI demands often follow other cycles in the corporation. For example, if CI supports those involved in developing annual plans, CI units find that they receive the bulk of their planning-related assignments within a very compressed time period.

Measuring Performance

How do you plan to measure a CI unit's performance, along with that of its staff? If you expect the unit to be 100 percent accurate all of the time, you are setting the stage for an ineffective unit. When you expect perfection, you are actually asking for the unit to provide you with CI and draw conclusions of such breadth and depth, subject to such qualifications, as to be virtually useless to you. Staff will cease to be aggressive for fear of being "wrong"; their results will cover *all* potential options. On the other hand, if you make it clear that perfection is not and cannot be expected from your CI unit, you may encourage it to take the small risks necessary to ensure consistent, quality, usable CI.

You should expect your CI unit to make some mistakes. Be wary if it does not.

Managing Your Own Program
■ ■ ■

To put it another way, not only should you *accept* the fact that the output from this unit cannot always be perfect but you should *expect* failures from time to time. In hospitals, for example, review groups look for improper medical practices by checking the records of surgeons. One group singled out for review is surgeons who appear to have a higher than average death rate for a particular operation. The concern is that they are taking too many risks. However, another group is also subject to the same review: surgeons who have a lower than average death rate for the same operation. If death rates are exceptionally low, the review body becomes concerned that patient care is suffering because these surgeons are too cautious and are not undertaking risky operations when they should. The lesson here is that if your CI unit does not have any failures or miscues, perhaps it is not taking enough risks in its analysis.

Performance should be measured against the stated mission of the unit, as described next. A sample mission statement appears in Exhibit 17.1.

Job Descriptions/Mission Statements
What form should job descriptions and mission statements take for CI units? You or the unit's manager generally creates an organizational mission statement for a CI unit as well as job descriptions for its personnel. Remember to consider related, supportive changes. For example, you should seek to modify the mission statements of other units—marketing, new business development, and strategic planning in particular—to require that they use CI in their planning work.

Also, you should seek to modify job descriptions of personnel in units such as purchasing, sales, and employee relations. Require that people holding these key positions must, as a part of their anticipated duties, provide raw data to the CI unit on an ongoing basis.

Financial Support
How will your CI unit be supported financially? Should you charge other units for the work that your CI unit provides to

---

Mission of the CI Unit

The unit's mission is to develop and to communicate an in-depth and current understanding of the following to senior management on a regular and as-needed basis:

- ■ *Current and future products/services of major competitors.*
- ■ *Current technologies underlying the activities of major competitors.*
- ■ *Current market activities of major competitors.*
- ■ *Current and future business strategies employed by major competitors.*
- ■ *Identity of potential new competitors.*

This competitive information will be used by officers and managers of the corporation in setting overall business strategies and making decisions on marketing, manufacturing, and distribution tactics.

Exhibit 17.1: Sample Mission Statement for an Internal CI Unit

them? Or will the CI unit receive funds from the same sources that support planning, legal, and related overhead functions?

Funding is a touchy issue. If you charge back other departments for CI, they may be reluctant to use the unit, clouding its future. Paying for a CI unit from an overhead budget will make it more attractive for other units to use it. Without charging back, however, you create a "free" resource. Experience shows that in a short time, "free" resources are overused without regard to cost-effectiveness, simply because they have no cost to the user. In turn, that means the CI unit must have some way other than charges to allocate its time among other corporate units. One option is to start a CI unit without using chargebacks to develop

349

a "market" for the services. Then, over time, gradually initiate some interdepartmental fee structure, whether direct or indirect.

The other difficulty with creating free resources is that they tend to be the first units that are cut back in a financial downturn. Because you need your CI unit more than ever when you are experiencing such a downturn, cutting back on it at that time can be disastrous.

Dealing with Success

How will you and the CI unit handle its success? To do so effectively, you must plan for it at the beginning. Experience shows that a successful CI unit is often flooded by assignments, requests, and demands beyond what its creators anticipated. Most units will seek to respond to these, because they rely on the good will of many managers making requests to provide raw data needed for other assignments.

The converse of this is to plan to deal with excessive amounts of raw data. Once departments using CI see its effectiveness, they will cooperate—perhaps too much—in providing needed raw data for the CI unit. It is most embarrassing to have to turn off the data flow after literally begging for it to start.

Remember too that past successes, just as past failures, can have an impact on how future CI reports are regarded. For example, as one observer has noted, "[T]he more successful an intelligence organization becomes, the less are its reports questioned and the greater the chance that it will fail."[4]

Integrating CI into the Decision-Making Process

CI Versus Policymaking

The key mission for a CI unit should be to provide needed information that will serve as a key element in your decision making. That means that those providing the CI must avoid having any preconceived position either for or against any specific policy or outcome that can be affected by their research.

There are two principal reasons for drawing and maintaining a line between CI and policymaking. The first is the need to keep CI unbiased. The second is the need to keep CI free from the appearance of special pleading. For example, if CI provided by your marketing unit stresses the need for additional distribution channels, that conclusion, even if valid, may be disregarded as special pleading by nonmarketing departments. Those with the operating responsibility must be the ones to recommend and ultimately carry out policy decisions.

However, you must not let the need to separate CI and policymaking impede effective planning and policymaking. For instance, it may be entirely appropriate for a CI report to examine the probable effects of alternative corporate policies, particularly when policies entail responses of a particular competitor to your initiatives. The division between policy and CI must not be so rigid that the CI unit is precluded from assessing fairly the impacts of policy decisions already made.

Conversely, the goal of CI is to provide the needed information and intelligence that will serve as a key element in decision making, so your internal CI suppliers must avoid having a preconceived position on any specific corporate policy that may bear on or be affected by the CI research they are conducting.

Integration by Participation
One way to bring CI into the decision-making process is to bring decision makers into the CI process. This is known as "integration by participation." An example of this can be seen in the operations of Xerox Corporation.

Xerox Corporation has had a corporate intelligence function for some 20 years. As we showed earlier, Xerox was not sensitive to emerging Japanese competition. Now Xerox's CI function shows it has evolved in many ways since it was established. For example, CI for design and technology planning now operates as follows:

351

Managing Your Own Program
■ ■ ■

■ CI takes the form of benchmarking, focusing on specific functions or processes that other firms—whether or not they are Xerox's competitors—do "extremely well." For example, Xerox has indicated that it "learned a great deal about material distribution from retailer L. L. Bean." Benchmarking is also focused on direct competitors. For example, CI disclosed that Xerox was spending twice as long as a top competitor in getting a product to market, using twice as much labor, and taking three times as long on tooling. These disclosures "led to some fundamental changes in product design, production, and delivery."

■ CI is no longer "just the job of those specifically assigned to the task." For example, "the people responsible for making [product] improvements gather intelligence as well."

■ CI's most valuable tools are visiting trade shows, reading periodicals, and "watching how competitors do business." For example, each year Xerox personnel from many disciplines visit Japan and other countries and then produce a study on their findings.

■ CI can involve reverse engineering of competitive products that are "attractive from a manufacturing or design standpoint." Such products are acquired, torn down, and then made available to Xerox's engineers. In turn, the engineers evaluate any patented technology that Xerox may be "up against." Also, they study those nonpatentable features as well as the applied engineering and manufacturing principles that reduce costs and improve quality.[5]

At Xerox, CI is closely integrated into both planning and product development, in no small measure by having personnel in those areas involved in a part of the CI process.

Requiring the Use of CI
In some cases, the most effective way to put CI to use is to require that every operating business unit, whether it is a small sales department or a large multinational subsidiary, include with its

annual plan an appraisal of current competition and the current marketplace. Experience shows that this is needed in addition to a strict requirement that the plans take competitors and competition into account.

> *Do not assume that everyone who should be using CI is doing so. Check it out.*

Put bluntly, if you cannot see the competitive information set forth separately, you have no guarantee that those preparing the plan have taken it into account or that they have even looked into it. Also, by seeing the CI that the unit has developed, you can evaluate its appropriateness and adequacy, and suggest additional sources. Further, you can supplement it with any CI you have developed on your own.

Table 17.1 summarizes the types of ongoing data collection and monitoring efforts your CI units can provide company wide that can become part of most departments' planning process.

A second stage would be to require the plan not only to indicate the current competitive environment but also to show how the unit perceives the future environment. From there, you can insist that the unit indicate *how* it intends to respond to changes in the competitive environment.

CI can be successfully injected at many stages other than the planning process. When you consider fundamental corporate decisions, such as an acquisition, a divestiture, a major capital investment, or the introduction of a new product, you can require that those involved both in considering and in advocating the transaction prepare a competitive analysis. The analysis should indicate how the planned action will assist your firm to respond to its competitors and how competitors may be expected to respond.

Table 17.1 Competitive Intelligence Unit Data Collection/Monitoring Efforts

Target	Focus	Effort	Suggested Methods

Top 5–10 Direct Industry Competitors	Long-term but limited to a set of key concepts	Continual	SDI.*
			Internal networking.
			Keep long-term background files.
			Get on mailing lists for:
			  House organs.
			  Annual report.
			  10-K.
			  Press releases.
			  Stockholders' meetings.
			Clip newspapers covering headquarters location.

Other Industry Leaders	Broad	Continual	Periodical scans;
			  Subscriptions.
			  SDI.
			Limited internal networking.
			Keep data a predetermined number of months.

Marketing and Promotion	New Trends New Concepts	Periodic	Subscriptions, such as Adweek. Limited SDI. Keep data for 3 months or less.
	Success Models	By Specific Request	Online databases. Interviews with special interest groups. Keep data only as long as needed.

*SDI: Selective dissemination of information. Essentially an automated way to survey new articles in selected publications on specific targets or topics using online databases. The results can be abstracts or just titles and are mailed to the user on a regular basis.

Managing Competitor Information: Forms

The first type of form for internal CI is the competitive intelligence audit form, a sample of which is shown in Exhibit 17.2. It helps you *solicit* CI data from staff who have contacts at competing businesses, are active in professional organizations with potential data sources, or formerly were employed by your competitor. Chapter 5 explains uses of the CI audit in detail.

Following are samples of three types of documents you can use to *distribute* the CI you collect: Competitor News, Competitor Report, and Competitor Profile.

Competitor News
From time to time, you may find that you wish to communicate raw, unevaluated data on a specific competitor quickly to a number of persons, as the data arrives. We call this Competitor News.

Exhibit 17.3 illustrates a typical form for communicating such materials.

Using the Competitor News form, you would insert the following under each heading:

■ *Competitor/Target:* Name of the firm you are tracking or a particular market in which you are interested.

■ *Subject:* Brief titles that permit you to narrow the focus of the message quickly, limiting it to subjects such as "marketing," "new products," or "pricing."

■ *Distributed To:* Names of those to whom this is sent. Showing all the names on the list helps avoid having those receiving the materials resend copies to interested people who have already received it. It also shows whether this data has not been delivered to a particular person who really needs to get it.

Competitive Intelligence Audit

Please take a moment to answer the following questions. This is an effort to identify competitive information assets inside of our firm on the [name] Industry.

Your complete answer to these questions will help us in our efforts to compete better in the future. If you have any questions, please call _____. When you are done, please return this directly to_____. Thank you.

1. Do you have frequent contact with consultants (including academics) or other research resources involved in our industry? Contact includes subscribing to publications or being on the mailing list for reports, newsletters, and so on. This group includes [examples]. If so, which ones? _____

_____

2. Do you monitor or cooperate with industry consumer or advocacy groups, such as [examples]? If so, which groups?___

_____

3. Are any of your personnel active in any industry trade or professional associations? This would include groups such as [examples]. "Active" includes not only going to meetings, but subscribing to publications or being on the mailing list for reports, newsletters, etc. If so, which associations? _____

_____

4. Have any of your employees previously worked for any of our direct competitors, including [list]? If so, please indicate that employee and his or her former affiliation.
    Name: *Former Employer:*
_____ _____

5. Are you regularly receiving any publications dealing with the following subjects [list, with examples of publications]? _____

_____

If so, which publications? _____

_____

Exhibit 17.2: Sample Competitive Intelligence Audit Form

356

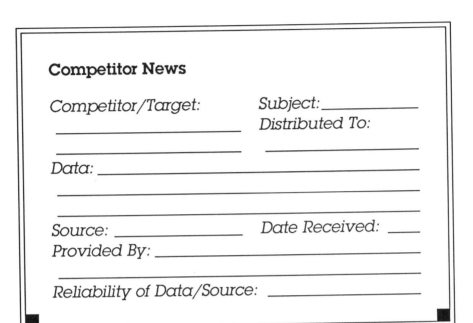

Competitor News

Competitor/Target: _____

_____

Subject:_____

Distributed To:

_____

Data: _____

_____

_____

Source: _____ Date Received: ____

Provided By: _____

_____

Reliability of Data/Source: _____

Exhibit 17.3: Sample of a Competitor News Form

- *Data:* A description of what you have found, such as the text of a local news story or a summary of an announcement at a trade show. It is captioned as "Data" so that those receiving it know that it is unevaluated.

- *Source:* The data's source, shown so that those reviewing it can decide its accuracy for themselves.

- *Date Received:* The date when you learned of this raw data. You can also indicate when the event probably occurred. This is to help remind those reviewing the Competitor News that such CI has a very short half-life.

- *Provided By:* Names of those persons and organizations helping your CI program; this helps future CI efforts by recognizing the participants' assistance. It also helps you track which units and people are most and least helpful to your CI unit.

■ *Reliability of Data/Source:* An estimate of how reliable the source and/or the data is. It is perfectly proper to indicate that the data is a rumor and that its reliability cannot be assessed.

Competitor Report

At the next level of detail and analysis is the Competitor Report. This differs from the Competitor News in that it is sent on a regular basis, perhaps weekly or monthly, and includes some analysis of the significance of the data being communicated. It can be seen as an accumulation of Competitor News publications, plus other raw data, all of which has then been subjected to preliminary, ongoing analysis.

Exhibit 17.4 illustrates a typical form for communicating such data.

Using this form, you would put the following under each heading:

■ *Competitor/Target:* Same as for Competitor News.

■ *Subject:* Same as for Competitor News.

■ *Distributed To:* Same as for Competitor News.

■ *Competitor Information:* A summary of what you have learned about the target competitor or market. This is not just an accumulation of pieces of raw data. It summarizes, thus reflecting evaluation and analysis.

■ *Significance of CI:* A brief description of what you believe this data means to the target and to your company.

■ *Sources:* Same as for Competitor News.

■ *Date Prepared:* The date, again to help remind those reviewing the form that such CI has a very short half-life.

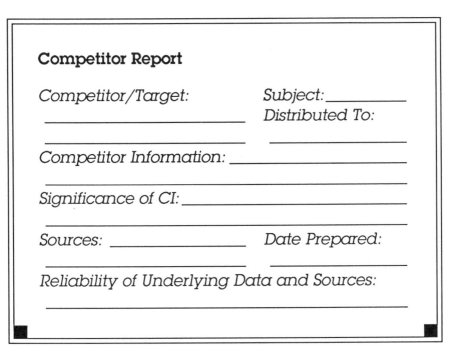

Competitor Report

Competitor/Target: *Subject:* _____
_____   *Distributed To:*
_____   _____

Competitor Information: _____

Significance of CI: _____

Sources: _____   *Date Prepared:*
_____   _____

Reliability of Underlying Data and Sources:
_____

Exhibit 17.4:   Sample of a Competitor Report Form

■   *Reliability of Underlying Data and Sources:* An estimate of how reliable you think each of the pieces of data and sources is. Usually, you can do this in the aggregate, noting something like "Based on past experience with these data sources, we believe that the data they provided is extremely accurate."

Competitor Profile
At the top of this pyramidal information system is the Competitor Profile, a document that stresses the analysis of raw data accumulated over time. A Competitor Profile may be distributed all at once; in sections, as discussed earlier; or kept in your CI unit to be referred to from time to time.

The sample Competitor Profile outline in Exhibit 17.5 has two key elements. First, it is arranged in a way that tracks, approximately, a firm's internal organization. Second, it is designed to force you to move upward from data to analysis.

359

Some of the highlights of the Competitor Profile are

■ Parts 1 through 4 are intended to contain analysis, whereas parts 5 and 6 are to contain data and raw materials. In fact, parts 5 and 6 are designed to capture the raw data supporting the analysis going into parts 1 through 4. For example, 1.1 is a summary of Part 2, 1.2 is a summary of Part 3, and so forth. In Part 4, 4.1's conclusion grows out of Part 5.1's data.

■ Parts 1 and 2 would be sent regularly to all senior officers. The final form of their contents depends on their own perceived needs.

■ In general, the senior officers, at the next level of detail, would only want the portions applicable to them. So, for example, the top marketing officer would get sections 3.3 and 4.3, and, if data was wanted in addition to analysis, section 5.3. Similarly, the chief officer in charge of engineering would get sections 3.1, 4.1, and 5.1. Of course, anyone could get any part, but managers probably prefer to tend to their own areas of responsibility.

■ The system provides a way to store raw data as it comes in. For example, information on the construction of a new facility would be filed under 5.2.1.6 (perhaps also a file category); a new test facility would be 5.4.3. It should also quickly show whether you are missing some key data on a particular competitor, because the category would be empty. In addition, if you have to generate a "snapshot" on some aspect of a particular competitor's plans or actions, a glance at the file would tell you whether there is anything to report or you have to start hunting for that data.

■ The section numbers also assist you in deciding on distribution. Ideally, you would identify recipients of each section with the section numbers. For example, data in 5.1.2, which is product development, should probably go automatically to the director of product development as well as to the next in line in your organization, the head of engineering and

TARGET COMPANY INC.

Organizational/Research/Dissemination Outline

Part 1. Executive Summary
> 1.1 Profile
> 1.2 Corporate, Management, and Organizational Structure
> 1.3 Overall Strategy
> 1.4 Operations

Part 2. Profile
> 2.1 Product Line
>> 2.1.1 Key Products
>> 2.1.2 Comparison with Our Products
> 2.2 Status in Industry
>> 2.2.1 Market Share and Rate of Growth
>> 2.2.2 Perceptions of Customers and of Other Competitors

Part 3. Corporate, Management, and Organizational Structure
> 3.1 Product Development and Engineering
> 3.2 Manufacturing
> 3.3 Marketing and Customer Service
> 3.4 Human and Physical Resources
> 3.5 Financial and Legal

Part 4. Overall Strategy
> 4.1 Product Development and Engineering
> 4.2 Manufacturing
> 4.3 Marketing and Customer Service
> 4.4 Human and Physical Resources
> 4.5 Financial and Legal

Part 5. Operations
> 5.1 Product Development and Engineering
>> 5.1.1 Product Specifications
>> 5.1.2 Product Development
>> 5.1.3 Current Technology
>> 5.1.4 Research and Development
> 5.2 Manufacturing
>> 5.2.1 Manufacturing Facilities

Exhibit 17.5: Sample of a Competitor Profile Outline

5.2.1.1 Location
5.2.1.2 Current Operations
5.2.1.3 Potential for Expansion
5.2.1.4 Expansion Plans
5.2.1.5 Closings
5.2.1.6 New Facilities
5.2.2 Operations
5.2.3 Materials Policies
5.2.4 Quality Control
5.2.5 Key Suppliers
5.2.6 Fiscal
5.2.6.1 Cost Structure
5.2.6.2 Capital Expenditures
5.2.6.3 Planned Improvements
5.3 Marketing and Customer Service
5.3.1 Customers
5.3.1.1 Key Customers
5.3.1.2 Status of Active Customers
5.3.2 Service
5.3.3 Distribution Systems
5.3.4 Pricing and Pricing Policies
5.3.5 Warranties
5.4 Human and Physical Resources
5.4.1 Key Executive and Management Personnel
5.4.2 Labor Force/Union Contracts
5.4.3 Nonmanufacturing Facilities, Such as Technology Centers
5.5 Financial and Legal
5.5.1 Current Financial Status
5.5.2 Financing of Distributors, Suppliers, and Customer Sales and Leases
5.5.3 Major Lawsuits and Regulatory Actions
Part 6. Materials from Target Company
6.1 Advertising Literature
6.2 Financial Statements
6.3 Price Lists
6.4 Specifications

Exhibit 17.5: *(continued)*

product development. In a way, you can think of the section numbers as "addresses" for a competitor news bulletin, telling you automatically to whom new data should go.

■ The numbers also enable you to classify the internal source of the data. Say data on a change in one competitor's quality control program (5.2.4) is given to you by your general manager of materials. In a sense, that manager's "address" is 5.2.3, "Materials Policies." So you could mark your competitor news bulletin 5.2.4/5.2.3. That would tell you who, in general terms, provided what information. You can also use this to show each unit how interdependent its information chains are and, conversely, who is not carrying his or her own weight. If you suspect the marketing department is not providing much raw data of use to the engineering department but is getting a lot from engineering, a quick check of 5.3 as the category and 5.1 as the source, as compared with 5.1 as the category and 5.3 as the source, rapidly reveals whether this is true.

Structuring, Disseminating, and Storing CI

Are you going to be able to disseminate CI in your firm as fast as you can develop it? Put another way, you have two basic options with raw and finished CI: storage and dissemination. Storage may be physical or electronic. Remember, however, that storage without an index or rapid access is not saving data, it is just wasting space.

If you are not distributing finished CI as it is being prepared, you may want to keep it in some intermediate form, such as a reference book about each competitor. The goal is to have needed data, in other than a raw state, at hand. If you do prepare the book, regularly review whether you are using all of these "intermediate products" in your work. If not, think seriously about eliminating them.

CI CLIP

"Knowledge is assumed to flow freely from place to place. The people making important decisions are supposed to have access to more or less the same body of information. Of course, pockets of ignorance or inside information remain here and there, but on the whole, once knowledge is public, ecomonists assume that it is known everywhere."

James Gleick.[6]

What Forms Can Finished CI Take?

Typically, your options are numerous, ranging from one-page bulletins to presentations, including reference books. In fact, some companies are experimenting with options as diverse as regular CI newsletters and "electronic mailboxes" to distribute their CI.

Your decision about the appropriate form or forms involves trade-offs between

■ Being current and providing some perspective.

■ Being easy to understand and perhaps less precise.

■ Being complete and thorough but subjecting the users to "information overload."

■ Being able to be absorbed rapidly, but lacking in detail.

■ Using "headlines" with short summaries and transmitting of careful analyses.

■ Providing free access to important CI and maintaining the confidentiality of the analysis and sources of raw data.

Forms in Which CI Is Made Available

Occasional Written Reports	*68%*
File Materials Available on Request	*60%*
Periodic Reports	*55%*
Occasional Presentations	*43%*
Newsletters	*29%*
In-house Electronic Database	*28%*
Periodic Presentations	*22%*[7]

The right form in which to present CI is, in part, determined by the need of the CI report to be useful and persuasive to the consumers. In presenting the results of a CI project, you should take care to avoid the following common problems:

■ One logjam is "group think," that is, the pressure among members of a group working on a project to find a common denominator and reach a consensus instead of stressing diversity where applicable. "Because judgments by consensus are the lowest common denominator, they are often of poor quality."[8]

■ Another roadblock is the "Sherwin Williams mentality" (taken from the paint company's advertising slogan, "We Cover the World"). That involves providing analysis on every conceivable aspect of a topic, whether the recipients have specifically asked for such CI or not.

Avoiding these traps can raise your credibility in the eyes of your end-users.

Managing Your Own Program
■ ■ ■

Know to Whom CI Is Going

You should identify the recipients and users of your finished CI *before* you begin any assignment. Knowing to whom the information is going helps you to determine what you need to find out, in what detail, and how to present it.

One key point often overlooked is to separate managers who *need* to know from those who merely *want* to know. By restricting your audience, you can better identify what data is to be collected and how your analysis is to be presented. In addition, the fewer people who have access to CI, the less severe will be potential security problems.

Another consideration arises as you distribute CI. When the raw data for your CI is provided by someone within your company, you may want to ensure that at least the raw data is distributed to that person's superiors, even if they are not necessarily appropriate consumers. A "pat on the head" to your supplier may work wonders in establishing cooperative data sources within a corporation.

Knowing to what use the finished CI may be put is important. Data and your conclusions should reflect and respond to the CI needs you established at the beginning of the project. Whether your consumers need recommendations for action or not is something you should establish at the beginning. If you cannot, find out before you prepare your final report.

> *Do not succumb to the temptation to put every-thing in your CI report.*

Format your results so that the final CI is readable, understandable, and useful to those to whom the CI is to go. A report on technological developments in an industry may go to the head of research and development. This type of report should differ in detail and form substantially from the same report going to the head of finance. Too often, those engaged in CI are tempted to present everything to everybody, just because they have collected all that data. Your audience, its sophistication, and its needs drive the form of your presentation. For example, AT&T created an "electronic intelligence network." Basically, it combines a daily competitive digest and an informal network approach to maintaining and sharing competitive information across the corporation.[9]

How do you handle CI that is "dated"? As we have already indicated, the half-life of some CI can be very short. Should you be protecting your associates from using dated CI? For example, should you recall old materials? That is not always a very rational solution. Is dating each page enough? Should you include in major reports an estimate of the half-life of the report? Should people receiving CI be briefed on its limits before you add them to a distribution list? Here again, knowing to whom the CI is going will help you determine the best way to present it.

Structuring Your Results
Your presentation of raw data and your CI analysis may not necessarily be a written report. For example, at Combustion Engineering Inc., planning and competitive intelligence are integrated on an ongoing basis. First, a competitor file is created and maintained by marketing or sales personnel. This serves as a reference tool to use in developing business plans as well as in answering one-time questions from all realms of the corporation.[10]

To handle structuring of your CI data and analysis, try to develop a format for the final report before you begin. For example, in developing a format for a regular CI report on each of a set of competitors, you have several options. The first is to use a form that can apply to all situations, such as an adaptation of some of the forms in this book. The second is to organize each report so that its structure parallels that of each company being tracked.

The third is to develop a report form that approximately tracks the users of your report, that is, the internal structure of your own firm. Such a report form may resemble the suggested Competitor Profile discussed earlier in this chapter.

The key benefit of the all-encompassing form option is that each report has the same structure. The disadvantage is that it may scatter data needed by one user into several categories.

The major benefit of the company-tracking form option is that each report can be prepared quickly by reference to the target company's own documents and reports. You do not have to skip from place to place to insert new raw data. The prime disadvantage is that, unless all of your competitors are structured and managed similarly, each report will differ, and it may be hard to find comparable data about each firm.

The major benefit of the user-tracking form option is that it provides a uniform format where each user knows exactly where to look for key data. The major problem with it is that such a form requires a substantial amount of effort to format. However, this option may be a key management tool in that it permits you to control the receipt and processing of raw data as well as of finished CI.

How to Disseminate CI

The next-to-last step in any CI project is dissemination of the results. Proper storage of data and results is your last step. For CI to be used, whether in planning or in any other context, it must be given to those who need it, in a suitable form, and in a timely manner.

The form you select for disseminating the CI should transmit the conclusions reached to the end-users in the most effective manner possible. There is no one right form. CI may be communicated orally, in writing, or in graphic form. The most common form of communication is the written report, but the most effective means of dissemination may involve using a combination of media and styles so that those receiving the CI are more likely to retain and understand the CI.

The method(s) you select depends on the need for clarity, accuracy, speed, and security. An oral presentation may be quick to prepare and present, but it may be difficult to have listeners grasp complex financial relationships merely by hearing a recitation of data. A graphic presentation can help clarify comparisons of data, but preparing complete and understandable graphics may require more time than is available. In CI, as in many other areas of business, timeliness determines whether information is useful. Precise information that arrives late may be less desirable than a rough approximation that is available on schedule.

Dissemination of the finished CI may be either limited or comprehensive. For example, if the director of new business development requests a CI report on a potential acquisition target, security and other considerations may require that the CI report be given directly to that person and only to that person. On the other hand, a CI report on a shadow market plan of a key competitor may have to be given to several individuals, such as your director of planning and your marketing manager. Each, in turn, may want to redistribute part or all of the CI you prepared or integrate the CI they received into reports or projects with which they and their staff are involved.

Ensuring Confidentiality

Last but not least, you should make sure that your CI results, as well as the sources of that CI, are kept confidential. The reasons for the secrecy about data are self-evident. If a competitor knows that you are conducting CI, that itself is valuable competitive information. If that same competitor knows the object of your CI efforts, it has gained an important insight into your probable strategy and plans.

The reasons for keeping the *sources* of data confidential are less clear. There are situations when secrecy could become critical. It would be embarrassing and potentially damaging if, for example, a list of distributors who cooperated in preparing a CI report reached the competitor targeted in your project. To minimize the chances of such a mishap, you may want to keep the list of cooperating sources separate from your report.

Determinations of what should be kept confidential and how that should be accomplished should be made, if possible, at the initiation of an assignment or even at the time you create a separate CI unit. If you do not do so then, at least review these issues *before* you distribute the results of your CI research and analysis.

Summary

Many decisions affect how you initiate and structure an ongoing CI program, including how to stage its development, how visible to make the program, ways to divide work loads between other departments and this unit, the reporting structure and level of staff, division of data gathering responsibilities, types of data that should not be collected and retained, procedures for testing data validity, keeping the demand for services within the unit's resources, measuring performance of the unit, developing appropriate job descriptions and missions, whether to charge other departments for the unit's services, and managing the data flow from internal sources.

CI providers should avoid taking positions on the policies and events for which they supply information. However, integrating that information into your business's overall planning efforts is vital and can be accomplished in part through requiring the use of CI in managerial responsibilities such as annual plans.

You can obtain CI data through internal interviews using the competitive intelligence audit, or any staff who formerly worked for or with your competitors can complete this informal form. Three additional forms that disseminate CI can be completed by people within the CI unit or any other department conducting CI: Competitor News, Competitor Report, and Competitor Profile.

Choose a form for your completed CI that best suits its priorities of being clear, understandable, useful, and timely. Oral, written, and graphic presentations all involve trade-offs between time and retention of data.

CI ALERT: What does this tell you?

"ASK MR. FOSTER TRAVEL SERVICE, North America's largest and oldest travel-management firm, has a rewarding career opportunity for the experienced manager with the skill and expertise to head the staff of our 30-person, $12-million-a-year San Ramon, CA, Commercial Business Center. This key branch is located in the San Francisco/East Bay area. Its primary client is a prestigious FORTUNE 500 Company."

Source: Advertisement, Business Travel News, January 15, 1990.

Notes

1. Brian Dumaine, "Corporate Spies Snoop to Conquer," *Fortune,* November 7, 1988, pp. 68-69, 72, 76.

2. Linda Koco, "Who Watches the Product Watchers?," *National Underwriter (Life & Health/Financial Services),* February 29, 1988, pp. 13, 30.

3. Ken Landis, "What Will You Do in 1992?," *Inside Business,* December 1988, pp. 1-6.

4. Richard H. Giza, "The Problems of the Intelligence Consumer," in Roy Godson (ed.), *Intelligence Requirements for the 1980s: Analysis and Estimates,* Washington, D.C.: National Strategy Information Center, Inc., 1986, pp. 189-206.

5. Edward S. Finein, "Why It Pays to Go Sleuthing," *Design News,* December 1, 1986.

6. James Gleick, *Chaos: Making a New Science,* New York: Viking Penguin Inc., 1987, p. 180.

7. The Conference Board, Inc., *Competitive Intelligence,* Research Report No. 913, 1988, p. 20.

8. Michael Handel, "Avoiding Political and Technological Surprise in the 1980s," in Roy Godson (ed.), *Intelligence Requirements for the 1980s: Analysis and Estimates*, Washington, D.C.: National Strategy Information Center, Inc., 1986, p. 103.

9. The Conference Board, Inc., *Competitive Intelligence,* Research Report No. 913, 1988, pp. 22-24.

10. The Conference Board, Inc., *Competitive Intelligence,* Research Report No. 913, 1988, pp. 37-38.

Appendix A

Glossary

90-10 Rule: A maxim that states that getting the last 10 percent of the data or information you are looking for may cost as much as or take as much time as getting the first 90 percent did.

Analogy: A tool for solving problems that involves the application of past experience to present problem solving. The key is an inference that certain observed similarities between two items or events means further similarities.

Anomaly: Data that does not fit; usually an indication that one's working assumptions are wrong or that an unknown factor is affecting results.

Benchmarking A process for comparing one company's operations against those of other firms, both in and out of the market. Typically, the comparison is made with those firms believed to exhibit the most efficient operations.

BI: Business intelligence. *See* Business Intelligence (BI).

Blowback: The contamination of your own intelligence channels or information by disinformation or misinformation that you have directed at your adversary. In the business context, it means being misled by your own disinformation.

Business Intelligence (BI): One synonym for competitive intelligence.

CI: Competitive intelligence or competitive information.

CI Audit: A review of your current operations to determine what you actually know about your current competitors and about their operations. A CI audit also helps you focus on what kind of CI you currently need.

CI Cycle: The process of establishing CI needs, collecting raw data, processing it into finished CI, and distributing it to the end-users.

Competitive Information: The result of competitive intelligence.

Competitive Intelligence: The use of public sources to locate and develop data that is then transformed into information, generally about competitors and/or the competition.

Competitive Scenario: An analysis of what one or more competitors can be expected to do in response to changes in market and other conditions affecting their activities. The analysis is based on a profile of the competitor, including estimations of its intentions and capabilities, stemming from a study of its past actions, and of the perceptions, style, and behavior of its present and future management. Each competitor's actions are studied against the same set of expected market conditions and changes.

Current Data: Facts that deal with a relatively short period of time, centered on the present. Examples of this might be sales figures for the past three-month period for one competitor.

Data: Raw, unevaluated material. Data may be numeric or textual. Data is the ultimate source of information, but becomes usable information only after it has been processed and analyzed. *See also* Current Data, Historic Data, Macro-level Data, and Micro-level Data.

Database: Systematically organized data, stored in a computer-readable form so that it can be updated, searched, and retrieved.

Deductive Methods: Problem-solving methods that involve reasoning from a known principle to an unknown, from the general to the specific, or from a premise to a logical conclusion.

Defensive CI: The process of monitoring and analyzing your own business's activities as your competitors and other outsiders see them.

Delphi Method: A forecasting procedure in which experts express formal judgments and opinions on the likelihood of future events. This is done anonymously and in several rounds, each of which involves a response to the opinions expressed by all participants in the prior round.

Disinformation: Incomplete or inaccurate information designed to mislead others about your intentions or abilities. When used in the arena of international politics, espionage, or intelligence, the term means the deliberate production and dissemination of falsehoods, fabrications, and forgeries aimed at misleading an opponent or those supporting an opponent.

End-Users: Persons or organizations who request and use information obtained from an online search or other source of CI.

Espionage: Either the collection of information by illegal means or the illegal collection of information. If the information has been collected from a government, this is a serious crime, such as treason. If it is from a business, it may be a theft offense.

False Confirmation: A data verification situation in which a second source of data appears to confirm the data from the first source but does not actually do so. Typically, this arises when the second source receives information from the first source, or both sources receive their data from another common source. They confirm each other, not because both are correct, but because both have the same origin.

False Negative: When a test gives an erroneous negative result instead of the correct positive result. The result is an erroneous indication that the condition being tested for is not present when it is in fact present.

False Positive: When a test gives an erroneous positive result instead of the correct negative result. The result is an erroneous indication that the condition being tested for is present when it is not in fact present.

FOIA: Freedom of Information Act. *See* Freedom of Information Act (FOIA).

Fraud: An act that involves distributing erroneous or false information with an intent to mislead or to take advantage of someone relying on that information.

Freedom of Information Act (FOIA):   Federal statute requiring that U.S. government agencies provide information to the public on request. Some agencies make no charge for producing information requested under the FOIA. Others may charge for the time involved as well as the cost of copying the files. Not every federal government record is subject to public disclosure under the FOIA. Important exceptions from disclosure include classified information, personnel files, and some material from private persons and companies that was given to the government but is confidential or proprietary in nature.

Half-Life: In scientific terms, the period of time after which a substance has lost 50 percent of any factor being measured, such as radioactive strength. In CI, it means the time after which CI has lost 50 percent of its relative value.

Historic Data: Data that covers a long period of time. It is designed to show long-term trends, such as gross sales in an industry over a five-year period. This may include projections made covering a long period of years.

Inductive Methods: Problem-solving methods that involve reasoning from particular facts or individual cases to a general conclusion.

Information: The material resulting from analyzing and evaluating raw data, reflecting both data and judgments. Information is an input to a finished CI evaluation.

Information Broker: A person involved in obtaining data on many subjects, including businesses, from public sources. The sources relied on are exclusively or predominantly public online databases. The data is provided without significant screening or analysis. The term originated because such businesses were seen as "brokering" the raw data found in online databases, by extracting it and reselling it to people who did not use these databases themselves.

Intelligence: Knowledge achieved by a logical analysis and integration of available information data on competitors or the competitive environment.

Libel: Something false that also defames another's reputation.

M & A: Mergers and acquisitions.

Macro-level Data: Data of a high level of aggregation, such as the size of a particular market or the overall rate of growth of the nation's economy.

Micro-level Data: Data of a low level of aggregation or even unaggregated data. This might be data, for example, on a competitor company's or division's sales of a particular product line.

Online Database: A computerized database that can be accessed from another computer and through which searches can be conducted from that computer. Typically this communication occurs over telephone lines.

Online Searching: Using a computer to locate specific information from an online database.

Planning: A process by which a business organization's mission is defined; its competitive strengths, including resources and liabilities, are evaluated; its goals are established; its alternative courses of action are identified; and selections are made from among them. Then the steps necessary to achieve those goals are set.

PR: Abbreviation for public relations. In business, this generally refers to the information released to the public by the business through the news media or in speeches. It can also refer to the office or firm responsible for releasing that information.

Protocol: The method of communicating commands to a database. This involves the way in which you contact and get into the database, the way you enter search and other commands, the form in which you write a search statement so that the database can execute it, how the system displays the results of a search, and how you sign off the database. Online databases vary in the types of commands that can be used and strategies that can be executed.

Reverse Engineering: The purchasing and dismantling of a product to identify how it was designed and constructed. This is usually done so that costs of making it as well as its relative quality can be estimated. It can provide information on how to produce a comparable, compatible, or competitive product.

Search Statement: A description of the specific kinds of data you seek to get from an online database. For example, you are seeking information on The Helicon Group, Ltd., and you are interested in its activities, if any, in 1990, in the area of CI. Your search statement, in English, might ask for documents containing all of the following concepts: Helicon Group and CI (or competitive intelligence) and the year 1990. You would then convert the search into a form that the database could use, using that database's particular protocols.

Shadow Market Plan: An estimate both of what a competitor is planning in its marketing efforts and of its capabilities. This is based on CI developed about the competitor, including an estimate of its intentions. People producing the shadow market plan often put themselves in the competitor's place and seek to re-create the competitor's market plan.

Shadow Market Planning: This involves an estimate of what a competitor is planning in its marketing efforts and an estimate of its capabilities. However, unlike a shadow market plan, this type of planning is an ongoing process and involves replicating what the competitor might do, given its capabilities, its personnel, its track record, and its view of market conditions.

SIC Code: The Standard Industrial Classification (SIC) code. This is a major statistical classification system used to promote the comparability of establishment data describing various facets of the U.S. economy.

Surveillance: A continuous and systematic watch over the actions of a competitor aimed at providing timely information for immediate responses to the competitor's actions.

Target: A specified competitor or one of its facilities, activities, or markets.

Appendix B

CI Resources

Books and Articles for Further Information

In addition to the notes' sources at the end of each chapter, the following books and articles may be of interest to you. For convenience, they are divided into groups to parallel the organization of the book.

Part I: The Big Picture

"Business Sharpens Its Spying Techniques." *Business Week* (August 4, 1975), pp. 60-63.

"Ethical Issues in Information-Finding Activities." *The Information Advisor* Vol. 1, No. 5 (February 1989), pp. 1-2.

Clayton, Mark. "The Usually Legal Business of Keeping Tabs on the Competition." *Christian Science Monitor* (October 26, 1987), p. 16.

———."When Gumshoes Go Too Far." *Christian Science Monitor* (October 28, 1987), p. 12.

Derra, Skip, and Ted Agres. "Competition Drives Market for Industrial Espionage." *Research & Development* (June 1987), pp. 63-64, 66, 70.

Greene, Richard. "Never Mind R&D, How About T&G?" *Forbes* (September 24, 1984), p. 142.

Appendixes and Index

Lasden, Martin. "MIS/DP Espionage: The Inside Story." *Computer Decisions* Vol. 18, No. 8 (April 8, 1986), pp. 66-71.

Miles, Gregory. "Information Thieves Are Now Corporate Enemy No. 1." *Business Week* (May 5, 1986), pp. 120-21, 123, 125.

Miller, Tim. "Staying Alive in the Jungle." *On-line Access Guide* (March/April 1987), pp. 44-57.

Olney, Clause W. "The Secret World of the Industrial Spy." *Business and Society Review*, Winter 1988, pp. 28-32.

Prescott, John E., and Daniel C. Smith. "Demystifying Competitive Analysis." *Planning Review* (September/October 1987), pp. 8-13.

Sammon, William L., Mark A. Kurland, and Robert Spitalnic. *Business Competitor Intelligence*. New York: Ronald Press, 1984.

Part II: Finding Information About Your Competitors

Abelson, Herbert I. "Focus Groups in Focus." *Marketing Communications* (February 1989), pp. 58-59, 61.

Alpert, William M. "What's On Tap?" *Barron's* (June 18, 1984), pp. 30, 32-33.

Clayton, Mark. "A Tackle Box of Sleuthing Tricks for Companies Out to Catch Rivals." *Christian Science Monitor* (October 27, 1987), p. 12.

Flam, Stephen. "How to Snoop on Your Competitors." *Fortune* (May 14, 1984), pp. 28-33.

Frank, Bob. "Brokers Are One Approach to Information Glut." *Legal Times* (May 19, 1986), pp. 24, 33.

Keiser, Barbie E. "Practical Competitor Intelligence." *Planning Review* (September/October 1987), pp. 14-18, 45.

Tyson, Kirk W. M. *Business Intelligence*. Lombard, Ill.: Leading Edge Publications, 1986.

Part III: Special Challenges

Crispell, Diane. "The On-Line Search." *American Demographics* (February 1986), pp. 46-47.

McKie, Peter. "Tracking Your Competition—The On-line Edge." *Personal Computing* (May 1986), pp. 93-103.

Scanlan, Jean M., Ulla de Stricker, and Anne Conway Fernald. *Business Online*. New York: John Wiley & Sons, 1989.

Vella, Carolyn M., and John J. McGonagle, Jr. *Competitive Intelligence in the Computer Age*. Westport, Conn.: Quorum Books, 1987.

Part IV: Turning Data into Actionable Information

"Business Planning." Small Business Consulting Practice Aid 6, New York: American Institute of Certified Public Accountants, 1986.

"Guard Your Garbage." *Fortune* (September 3, 1984), p. 9.

"How to Use Competitive Intelligence in a Restructuring Program." *Corporate Restructuring* (June 1988), pp. 8-9.

"Some Need 'Info' Before Investing in Stocks." *Business Digest of Lehigh Valley* (June 1989), pp. 15, 17.

American Institute of Certified Public Accountants. "What Else Can Financial Statements Tell You?" 1987.

Andriole, Stephen J. *Handbook of Problem Solving*. New York: Petrocelli Books, 1983.

Attanasio, Dominick. "The Multiple Benefits of Competitor Intelligence." *The Journal of Business Strategy* (May/June 1988), pp. 16-19.

Ball, Richard. "Assessing Your Competitor's People and Organization." *Long Range Planning* (April 1987), pp. 32-41.

Bennett, Steven J., and Michael Snell. "A Corporate Spy on Your Own Team." *Sales & Marketing Management* (February 1988), pp. 60-65.

Blumenthal, Philip L., Jr. "Financial Model Preparation." Technical Consulting Practice Aid 2, New York: American Institute of Certified Public Accountants, 1983.

Carey, E. Raymond. "Marketing Strategy—An Overview." Harvard Business School Case 579-054, Cambridge: HBS Case Services, 1978.

Eels, Richard, and Peter Nehemkis. *Corporate Intelligence and Espionage*. New York: Macmillan Publishing Co., 1984.

Fuld, Leonard M. *Competitor Intelligence*. New York: John Wiley & Sons, 1985.

Garvin, Andrew, and Hubert Bermont. *How to Win with Information or Lose Without It*. Washington, D.C.: Bermont Books, 1980.

Holmes, John. "Cure Sought for Doctored Research." *Insight* (March 23, 1987), pp. 56-57.

Hyatt, Joshua. "Cat Fight." *Inc.* (November 1986), pp. 82-86.

Johnson, Robert. "The Case of Marc Feith Shows Corporate Spies Aren't Just High-Tech." *The Wall Street Journal* (January 9, 1987), pp. 1, 12.

Kelly, John M. *How to Check Out Your Competition*. New York: John Wiley & Sons, 1987.

Kovach, Jeffery. "Spies on the Payroll." *Industry Week* (May 13, 1985), pp. 75-77.

Lieberstein, Stanley H. *Who Owns What Is in Your Head?* New York: Hawthorn Books, 1979.

Lovelock, Christopher H. "Conducting and Interpreting a Marketing Research Study." Harvard Business School Note 9-582-152, Cambridge: HBS Case Services, 1982.

Markowitz, Zane N. "Hidden Sector Competitor Analysis." *Planning Review* (September/October 1987), pp. 20, 24, 46.

Metzler, Morton F. *Information: The Ultimate Management Resource*. New York: AMACOM, a division of American Management Associations, 1981.

Miller, Cyndee. "Intelligence Systems." *Marketing News* (May 9, 1988), pp. 2, 11.

Monk, J. Thomas, and Kenneth M. Landis. "M&A Sleuthing Easier with On-line Clues." *Cashflow* (March 1988), pp. 53-54.

379

Appendixes and Index

Park, C. Whan, and Daniel C. Smith. "Competitors as Sources of Innovative Marketing Strategies." Working Paper 86-109, Marketing Science Institute, 1986.

Penzias, Arno. *Ideas and Information: Managing in a High Tech World.* New York: Simon and Schuster, 1990.

Porter, Michael E. "How Competitive Forces Shape Strategy." *Harvard Business Review* (March/April 1979), pp. 137-45.

Prescott, John E. "A Process for Applying Analytic Models in Competitive Analysis." In William R. King and David T. Cleland (ed.). *Strategic Planning and Management Handbook.* New York: Van Nostrand Reinhold Co., 1986, pp. 222-50.

Prescott, John E., and Daniel C. Smith. "A Project-Based Approach to Competitive Analysis." *Strategic Management Journal* (September/October 1987), pp. 411-24.

Saunders, Michael. *Protecting Your Business Secrets.* New York: Nichols, 1985.

Schmid, Robert E., Jr. "Reverse Engineering a Service Product." *Planning Review* (September/October 1987), pp. 33-35.

Stevenson, Howard H. "Resource Assessment: Identifying Corporate Strengths and Weaknesses." In William D. Guth (ed.). *Handbook of Business Strategy.* Boston: Warren, Gorham & Lamont, 1985.

Wurman, Richard S. *Information Anxiety.* New York: Doubleday, 1989.

Zinkhan, George M., and Betsy D. Gelb. "Competitive Intelligence Practices of Industrial Marketers." *Industrial Marketing Management* Vol. 14, No. 4, 1985, pp. 269-75.

Part V: Managing Your Own Program

"Charge-back: From Free Access to Fee Access." *Information Center* (June 1989), p. 13.

Ghoshal, Sumantra, and Seok Ki Kim. "Building Effective Systems for Competitive Advantage." *Sloan Management Review,* Fall 1986, pp. 49-58.

Herring, Jan P. "Building a Business Intelligence System." *Journal of Business Strategy* (May/June 1988), pp. 4-9.

McGonagle, John J., Jr. *Managing The Consultant—A Corporate Guide.* Radnor, Pa: Chilton Book Co., 1981.

O'Riordan, P. Declan. "The Emerging Role of the Chief Information Officer." *Information Strategy: The Executive's Journal* Vol. 2, No. 2 (Winter 1986), pp. 8-11.

Pipkin, Al. "The 21st Century Controller." *Management Accounting* (February 1989), pp. 21-25.

Stern, Bruce, and Scott Dawson. "How to Select a Market Research Firm." *American Demographics* (March 1989), pp. 44, 46.

Symonds, Curtis. *A Design for Business Intelligence.* New York: American Management Association, Inc., 1971.

Research and Reference Resources

Note: The citation of any publication or organization is not a recommendation or endorsement of any sort. This information is provided to illustrate the wide variety of resources available to you.

General CI Issues

Books and Directories

Daniells, Lorna M. *Business Information Sources*. Berkeley, Calif.: University of California Press, 1985 (revised edition).

Horowitz, Lois. *Knowing Where to Look*. Cincinnati, Ohio: Writers Digest Books, 1984.

IRS Corporate Financial Ratios. Evanston, Ill.: Schonfeld & Associates, Inc. (annual). (2350 Crawford Avenue, Evanston, IL 60201)

Lesko, Matthew, *Information U.S.A.* New York: Penguin Books, Revised Edition, 1986.

_____. *Lesko's New Tech Sourcebook*. New York: Harper & Row, 1986.

Washington Information Directory. Washington, D.C.: Congressional Quarterly Inc. (annual) (1414 22nd Street, N.W., Washington, DC 20067).

Yearbook of Experts, Authorities, and Spokespersons. Washington, D.C.: Broadcast Interview Source (annual) (2233 Wisconsin Avenue, N.W., Washington, D.C. 20007-4104).

Periodicals

The following lists some of the many business and trade publications we mentioned in the text. They are just a sample of the wide variety available.

Advertising Age: Crain Communications Inc., 740 Rush Street, Chicago, IL 60611.

American Banker: American Banker-Bond Buyer, One State Street Plaza, New York, NY 10004.

Institutional Investor: Institutional Investor Inc., 488 Madison Avenue, New York, NY 10022.

Journal of Advertising Research: Advertising Research Foundation, 3 East 54th Street, New York, NY 10022.

Life Insurance Selling: Commerce Publishing Company, 408 Olive Street, St. Louis, MO 63102.

Marketing Communications: Media Horizons Inc., 228 East 45th Street, New York, NY 10017.

Modern Maturity: American Association of Retired Persons, 3200 East Carson Street, Lakewood, CA 90712-4038.

The Information Advisor: The Winters Group, 14 Franklin Street, Rochester, NY 14604.

Wall Street Transcript: Wall Street Transcript, Inc., 99 Water Street, New York, NY 10005-4393.

Appendixes and Index

For information on others, see reference publications such as *Standard Rate & Data Service Business Publication Rates and Data:* Standard Rate & Data Service, Inc., 3004 Glenview Road, Wilmette, IL 60091.

Database Vendors
You can access the databases mentioned in the text, as well as thousands of others from one or more of these vendors:

BRS Information Technologies Inc., 8000 Westpark Drive, McLean, VA 22102. 800/442-0900

CompuServe Inc., P.O. Box 20212, Columbus, OH 43220 800/848-8990

Datastar/D-S Marketing, Inc., 485 Devon Park Drive, Wayne, PA 19087. 800/221-7754

Dialog Information Services, Inc., 3460 Hillview Avenue, Palo Alto, CA 94304-1396. 800/334-2564

Dow Jones & Company, Inc., P.O. Box 300, Princeton, NJ 08543-0300. 800/832-1234

InvesText, 11 Farnsworth Street, Boston, MA 02210. 800/662-7878

Mead Data Central Inc., 9393 Springboro Pike, Dayton, OH 45401. 800/543-2744

Mergers & Acquisitions, 229 South 18th Street, Philadelphia, PA 19103. 215/875-2330

Mistui & Co. (USA), Inc., 200 Park Avenue, New York, NY 10166-0130. 212 878-4000

ORBIT Search Service, 8000 Westpark Drive, McLean, VA 22102. 800/45-ORBIT

VU/TEXT Information Services, Inc., 325 Chestnut Street, Philadelphia, PA 19106. 800/323-2940

West Publishing Company, 50 West Kellog Blvd., Eagan, MN 55102-1611. 800/937-8529

Guides to Databases
For information on what specific databases contain, and from whom they are available, you can refer to works such as the following:

Books and Periodicals Online. Medford, N.J.: Learned Information, Inc. (annual) (143 Old Marlton Pike, Medford, NJ 08055-8707).

Database Directory. White Plains, N.Y.: Knowledge Industry Publications, Inc. (annual) (701 Westchester Avenue, White Plains, NY 10604).

Directory of Online Business Databases. Auburn, Maine: W.B. McCarthy Associates (annual) (P. O. Box 1537, Auburn, ME 04211-1537).

Directory of Online Databases. New York: Cuadra/Elsevier (quarterly) (P.O. Box 872, Madison Square Station, New York, NY 10159).

Fulltext Sources Online. Needham Height, Mass.: Bibliodata (semiannual) (P.O. Box 61, Needham Heights, MA 02194).

Organizations
The range of business, service, and trade organizations is almost impossible to contemplate. Among the specific ones mentioned in the text are

Bank Marketing Association, an affiliate of the American Bankers Association, 309 West Washington Street, Chicago, IL 60606. 800/433-9013

National Association of State Development Agencies, 444 North Capitol Street, Washington, DC 20001. 202/624-5411

Society of Competitor Intelligence Professionals, 8375 Leesburg Pike, Vienna, VA 22180.

U.S. Customs Service, Washington, D.C. 202/566-8047.

Guides to Organizations

The following references can help you locate many others:

Directory of Fee-Based Information Services. Houston: Burwell Enterprises (annual) (5106 FM 1960 W., Suite 349, Houston, TX 77069).

Directory of Special Libraries and Information Centers. Detroit: Aslib-Gale Research Company (annual) (The Book Tower, Detroit, MI 48226).

Encyclopedia of Associations and Organizations. Detroit: Aslib-Gale Research Company (annual) (The Book Tower, Detroit, MI 48226).

Makower, Joel, and Alan Green. *Instant Information.* New York: Prentice-Hall Press, 1987.

National Trade and Professional Associations of the United States (annual), available from Columbia Books Inc., 1350 New York Avenue, N.W., Washington, DC 20005.

Services

Several commercial services can help you get copies of documents filed with the U.S. Securities and Exchange Commission. Two of them are:

Bechtel Information Services, 9430 Key West Avenue, Rockville, MD 20850-3324. 301/258-4300

Disclosure Inc., 5161 River Road, Bethesda, MD 20816-1584. 301/951-1300

Numerous services can help you get copies of articles from magazines and newspapers. Some are highly specialized. Others cover a wide variety of industries. Among the more general services are the following:

FIND/SVP Inc., 625 Avenue of the Americas, New York, NY 10011-2002. 212/645-4500

Information on Demand, Inc., P.O. Box 1370, Berkeley, CA 94701. 800/227-0750

INQUIRE, The George Washington University, The Gelman Library, 2130 H Street, NW, Washington, DC 20052. 202/994-6973

International Resources

Many of the resources listed earlier, such as database suppliers and reference works, can provide access to international information. In addition, the following publications and catalogs can help you get started in developing your own international CI resources:

"The 1989 Corporate Finance International Register." *Corporate Finance* (January 1989), pp. 61-104.

"The Global 1000." *Business Week* (July 17, 1989), pp. 139-178.

EuroMarket Catalog, available from UNIPUB™, 4611-F, Assembly Drive, Lanham, MD 20706.

Appendixes and Index

Euromonitor Quarterly Catalogue, available from Euromonitor, 87-88 Turnmill Street, London EC1M 5QU, U.K.

The European Community as a Publisher, available from the Office for Official Publications of the European Communities, L-2985 Luxembourg.

Fuld, Leonard M. "How to Gather Foreign Intelligence Without Leaving Home." *Marketing News* (January 4, 1988), pp. 24, 27.

Information Gathering on Japan: A Primer. Washington, D.C.: Search Associates Inc., 1988 (3422 Q Street, NW, Washington, DC 20007).

Japan External Trade Organization, "JETRO Publications." Available from JETRO, 2-5 Toramomon 2-chome, Minato-ku, Tokyo 105, Japan.

Japanese Science & Technology (2nd edition 1988). U.S. Department of Commerce, National Technical Information Service, Springfield, VA 22161.

Land, Brian, *Sources of Information for Canadian Business*. Ottawa, Ontario: The Canadian Chamber of Commerce, 1985 (4th ed.).

Organisation for Economic Co-operation and Development. *OECD Publications*, available from OECD Publications and Information Center, 2001 L Street, NW, Washington, DC 20006-4095.

Singapore Economic Development Board & the Singapore Trade Development Board, *Major Supporting Industries in Singapore*. 1989, available from Singapore Economic Development Board, 250 North Bridge Road, #24-00, Raffles City Tower, Singapore 0617.

Worldwide Chamber of Commerce Directory. Loveland, Colo: Worldwide Chamber of Commerce Directory, Inc. (annual) (P.O. Box 1029, Loveland, CO 80539).

Appendixes and Index
■ ■ ■